UNIVERSITY COLLEGE OF THE
FRASER VALLEY
P9-EDU-715

The Citizen's Guide to Planning

DATE DUE			
MAR 15 2000			
MAR 29 2000			
APR 17 2000			
SEP 11 2000			
MAY - 6 2004			

DISCARDED

201-9500 PRINTED IN U.S.A.

The citizen's guide to
planning /

UNIVERSITY COLLEGE OF THE FRASER VALLEY
2 6025 00445 472 1

c. 1 Ab

The Citizen's Guide to Planning

Third Edition

By Herbert H. Smith

UNIVERSITY COLLEGE OF THE FRASER VALLEY
LIBRARY

PLANNERS PRESS
AMERICAN PLANNING ASSOCIATION
Chicago, Illinois
Washington, D.C.

Third Edition MAY 11 1999 a111326
Copyright 1993 by the American Planning Association
1313 E. 60th St.
Chicago, IL 60637
ISBN (paperback edition): 0-918286-83-2
ISBN (hardbound edition): 0-918286-84-0
Library of Congress Catalog Number: 92-76067

Originally published in 1961 as *The Citizen's Guide to Planning,*
© 1961 Chandler-Davis Publishing Company.

First Edition
First printing, 1961; second printing, 1962; third printing, 1963;
fourth printing, 1964; fifth printing, 1967; sixth printing, 1969;
seventh printing, 1972.

Second Edition
First printing, 1979; second printing, 1980;
third printing, 1984; fourth printing, 1989.
Copyright to the original edition assigned to Herbert H. Smith, July 1976.

Printed in the United States of America
All rights reserved

To each of the several hundred planning graduate students whose paths crossed mine during my 12 years as a teacher, thus making my life brighter and more fulfilling from having known them. May they continue to be faithful to the cause and have great success in their professional careers.

Contents

Acknowledgments

My deep gratitude goes to all those who have provided me assistance in any form and encouragement in the preparation of this, the Third Edition. Appreciation also goes to all of those who have been interested enough to purchase and read either one of the first two editions to the extent that justified this revision and update. It would be remiss of me not to single out some of those who substantially contributed to my research and the production of this edition. To the following I particularly owe my sincere thanks:

Robert Baldwin, AICP, Principal Planner, Zoning, Department of Planning and Development, a most cooperative provider of helpful details on Houston's zoning effort.

Professor Earnest R. Bartley, AICP, University of Florida, for going far above the call of duty in providing me with the interpretive information and comments on the 1985 Florida Local Government Comprehensive Planning and Land Development Regulation Act.

Dixi Gloystein, computer teacher and consultant extraordinary, without whom, probably, I would not have undertaken this task.

Hal Gloystein, whose patient and painstaking mechanical assistance made it possible for the first complete, comprehensive manuscript to come into being.

Mary Lou Henry, AICP, Vice President, Vernon G. Henry, Inc., Houston, Texas, for her most helpful information about the process and prospects for Houston's first zoning ordinance.

Robert F. Hintz, AICP, Planning Consultant, Seattle, Washington, for providing information on the Washington State Growth Management Act.

James A. Jacobs, Director of Research, Colorado Public Expenditure Council, who provided statistical information on state and local taxation.

Thomas J. Peterson, AICP, Planning Director, Fort Collins, Colorado, who provided valuable assistance regarding the Fort Collins Land Development Guidance System.

Rita R. Robison, Growth Management Information Specialist, Department of Community Development, for supplying informational material on the Washington State Growth Management Act.

Mitch Rohse, AICP, Oregon Department of Land Conservation and Development, and Michael P. Saba, AICP, Portland Planning Bureau, for seeing that I had the complete Oregon planning program story to draw from.

Roger A. Wilburn, Florida Department of Community Affairs, and Ronald Villella, Florida Attorney General's Office, for supplying a wealth of information on the Florida planning legislation and administrative code.

Professor Edward Ziegler, University of Denver Law School, whose consultation regarding legal aspects of U.S. Supreme Court decisions re taking cases was most helpful.

Finally, but most importantly of all, my loving gratitude goes to my partner and friend, my wife Nancy, who kept me going with her encouragement and love and whose dedicated editing of the first and final manuscripts was an outstanding contribution to the quality of the writing.

Foreword

Thirty-one years ago, the first edition of this book was dictated on an old-fashioned Dictaphone recorder to be transcribed by my secretary. In that same year, 1961, it was published by Chandler-Davis Publishing Company. Fourteen years ago, the second edition was typed by me on a Royal typewriter, somewhat of an antique even then, to be retyped in manuscript form by a professional typist. This was published by the American Planning Association in 1979. Between the two publishers, approximately 60,000 copies have been sold. What a difference in technology a few years can make: as this Third Edition was punched out it was written on a personal computer, a gadget that not more than five years ago I vowed I would never touch.

Now it is time to revise and update the book's contents in this third edition, hopefully keeping the objective that has always been my primary purpose. That is: to explain the planning process in such a way that *anyone* the least bit interested in the future of their hamlet, village, town, or city can understand how democratic, comprehensive planning is able to provide the means of protecting and improving that future and can be motivated to do something about it. Perhaps, of even more importance, that individual concern could be extended to include the future of our society and our country. It is an inescapable certainty that as we build our individual urban units we are creating the environment and physical character of our nation.

When this revision was started, a quandary arose as to what to do about the previously written forewords. Should both be deleted, should they be revised, or will their retention serve a purpose? After reading them several times, I decided to include them in this edition. The reason for this decision is to emphasize most emphatically that we have learned very little over the elapsed years about how better to shape the urban form. We continue to destroy our natural assets under the banner of "economic development," fail to adopt and enforce effective land-use and design standards, and elect politicians with no sense of the future whose only concern is how to get reelected in two, four, or six years. In others words, we have talked a good game about environmental concerns, the planning process, building a better future in human settlement form, but have failed miserably in taking the necessary action to make any of the processes to accomplish these goals really effective.

This rather pessimistic conclusion certainly was more than justified from my site visits and interviews in 15 cities across the country that were the basis of *Planning America's Communities: Paradise Found? Paradise Lost,* my book published by APA's Planners Press in 1991. In only three cities did I find that the planning process was truly working because of the "planning attitude" of citizens and elected officials. Two others had a past history of highly successful planning, but both, due to a changed form of government, lost their sense of comprehensive planning evident in prior years. In almost all of the other 10, planning tended to be largely "lip service" on the part of the elected officials. Merging this observation with the rest of my 44 years experience as a planning professional somewhat familiar with numerous towns and cities causes me—while recognizing that these selected cities were only a sample—to conclude that they reasonably reflect what is true nationwide.

So, because this and the earlier forewords combined are reflective of my frustration throughout my life after I entered into planning as a profession, the others are again included. At the same time, they show that I am stubborn, persistent, concerned, and determined never to abandon the hope that a way can be found, call it a miracle if you must, to inculcate the importance of collectively adopting a "planning attitude" about our urban form and, further, working to make long-range comprehensive planning an essential element in our society.

Almost as a footnote to the above, I cannot avoid adding another frustration that must be felt today by any writer of books other than fiction novels. There is no way in today's rapid change that one can go through the organization, writing, review, editing, and publication of an informative, analytical, or technical book so that it arrives in the hands of readers and still is considered completely current. In effect, we are writing history when such publication requires about three years from conception to completion. The best hope is that we can learn from that which has passed and be better equipped to adjust to and effectively utilize that which has changed since the author, with the best of intentions, struggled to gather data and information then current and relate it to his or her readers. Perhaps knowing about the planning process's most recent history will help both professional planners and interested laypersons to understand the problems of the past and be better prepared to cope with the sonic speed of changes ahead.

Herbert H. Smith
1992

Second Edition Foreword—1979

When I started this revision of *The Citizen's Guide to Planning,* my intention was to replace my original foreword as outdated. After reflecting about it, I decided, instead, to leave it intact and to comment on it. Rereading what I had written back in 1961 caused me to consider a whole series of questions about our society and our system and about the status of things as they are now compared to our attitudes and condition 10 or 15 years ago. Have we made a better country or a better world? Have we learned from past mistakes, or are we merely repeating our previous ones? Do we have any better understanding of the value of precious resources, the environment, social justice, and orderly development? Have we reached the point at which we understand the difference between exploitation and deriving a fair and just return on private investment that does not demand public subsidy for undue enrichment or selfish interests? Are we able to point with pride to informed, concerned, and responsive leaders and elected officials who put community good above personal interests?

From an entirely cynical viewpoint, one could answer all such questions with a resounding "No," although that might be an unfair generalization. Nevertheless, even the most optimistic among us would have to admit realistically that, while we have made progress in some of the areas of concern, we, the American public, have been "weighed in the balance and found wanting." We have continued to take too much for granted, to assume that technology will solve all of our problems, to consider those who cry out about the rape of our landscape and our resources as "kooks," and to lull ourselves complacently into a false sense of security while being anesthetized by an electronic marvel that projects pictures and sound and succeeds only in turning life into a spectator sport.

It is a certainty that neither this book nor any other is going to change either human nature or a great many attitudes. Even so, after 30 years of frequent frustration over our lack of concern, I continue to hope for the future and have faith in our system and our people. Many have grown in awareness and the voices of our concerned citizens, now much louder, are being heard. Neighborhoods are becoming a rallying point for organization, involvement, and legitimate demands for effective community development and planning. Citizen action groups are finding that well-stated and well-supported positions can be convincingly put forth to affect planned change based upon genuine community interest. In short, there are winds of change—change for the better—blowing on the American scene. It is my hope that my small effort in revising this book can help to keep those winds blowing.

Therefore, I have broadened the purpose of this second edition. While initially I have wanted *The Citizen's Guide to Planning* to be useful to all interested citizens, I directed my first edition largely toward members of planning boards. With the changes that have now taken place in our cities and rural areas, with the shift in the direction of planning and, especially, of the federal programs that have been to a large measure the supporting financial base, all of us—not just the members of our elected or appointed bodies—must be informed. We need civic leaders, neighborhood organizers, educators, and young people who are aware that the future, their future, is too important to leave to the work of others or to chance. This book is intended to provide some thought and encouragement to any concerned person who is resolved to be more a part of the future.

At the time I first wrote the book, after having been a practicing planner in both the public and private sectors for 13 years, I am afraid I was convinced there were not many of the "whys" and "wherefores" of planning that I didn't know. It was my belief then, however, and still is now, that planners spend altogether too much time talking to each other and far too little time trying to explain the importance of meaningful planning to the general public. I may never know whether my attempt to present what I then thought I knew was successful at all, even though the book went through seven printings. I do know, having added another 16 years to my professional experience (in private practice and as a city planning director, city manager, and planning educator), that I have come to a stage in life when I realize how little I knew earlier. I also know that I probably have even fewer answers to the question of how effective planning can and should be done now. Hopefully, this can be taken as a sign of maturing. Nevertheless, there is one thing that I knew in 1961 but now know more factually and with an even deeper conviction than I have ever known it: there is no more important problem facing the American people than that of how to make community planning effective in a democratic society.

Original Foreword—1961

As communities are increasingly beset by problems of growth and development, as they struggle to provide essential municipal services without bankrupting themselves, as the great metropolitan areas sprawl ever outward, the realization grows that we must adjust our attitudes toward community organization if we are to preserve traditional values. The word "planning" is increasingly bandied about—but what does it mean?

Unfortunately, there is a lack of common understanding of the meaning of the word. In the minds of most of our citizens, it evokes no clear-cut concept: in the jargon of the advertising agency, no image is created. Until very recently, planning activities have too often been confined to mere academic exercises undertaken by professionals, and understood—if at all—only by other professionals. As the emphasis on the rebuilding of the cities and the planning of suburban towns continues to increase, more and more citizens find themselves appointed to planning boards or commissions. Often armed only with good intentions, a vague idea of what planning is all about, and a willingness to learn, the member of the planning board (the term "planning board" will be used hereafter as synonymous with "planning commission") needs a source of information written in plain language. The purpose of this book is to set forth the meaning of planning in terms understandable by all interested laymen.

It has been my intention to write a book primarily for the newly appointed member of a planning board or a newly interested private citizen, and the book has been organized to cover the areas of planning most likely to be encountered by such a person. To the greatest extent possible, I have avoided technical terminology, statistical formulas, and detailed study outlines. The book is based upon my personal experience and sets forth information obtained and conclusions reached during my participation in some 200 municipal planning programs, a number of county and regional planning projects, and a state planning program.

The observations which follow are based upon the sincere belief that planning is an extremely desirable governmental function, and that the prospects for communities which attempt to face the future without sound planning are frightening to behold. We can and must be better informed on this subject if our efforts to build better communities are not to be wasted.

CHAPTER

1

The Reasons for Planning

We can no longer say that we do not foresee the consequence of our actions. It is perfectly clear that because of the things that today we do to the land and to the water and to the air around us, we are laying up a store of troubles, a store of expenses, a store of injury and an abundance of shortages for future generations. Yet our public philosophy does nothing much more than click its tongue at the offenders. This is a philosophy which needs changing.[1]

Hundreds of thousands of words are written yearly about human exploitation of natural resources, our misuse of the land, and the increasingly complex organization of our urban communities. Again and again the same conclusion is reached: if order is to be created out of chaos, the solution will be found in the process of planning. Certainly no acceptable and workable alternative has been found permitting us to overcome the myriad problems we have created for ourselves in environment, land development, economic conditions, and quality of life. Yet mere observance provides overwhelming evidence that we as a society have not accepted this maxim that organized planning is the only way in a capitalistic, "democratic" society that the damage we have done, and are doing to ourselves, can be stopped and perhaps corrected.

Community building of a physical form is done largely by private individuals on private land, but based upon public provision of infrastructure, cultural quality, recreation facilities and open space. However, we have not been willing to act: to accept the fact that the amenities provided by the public sector create a community interest in how each piece of land is to be used and developed equal to or even exceeding that of the private interest or "private right." Until we do understand this and take appropriate steps to control our land resources for the societal interest, we will continue to create chaos—costly, inefficient, unsightly, and destructive of quality of life.

Here is just a quick look at some of the things with which we have failed to deal dynamically and effectively. With the development of the automobile, people have gained vastly increased freedom of movement. Their desire to escape from crowded and deteriorating cities has become manifest in the horizontal metropolises of the automobile age. Starting from the central cores of established cities, Americans have expanded outward, first in concentric rings and then along the corridors of major roadways in the pattern often called urban sprawl. In the flight from the city, however, the suburban dweller does not leave behind an acquired taste for the conveniences of city life and desire for organized (and expensive) municipal services. The suburban family wants its children's schools to be well-staffed and efficient. They expect round-the-clock police and fire protection. If garbage and trash are not collected once a week, they become extremely upset. Frequently, they find themselves so closely crowded against neighbors in an area that recently was rural that public water and sewerage facilities must be installed to protect the public health. More often than not, new recruits to the open spaces will want the convenience of nearby shopping facilities as well, provided, of course, that the gasoline station or delicatessen isn't built next door to their house.

In the meantime, city dwellers face increasing problems of their own. No longer do they have a stable tax base that permits the provision of adequate municipal services. No longer do they live in the midst of a large residential complex of solid citizens interested in their community and filled with civic pride. The central business district becomes more difficult to maintain as trade is lost to suburban shopping centers. There seems to be no end to the number of cars for which adequate parking spaces must be found; automobiles clog every major street. Older residential areas suddenly seem outmoded, deteriorated, even blighted. Costly corrective measures must be taken, and urban renewal projects involving the relocation of families, the acquisition of properties, and the clearance and rebuilding of whole blocks at a time seem the only solution.

IF YOU DANCE, YOU GOTTA PAY THE PIPER

Whether we live in the suburbs or in the city, we are faced with soaring taxes, an inadequate supply of available housing for all economic groups, rising crime rates, increasing pollution, inadequate streets and roads, decreasing services, decaying municipal facilities, and insufficient and inefficient school systems. There is only one way that the means of meeting the costs of improving the situation can be found: these funds must come from the money you and I pay in federal, state, and local taxes.

During the period from 1950 to 1980, federal funding increased greatly to assist in paying for some of these essential facilities and services and we became too dependent upon this source, even though it came from taxes we as individuals paid. Since 1980, there has been a complete reversal with the change of federal policy to limit spending and pass on to the states the responsibility of providing funding or finding a solution. Many state legislatures, such as the one in Colorado, have failed or been unable, due to their own tight financial situation, to step in to fill this gap. That still leaves us with the factual, inescapable reality that there is only one way to meet the costs of improving the situation—that is from the taxes we pay. Now, more than ever, we must accept that satisfactory services and desirable amenities, the things distinguishing a good community from just another blot on the landscape, must come from the municipal tax base. Unless this tax base is sound and continually improves, the ever-rising demand for services cannot be met.

This leaves local governments searching for every kind of tax, fee, service charge or any other possible source of revenue such as increased ratables (more taxable development) to just keep up with maintenance and prevent total deterioration. They find themselves in a real dilemma with the growing numbers of "tax revolt"-minded residents who insist that they will not accept *any* increase in the tax rate or real estate reevaluation. As has been the case over the years, the real estate property tax provides a large portion of the total tax bill we pay, with somewhat less dependency on property tax as was true during the days of myriad federal funding programs, local officials find that they must "bite the bullet" and, once again, begin to increase this very obvious and unpopular tax. Not something that any of them looking forward to an election have the courage or the desire to do.

Unfortunately, we have been told that the only way the tax base can be improved or even maintained is if we encourage all forms of growth, adopt no regulations or restrictions that will hamper "free enterprise" in any way, and, certainly, never demand that development be anything more than mediocre. To do otherwise, we are told, simply will drive away economic opportunities and preclude the creation of jobs for our people. But will it really?

In an analysis entitled, "Does Development Really Pay for Itself?" in Public Investment, published September 1991 by the American Planning Association, it was reported by the county's regional planning commissioner that the impacts of development on DuPage County, Illinois, may actually cause property taxes to rise. DuPage County, west of Chicago, has enjoyed a period of rapid and substantial growth encouraged by both residents and political leaders, who sought to bring about a higher quality of life and an enhanced tax base that would pay for better schools, public services, and roads. This empirical study found that the relationship between taxation rates and new development was *positive*; one underlying reason may be that current fiscal impact analyses may be too narrowly focused on one school or fire or police district rather than on cumulative impacts. The study found that the increased land value brought on by development is not paying for the development-caused burdens on public infrastructure and services.[2]

In thinking about desirable, attractive cities or neighborhoods you have seen—the places that made you think, "How nice it would be to live there"—what about them did you find attractive? Was it that their people had no sense of purpose and direction and left things to chance, being satisfied with whatever happened; or was it because someone cared, someone bothered to plan, and those involved recognized that quality and excellence are important and can be achieved? If the truth were known, it would be that the residents of desirable neighborhoods have discovered that quality breeds excellence and that the higher you set your standards, the more you are sought out by those looking to make sound economic investments.

The city of Albuquerque, New Mexico, with which I was once associated, should have learned this the hard way some time ago. Its officials made a zoning change in violation of an adopted future land-use plan so that a major industry could locate in an expanding residential area. The space should have been used for a school and open space to add stability to the residences; but the company wanted "freeway exposure," refused to consider other sites in an excellent industrial park already zoned, and threatened to go to another community if it didn't get its way. The change was made, and the plant is now surrounded by a KOA campground and some rather ill-conceived mobile-home parks.

Having revisited Albuquerque during the research for *Planning America's Communities,* it was obvious that not much had been learned from that experience, and planning for the future still is permitted to be ineffectual.

The better cities and the better neighborhoods (and this does not simply mean more wealthy) know that Dr. John R. Silber, president of Boston University, was right when he said in an article on excellence in *Harper's* magazine:

> The only standard of performance that can sustain a free society is excellence. It is increasingly claimed, however, that excellence is at odds with democracy; increasingly we are urged to offer a dangerous embrace to mere adequacy. . . . Our flight from excellence is profoundly philosophical. Out of a well-intentioned but inept concern with quality of opportunity, we have begun to reject anything that exceeds anyone's grasp. Some might argue that it is our right to engage in this curious flight, and so it is, the right of free men to be fools. But do we have the right as citizens in a free society to reject excellence on behalf of others who may not be so foolish?

Thus, if we are really honest with ourselves, we know that in the area of land and resource utilization, people, if left to their individual devices, will be seduced by the siren of exploitation in our erstwhile "free enterprise" system. Collective society's use of the planning process is the only way that this can be overcome, excellence achieved, the errors of the past corrected, current mistakes avoided, and future misjudgments held to a minimum.

A very simple analogy can be drawn between putting together an old fashioned jigsaw puzzle and the formation, growth, and development of a village, town, or city. In the puzzle, the task is to find a corner with which to start: look for the right shape, right color, and image that will fit nicely into that corner. The puzzle is then completed by continuing to find the next right piece until the picture or design lies beautifully on the table as a finished picture. That is exactly the way a community of whatever size is built. As each piece of property is developed or each new subdivision of land and its development occurs—whether it be for residential, commercial, or industrial purposes—as streets and utilities are installed, the community of the future takes shape a piece at a time.

The use made of the land, the physical organization of the developed area, the resulting population density and the quality, good or bad, after development are the primary determinants of the need for municipal facilities and services. When the costs for these are added, together with schools, libraries, public buildings, etc., you get the total amount of revenue that needs to be derived from the taxes, fees, and other sources of revenue available to the community. A most important factor to remember is that the quality of any new development and the existing development of land becomes the base for the net valuation taxable from which the real estate property tax is obtained.

Tax assessments are based upon values of land and real property improvements, which, in turn, are a reflection of the standards and characteristics of any given area. The logic of insisting upon quality development in these times of municipal financial crisis would appear to be beyond question, except to those whose only objective is speculative personal enrichment. Thus the role of the planning process, the leadership of the planners and the elected officials, becomes increasingly important in seeing that orderly, economically sound development is what results from each piece of that community-building jigsaw puzzle. A well-supported, citizen-based municipal planning program is the only way, however, that the wisdom of this logic can be applied to governmental structure. Planning for the future development of any community is not only good sense, it is good business.

Although the percentage of total local and state revenue derived from the real estate property tax has been declining, the overall amount continues to increase and remains a large portion of that which supports governmental services. As shown in Table 1 on page 8, there are three major tax sources available to state and local governments. These are property, sales, and income taxes. Good planning can, or should, be the way in which any government, especially municipal government, sees that costs are properly contained. These revenue sources, as a result of the quality of the community, can remain stable while not being punitive. To emphasize the way in which all taxes have geometrically increased, statistics are included for 1978-79 and 1988-89.

The U.S. Census Bureau reports that of the $67.5 billion that local governments collected in 1976, 81 percent came from property taxes—about nine percent of each American's income. The average paid was $266 per property, as compared with $160—an increase of 60 percent from the previous year. It was just such statistics that induced Californians to go to the polls in June 1978 and pass Proposition 13 by better than a two-to-one vote and constitutionally limit the taxation on real estate. The taxpayer revolt was off and running. (See Chapter 13, Some Things to Think About)

As a result of the taxpayers' revolt, including an impetus such as California's Proposition 13 (the "Mother of All Tax Limitations"), all elected officials have become even more hesitant to increase any tax as clearly visible as the real estate property tax. Instead they turn to the revenue sources that most closely meet the classification of "hidden tax," such as those mentioned above. Unfortunately, the unpropitious revenue situation has also motivated a greater use of the most regressive tax of all, the sales tax. When viewed in a broader perspective, regardless of the varied tax sources and taxpayers' revolts, figures showing the amount of increased taxation are more than just a bit astounding.

More recent analyses of the sources of taxation, as shown on Table 1, indicates that while income tax collections have risen more than those of property taxes, there remains a major dependence on the real estate property tax. Nationally, between 1979 and 1989, property tax receipts increased at a lower rate, up 119.5 percent, than either general sales, up 141.8 percent, or income, up 152.2 percent. In Colorado, this national decrease of reliance on the property tax is not as obvious as shown by the 132.87 percent increase in this tax, yet the 153.62 percent rise in sales tax collections is almost the same as nationally. This situation may well indicate support for the conclusion that, since 1976, government in Colorado has been taken for a ride by the purveyors of the philosophy that all growth is good if it purports to bring any increase in the real estate property tax, even if it later becomes more of a problem than a benefit. Along with this has come a significant decrease in local officials' support for meaningful planning and zoning when the exact opposite should have been the case.

A PENNY SAVED IS A PENNY EARNED

Logical patterns of land use based upon the needs and desires of individual communities can be established through planning and enforced through zoning. Attractive, carefully developed, orderly communities have inherently sound economic foundations. When we permit haphazard, disorganized, and unattractive development, we allow the destruction of the very essence of sound community life. In effect, we require those citizens who take pride in their property to

Table 1. State and Local Taxes and Selected Spending (Millions)

	1978–79	1988–89	Increase	% Change
United States				
Taxes				
Property	64,944	142,525	77,581	119.46%
General Sales	46,599	112,598	66,093	141.84%
Income	49,060	123,729	74,669	152.20%
Other	44,951	89,795	44,844	99.76%
Total	205,554	468,647	263,133	128.01%
Own Source General Revenue	268,115	660,020	391,905	146.17%
Colorado				
Taxes				
Property	904.7	2,106.8	1,202.1	132.87%
General Sales	797.1	1,521.8	724.7	90.92%
Income	569.4	1,444.1	874.7	153.62%
Other	423.9	866.9	443.0	104.51%
Total	2,695.1	5,939.6	3,244.5	120.39%
Own Source General Revenue	3,696.8	8,810.3	5,113.5	138.32%
Selected Expenditures				
United States				
K–12 Education	83,385	185,171	101,786	122.07%
Higher Education	30,059	67,550	37,491	124.72%
Social Services*	41,898	97,879	55,981	133.61%
Transportation	28,440	58,093	29,653	104.27%
Total General Expenditures	327,517	762,311	434,794	132.75%
Colorado				
K–12 Education	1,170.6	2,543.1	1,372.5	117.25%
Higher Education	574.6	979.6	375.0	65.26%
Social Services*	385.7	951.0	565.3	146.56%
Transportation	397.7	935.8	556.1	146.46%
Total General Expenditures	4,153.7	9,868.9	5,715.2	137.59%

* Includes Maintenance

Source: U.S. Census Bureau, Government Finances, 1978–79/1988–89.

subsidize the exploitation of the community by the entrepreneur whose sole interest is in a maximum profit from real estate development.

Many examples can be cited to substantiate the practical wisdom of planning for the future. During my private consulting days, a municipality saved tens of thousands of dollars through its planning program by anticipating the extension of the municipal sewer system in advance of the construction of a railroad overpass. By arranging for the installation of the necessary sewer pipes (even though they were not to be used immediately) at the time of the construction of the overpass, the municipality saved not only a sizable amount of money but also a great deal of inconvenience.

In another community in which I worked for a number of years, several hundred thousand dollars were saved by the careful study and redesign of proposed subdivisions. In many cases, it was possible to reduce the length of streets, resulting in both a lower initial cost for the developer and lower maintenance costs for the municipality. By relating proposed subdivisions to a master plan for future development, the right-of-way for a projected major street was assembled through dedication, at no cost to the municipality.

On the other side of the coin, I saw a city pay $12,000 for a small parcel of land essential to the improvement of a street intersection. Nine years before, the city had acquired the very same parcel through tax delinquency but, in its anxiety to return it to the tax rolls (and in the absence of any long-range plan), the city had sold the land for $360.

More recently, Albuquerque, in order to preserve a scenic mountain backdrop for the public and prevent developers from dotting it with housing, paid $3,000 an acre for 520 acres of land most suited for mountain goats. The irony of this is that, only about 15 years before, this same land had been sold for delinquent taxes for about $50 per acre, the buyers having to pay nothing down, nothing on the principal over the years, and only a very nominal interest rate. The city was not planning-conscious at the time and saw no reason to be concerned. Incidentally, the land buyers, most of whom were "pillars" of the community, wanted $7,500 an acre for the land from the city, and it was only by some strong-arm tactics and the threat of public reaction that they were "encouraged" to allow the purchase at the "bargain" price. Endless examples of this kind could be cited, many of them far more expensive to the taxpayer.

No thinking person, I suppose, doubts that a community can save money through sound planning, but one of the most important reasons for planning is intangible. Few of us can say honestly that we are satisfied with the kind of environment we are creating in and around our communities. If we look at the general aspect of our cities, towns, and suburbs, what do we see? Have they been improving, and is life being made more pleasant, enjoyable, sensible, and orderly for our people? Are we eliminating the sore spots of obsolescence and decay, strengthening our central business cores, and overcoming the bottlenecks of traffic and parking? Are we conserving our open space and providing future generations with an opportunity to experience the pleasures of light, green areas, or, even more importantly, decent air to breathe? Or are we continuing to make the same mistake with respect to these essential elements that we have made in the past? Unfortunately, the evidence seems to indicate that where we don't have planning, or in some of our floundering approaches to planning, we are missing a golden opportunity to improve our environment and the quality of the places in which we live. One gets the impression, in fact, that in many cases we are not only repeating these mistakes but are compounding them in our haste to pursue economic gain.

This is not to take away from the admirable efforts that have been made in some quarters or to deny that we have perhaps prevented the situation from being worse than it is. I find it hard to believe, however, that we have done the best that we can do. One needs only to drive some of our major land-service highways with a sense of awareness to realize that all of that despicable highway clutter was not built before the advent of supposedly advanced thinking in planning and zoning. We still accept the preposterous notion that the ownership of highway frontage endows an individual with the right to capitalize on every possible opportunity for economic self-betterment at the expense of the public. We still permit entrepreneurs and developers, in their anxiety to build hot dog stands, gas stations, fast food outlets, discount marts, and ill-conceived shopping centers, to assure us that no one is willing to live next to a highway and that the idea of open space or green areas went out with the horse and buggy. Yet for years some of the most sought after residential sites have been those with reverse frontage along highways such as the Merritt Parkway in Connecticut and the Garden State Parkway in New Jersey. Nor is this exploitation confined to our highways. An examination of our cities will show that, while more and more of us are talking about the importance of planning and zoning, some of the politicians still ignore plans, making destructive zoning changes under the guise of increasing tax ratables and granting zoning variances that eat the very heart out of the principles of planning and zoning.

As a result of recession conditions, the drastic cut in federal domestic aid, and the resultant need for local governments to fight for economic survival the term "economic development" has become even more the "in thing." Before going further, let it be made clear that I am all for *good* economic development. Unfortunately, there is no standard for the term and very few understand that there is a difference between good and *bad* economic development. This is vividly reflected by the fact that the most deceptive, misleading words in vogue today are "economic development" as they are mistakenly applied and accepted by people and elected officials in communities everywhere.

As far as cities are concerned, these two words are being turned into something just as life threatening as cancer or being hooked on crack or any form of dope. Everything labeled "economic development" is not necessarily good economic growth and, in many cases is unsound, speculative "schlock." Unfortunately, planning standards and zoning regulations are being thrown out the window in our eagerness to cater to exploitative developers who tell us that what they propose will create new jobs and tax ratables; however, the community's well thought out standards must be relaxed "a little bit" or else they will go to some other place with their "prize economic development package." In this case, the best possible answer is to tell them *to please do so!*

Once again our communities—villages, towns, or cities—have reached the point where they must make a choice. That choice is whether we allow ourselves to be suckered by believing that economic development provides surviving competitiveness or whether we choose to believe that the importance of maintaining quality is what really pays off and insist that this latter will be the path we will follow. Which of these choices our communities decide to make will determine the future of America's character and quality of life.

Communities which, and people who, consider economic development to be anything purporting to provide jobs and stimulate tax revenues and who think that a piecemeal approach is the panacea for solving problems are deluding themselves badly. Without fail, when a municipality ignores its master plan or doesn't have one, changes its plan, changes a zoning ordinance, or grants a variance to allow something to happen as a result of being sold economic development by that smooth-talking developer or pressure from a few misguided citizens, the results are more problems created than any tax revenue generated can pay for or correct. This conclusion certainly is verified by the DuPage County report to which reference has been made.

THE LAND OF PLENTY—WITH SO MUCH NEED

Why is this so? Why have we failed to get the most out of the planning process and do as well as other countries such as Great Britain, Sweden, and Norway in building new towns and getting the most out of our existing cities? We have more of everything—more land, more cars, more money, more schools, more television, and more chances for advancing our society—but, by all standards of quality and sensibility, we seem determined to fail. I suggest that there may be four basic reasons for this. The first, and probably the most fundamental, is the existence of widespread apathy based upon a frighteningly materialistic attitude. We have been "Madison Avenue'd" to the point that ideals and principles have become entirely secondary to things, goods, products, and a rising standard of living. This has resulted in an unconcern on the part of the general public toward supporting sound principles of objective planning. It can be summed up by the rather callous attitude, not often openly expressed, that seems to prevail in a lot of us: "I don't care what you do to my town or how much you put in your pocket so long as I get mine."

The second reason for failure is the fact that our society lacks almost totally a clear concept of the meaning of good planning and zoning. It might even be said that we have no clear concept of what a really good city should be for our day and age. We certainly haven't seen many, and it is, therefore, hard to picture what good planning could do for us. Try, for example, running a little survey of your own. Stop 10 people on the street and ask them to describe city planning for you. If you can get any of them even to attempt it, which is doubtful, you will get as many different descriptions as there are people who respond. (As a matter of fact, I still have trouble when people ask me what I "do." When I say I am a planner, the usual response is, "Oh, that's nice. What do you plant?") Our people are not informed on the subject and thus cannot be expected to have a concept. The general public is unaware of any objective standard by which to judge results. People put up with poor planning because they are told it is good and they have no way of knowing otherwise.

Thirdly, and as a corollary, we are suffering from an undisciplined approach to the techniques of planning. If one wishes to be a doctor, lawyer, or scientist, one pursues a reasonably standard course of study, exercising much the same organized perseverance regardless of the school one chooses. In many instances, one then submits to examination, obtains a license, procures a registration, or establishes oneself in a profession. Not so in planning. Anybody can be an expert, and anyone who has read an article on the subject of planning or held up his or her hand to be sworn in on a planning board can develop the expert complex. As a result, the function of planning suffers, and so do our communities.

Finally, as is true in so many other areas of our complicated social structure, we are suffering from a lack of aggressive, imaginative, and inspiring leadership. This ties in with the first of these reasons for our planning difficulties. When people are unconcerned, when affairs of government are left to others, when business leaders live in the suburbs to escape city problems, when financial forces are little interested in the true economic health of the community that is essentially their lifeblood, we will have lackeys and hacks in positions of importance and lackluster leadership will prevail.

If our cities are to survive, if we are ever to have well-planned and well-developed communities, we must begin to recognize that the way to achieve these objectives will depend entirely on a changing public attitude that will demand inspired and inspiring leadership. This leadership qualification should apply to mayors, every elected official, planning commission chairpersons, and, as much as possible, to the entire administrative system. Experience has shown that, given a mayor who is a true leader, things can be made to happen, the inspirational example can, and does, filter through not only to other governmental positions, but to the business community and the private sector as well. Such leadership inspires a sense of place, a sense of pride, and an interest by individual residents in becoming more involved personally. This occurs because they feel that their efforts won't be wasted, that someone will listen to them and that things can be made to happen. One such inspired leader, former Mayor Neil Goldschmidt, was the cause of a complete turnaround leading to the revitalization of the city of Portland, Oregon. This same interest in the community and the pride of place continues on there today, long after that mayor went on to higher political office.

How can the public attitude be changed so that such leadership becomes the expected, not just accidental good fortune when, and if, by a fortuitous circumstance it happens? There is no doubt that in today's society this is a most difficult, but not impossible, task. It can be done in one of two ways. The first can be the basis for people to become involved and insist on better leadership, but this is not the pleasant or desirable way. That is, things can get so bad that a serious crisis occurs concerning police or fire protection, delivery of services, commission of crimes, lack of good planning and zoning, or a great variety of other mishaps. The other way, the desirable one, is for one or more small groups of people with a planning attitude and a concern for the future to determine to inform and educate others about how much better their community could be with the right kind of elected leadership. Along with this must go the understanding that this is all to be based on more effective long-range planning and the goal of building a better town or city.

The objective should be to sufficiently inform as many people as possible within the community to the point that they recognize the necessity of electing capable leaders at the next election. A small group should be created that will accept the responsibility for a thorough search of voting records, involvement in meetings, actions initiated and successfully completed by all those presently holding public elected office. This information should then be made widely available. The next step would be to encourage people to demand discussions of the issues—not negative campaigning—and a clear statement of each candidate's platform and program for the future. Anyone approached by a candidate should ask that person for a copy of these position statements and demand that they state how they stand, if elected, regarding stronger and better long-range planning and support for effectuating action to carry that planning forward. The key is to get a firm commitment (if such is possible from any politician today).

With this kind of information, small or large groups, neighborhood organizations, or other civic groups can arrange to meet together and exchange information, then decide if any of the declared candidates can provide the kind of leadership sought. If not, then look for someone in the community who can, and pledge to support and work for them to get elected. Such grassroots groundswells have successfully turned inertia-plagued governments around in the past and still can do so even in these apathetic times. There is nothing more important than dynamic leadership to a community, county, state or national government in determining the future which we now face and that following generations will inherit.

THERE IS NO SUCH THING AS THE "RIGHT OF EXPLOITATION"

If things are not as rosy as they should be, perhaps we should ask ourselves if it isn't time for more effective action; that is, if we believe that the argument for the desirability of conserving and, yes, even saving our American cities, can be and should be one of the most convincing arguments of our times. I am equally convinced that we cannot save our cities without effective planning and zoning. Our past has proved that we need organized planning to improve conditions for societal living and for mankind, even though it carries with it restriction and regulation. It has been said that people are never more inconsiderate in their dealings with their neighbors than when it comes to land utilization. If this is true—and a poorly planned city is the best possible evidence—it is certainly unfortunate. To ignore the fact that cities can be improved through the development of an orderly sense of purpose and objective is to admit that we cannot learn and instead are doomed to ultimate stagnation by our obstinate unwillingness to change or improve.

We need effective planning to make better economic sense out of our cities and our counties. Land and its resources are our most important assets, and the wise utilization of them our greatest opportunity for continuing a sound economy. Exploitation and the misuse of land can result in dire economic consequences for us all. Where, in all of our history and legal precepts, has it been said that a system of public subsidy for personal enrichment—for those clever enough to take full advantage of the opportunity—is the system sanctioned, made sacred, and not to be questioned in a democratic society? Where can it be found in constitutions, laws, or precedents that a collective group of people as a society must accept placidly the idea that resources and land, regardless of ownership, carry with them the right of speculation and wealth, notwithstanding the effect such "rights" may have upon genuine public interest?

This public interest, which no one with any understanding of our constitutional law can deny exists, is the basis for the term "community interest" mentioned at the beginning of this chapter. An irony exists in that it can be best defined and defended by real estate brokers' timeworn answer to the question of what three things determine the value of property—*location, location, location.* This is true, but what determines the value of any "location"? Tour your community and pick out what you consider to be the most valuable and desirable residential property. Study what is around it in the way of neighborhood character. Notice the paved street, sidewalks, fire hydrant, street trees and consider the nearby school, the other public amenities of the community, the police and fire protection, and even the garbage collection—all provided with public funds.

Now in your mind pick up that structure (and it could be a commercial or industrial property) and place it in the most remote area imaginable, such as a Colorado valley or plateau west of the Continental Divide. What has happened then to its value once the location has lost what the public sector and community quality have contributed? We now have a very clear illustration of why there is a legal claim that "community interest" exists in the development, even the maintenance, of every piece of land. Yet, we still allow ourselves to be duped by the "growth is progress" and "anything purporting to be economic development is good" spellbinders (frequently empowered by those who have taken successfully from the land and the community and never given back).

Planning is necessary for the sheer survival of our society in the form that we deem desirable. This never was more glaringly true than it is today with economic recession, the constant threat of an energy crisis, rampant pollution, water shortages in many places, the presence of hazardous wastes, environmental destruction, increasing homelessness, and the overall social crisis in our cities. Improved communities, housing conditions, open spaces, recreational areas, and other aspects of workable city structure are essential to our mental as well as to our economic health. We cannot go on destroying our natural resources, obliterating our landscapes, or planting our fields with 2-by-4 cracker boxes called houses in a dreary, discouraging atmosphere and expect to maintain any kind of a sound social structure.

We desperately need to remember the philosophy of the early native American Indians in their reverence of the land, including the belief that it was not theirs to harm as they saw fit, but rather, their use of it was only a form of stewardship. This meant that they were to respect, preserve, and enhance it to pass it on to their children's children in better condition that when they assumed their stewardship responsibility. Today, more than ever before, as our society becomes more complicated and complex, each of us must recognize that we have an individual moral responsibility to do our best to improve our community, large or small, as well as our total environment. In accepting this responsibility we must exert an effort to support the causes that will permit us collectively to achieve improvement and the preservation of our quality of life.

Planning for our cities, towns, and villages is the major means by which the environment, community character, and our own individual way of life can be improved and our responsibility met. Along with this go two fundamental principles to keep in mind, both while reading this book and long afterwards. The first is that good planning can occur only from citizen concern, commitment, and contribution in the way of involvement. The second is that, to be successful, planning has to be made a meaningful part of our political process. Electing anyone who has not made it clear that he or she stands foursquare for effective community planning is like inviting the fox into the chicken coop. If our communities are not to be bankrupted by wasteful and uncoordinated development, we must have workable, practical plans for the future. If we are not to be overwhelmed by man-made ugliness, inefficient and uneconomical community structures, we must see to it that our plans are implemented and that they work.

> I believe that planning is best described as an attitude. It is recognition and acceptance of change. It is faith in the future, not starry-eyed worship but belief based on a realistic appraisal.
>
> It is faith in the ability of men working through democracy to meet and solve the problems of the future. It is willingness to try and to keep trying to work out common problems as honestly, as efficiently, as sympathetically as we possibly can.
>
> Above all, it a shared belief in democracy—shared alike by citizens and officials. Unless we make common cause, we are lost.[3]

NOTES

1. Marjorie S. Berger, ed., *Dennis O'Harrow: Plain Talk and Plan Talk,* (Chicago: Planners Press, American Planning Association, 1981), p. 39.

2. *Public Investment* (September 1991), pp. 1-3.

3. Berger, p. 5.

CHAPTER

2

The Development of Planning

Whether we realize it or not, governmental planning at the federal, state, county, and local levels is all around us; some aspects of our day-to-day lives are constantly being planned or, perhaps, programmed or effectuated. While there are those who disagree in principle with this fact, as our social structure has become more and more complex, it has become a necessary process if we are to preserve our resources and assets and avoid ever greater chaos in the future. This is especially true for our communities, both large and small. The major cutbacks in federal aid programs have been combined with the unwillingness, or inability, of some states to assume a greater financial role to help local government deal with the rising costs of meeting requirements mandated by these same states and the federal government. These factors, together with the maintenance of their infrastructure and public service, have caused cities and towns to face one of the greatest challenges ever—economic survival. The real concern we should have and the questions we should ask are not whether planning is being done, but rather are we sure that it is desirable, is it the best planning possible and, most importantly, are we playing a part in that planning process? It is certain that we will never know unless we accept our responsibility as citizens and become involved instead of sitting back and complaining about what "they" are doing or have done.

Planning as a process has progressed from the largely theoretical and frequently impractical ivory-tower approach to today's deliberate, hardheaded analysis of all aspects of city, community, and regional problems, whether they be physical, social, economic, or environmental. No longer is the planner concerned merely with the physical design or growth of a given area. Now he or she deals with the sometimes staggering issues of housing, social programs, downtown rebuilding, parks and open space, schools, sewers, employment potentials, street and road improvement—all of the municipal needs and facilities that must be supported by taxes and that hit the taxpayers where they feel it most: in their pocketbooks.

Today, any municipality in any state can organize a planning program as a governmental function. Your community may have already done so. Not only do state statutes allow municipalities to engage in planning activities, but in most states planning is encouraged at county and regional levels. Specific procedures are established by this state legislation, frequently referred to as an "enabling act." Such acts include not only the creation process for a planning commission by local governing bodies, but also the duties, responsibilities, and procedures that each commission must follow. Especially important is the section (or sections) dealing with the conduct of required public hearings before action can be taken on certain matters. The reader is urged to obtain a copy of her or his state enabling act and become familiar with it as this provides the framework for helping to determine the effectiveness of the planning process in your community. Doing so may even help to encourage more individual involvement in the planning process.

EVOLUTION IS INESCAPABLE

While no attempt will be made in this book to explore thoroughly all the influences of the past and the complete historic evolution of communities and urban form, a quick review of some of the major milestones is important to understanding today's problems and current planning endeavors. Cities have been "planned" to one extent or another for almost as long as they have been built. Even the earliest prehistoric villages and ancient cities had preconceived form as well as controls designed to achieve that form. From the earliest time of the grouping together of people into communities, there have been fundamental reasons for cities other than what may be described as an inherent need for societal living. These reasons have included dictates and desires of rulers, protection, availability of resources, culture, education, commerce, trade, and economic betterment. In order to respond to these various requisites, cities were located in particular places because of the topography, climate, available water, or tactical advantages that made communal living possible, desirable, or sensible. Bodies of water, the confluence of rivers, and river valleys, for example, became the points of origination for many cities.

Many features of these early cities carried over into our cities today, and we have learned much from the city builders and "planners" of Egypt, Greece, Italy, France, Sweden, and Great Britain. The major milestones that have affected American city form and planning up to the 20th century, however, are chiefly these:

1. The rectilinear (gridiron) city plan credited to Hippodamus of Miletus in the 5th century B.C.

2. The invention and spread of gunpowder, beginning in the early 14th century, which made the walled city obsolete and resulted in the spreading out of the urban form.

3. The Renaissance Baroque design form, which gave flexibility to the designer for free-flowing and open city planning.

4. The Industrial Revolution and its technological developments, which changed life-styles and ideas of a standard of living.

5. Colonialism, with its resulting development of commerce and trade and the formation of new settlements and cities.

6. Frontierism and western expansion in the U.S.

7. The English Garden City movement, bringing with it an appreciation of a degree of open space and green living environment.

8. The 1893 World's Columbian Exposition in Chicago and the birth of a neoclassic design style in the U.S.

When one reflects on the cities in which we live today, it is easy to see the influences over the years of these events and their legacies. It is also easy to recognize that none of the above, founded in the technology of their times, anticipated the monstrous effect of the internal-combustion engine, the automobile, and our 20th century subservience to it. Much credit for what we now call urban sprawl and the degradation of our inner cities can be given this obsession to which we have succumbed. Not only are we burdened with the problem of scatteration of new development and the inherent difficulties arising from it, but an even greater planning problem lies in our older cities where it is almost impossible to adapt long-established urban physical structure to 20th- and 21st-century living patterns.

For most people, the start of modern-day city planning is considered to be the 1893 World's Columbian Exposition in Chicago. While it is true that plans for development of many cities had been prepared prior to 1893, the attempt made in Chicago to breathe a bit of aesthetics and social consciousness into urban life was felt strongly during the 36 years between the exposition and the 1929 stock market crash. Some of the best known earlier plans that should be noted were those for Williamsburg, Virginia (settled in 1633); Philadelphia (1682); Savannah, Georgia (1733); Washington, D.C. (1791); Buffalo, New York (1804); and Detroit (1807). The New York City Commission Plan of 1811 should be included as well. As we view these cities today, it is easy to be overly critical about the lack of foresight and the dominance of economic consideration over physical and social amenities, but aren't we still making the same type of shortsighted decisions today in building our urban form?

While many of these plans were lacking in concern for people, especially future generations, nowhere is criticism seemingly more justified than in analyzing the inherited plight of New York City. After rejecting a previous plan by Joseph Mangin, an architect and surveyor, the designated commission was led by the pressures of exploitive interests and economic gain for a few simply to superimpose on Manhattan Island the unimaginative and uninspiring plan we see today.

In their book *The Urban Pattern,* Arthur B. Gallion and Simon Eisner sum it up well:

> The position of the commission was quite clear: "Straight-sided and right-angled houses," they reported, "are the most cheap to build and the most convenient to live in." The matter of economy obviously guided the commission in its deliberations and dictated its conclusions. They found that "the price of land is so uncommonly great" and their proposal for retention of open space was indeed frugal... (it was not until 1856 that the city acquired the land for Central Park at a cost to the citizens of $5,500,000 for the 800 acres.) But it is the economy of the commission that poses the most pertinent issue because it bears strong resemblance to that practiced in later and less happy days of urban planning.... The commission surely expected the city to continue the growth it was then enjoying: They obviously did for they so mapped it for subdivision and sale.... This is the variety of economy that distorts the planning of our cities today ... There were those who protested the formlessness of the commission's plan. Many agreed with Henry R. Aldrich when he claimed its inspiration was "the great facility which it provides for gambling in land values and ready purchase and sale of building blocks" which had "wrought incalculable mischief." It was an omen of the fate to befall the American city in subsequent years.[1]

WHERE THERE IS MUCK, YOU CAN ALWAYS FIND A RAKE

By 1893, the results of such shortsightedness and greed could be seen clearly, not only in New York City but also in many other cities. Tenement houses, slums, filth, and disparaging conditions were rampant. A few socially conscious journalists such as Lincoln Steffens, then referred to as "muckrakers," had begun to call the public's attention to these ills. The stage was set for a reaction. This took the form of the White City, or as it was to become known, the "City Beautiful," which was the theme of that year's Chicago exposition. Beautiful white facades, dazzling esplanades, and bubbling fountains offered urban dwellers some escape from what our cities had become and, at the same time, served to inspire many visitors to return home and try to do something about "beautifying" their own drab urban environment. In his book *American City Planning,* Mel Scott says:

> . . . the brilliant image of symmetrical edifices, colossal statues, and stupendous domes burned in memory long after the summer pilgrims had returned to their lackluster commercial cities, dreary mill towns, and homely prairie villages. Plastic fantasy that it was, the World's Columbian Exposition touched the deep longing of a nation suffering from a loss of continuity with history for visual assurance of maturity and success. Not the creative and original office blocks in downtown Chicago, but the specious classicism of the fair satisfied the hunger for cultural security and self-approbation.[2]

Thus was born the City Beautiful movement and, in effect, the basis of the theory that urban form, if left to individual motivations, might not be always the best and that the viability of the city was a matter of public as well as private concern. Following the turn of the century, many communities undertook "city beautifying" projects. Civic centers, public plazas, and massive monumental structures in classical styles were advocated, initiated, and accomplished by governments, civic leaders, and citizen groups—all, unfortunately, showing little regard for the social and economic problems of the people. Nevertheless, the ignition of the spark of human concern and sense of the interrelation of social and economic factors to physical form was achieved, and the flame slowly spread.

While cities had begun to utilize the "police power" inherent in governmental regulation of land use (primarily this took the form of restrictions against use of a nuisance variety), it was not until 1916 that zoning was shaped into the form we know it today. (See Chapter 6—

The Relationship of Zoning to Planning.) In the meantime, the word "planning" began to be bandied about more and more as a government function. Cities recognized the need for a sense of direction, a comprehensive overview of where they were and where they were heading. Daniel Burnham, one of the principal architects of the Chicago exposition, was asked to develop a plan for the lakefront, which grew into a plan for the entire Chicago region. In 1907, Hartford, Connecticut, became the first city to establish an official planning commission and was followed quickly by Milwaukee (1908) and Chicago (1909). In 1909, the First National Conference on City Planning was held in Washington. Also in 1909, Wisconsin enacted a state enabling act authorizing cities of the second and third class to create planning commissions. The state of Massachusetts, in 1913, went further by requiring all cities over 10,000 in population to have planning commissions.

AS TOPSY GREW, SO DID ZONING

As planning efforts on the part of governments grew, the realization also grew that the advisory nature of plans needed methods and tools of enforcement. Early efforts at land-use regulation were put into a comprehensive zoning ordinance in New York City in 1916. Here was the first attempt to combine, in one police-power ordinance, restrictions on and regulations for land use, height and bulk of buildings, as well as the density of population and development. Much of the credit for this work is given to Frank M. Bassett, a prominent New York lawyer in his time. Following this action, cities all over the country began to climb on the zoning bandwagon. (See Chapter 6.)

Progress was interrupted by the outbreak of World War I, but with its end and the resumption of the pursuit of the great American dream, growth of cities again received attention. Zoning became more popular; but as there was little for guidance other than the New York City ordinance and some state enabling acts, which varied greatly, a federal agency undertook to provide some degree of standardization. The United States Department of Commerce, under Secretary Herbert Hoover, in 1922 developed "A Standard State Zoning Enabling Act" which was followed in 1928 by "A Standard State Planning Enabling Act." While there have been many changes in our concerns, problems, and approaches since then, some of the language of these models will still be found in the enabling legislation of most states pertaining to zoning and planning. They are discussed further in Chapter 4.

Following the crash of the stock market in 1929, every state and federal agency became involved in dealing with the Great Depression and restoring the economy. As private construction came to a virtual halt, public works planning and projects became the thing of the hour. Using the model acts as formats, many states adopted planning legislation, and by 1936 almost all states had created state planning boards. These agencies not only busied themselves with proposals for public facilities but also did excellent work in areas of statewide land use, natural resources inventory, transportation projects, and public open-space preservation. As a means of recovery from the devastating depression, President Franklin Delano Roosevelt began what has become known as the "federal alphabet soup days." After first gaining congressional concurrence with the idea of granting him emergency powers, he created a great number of special agencies and programs designed to overcome the massive unemployment that existed throughout the country. The more notable among them were the National Recovery Act (NRA), the umbrella legislation under which operated the individual programs, including the Reconstruction Finance Corporation (RFC), Works Progress Administration (WPA), Public Works Administration (PWA), and Civilian Conservation Corps (CCC).

These last three were created to provide some type of employment for those standing in bread lines and haunting soup kitchens to survive. Through them some outstanding public works were accomplished. Schools, utility systems, roads and highways, park development, public buildings, and conservation programs were spinoff contributions to the quality of life while providing millions of much needed jobs. As an example, it was during this time that the now famous Riverwalk (Paseo del Rio) in San Antonio was started, together with many other public projects we can still enjoy and admire today. Another fortunate aspect of the federal recovery programs was the accompanying increase in interest regarding the idea of comprehensive planning and a greater realization that the shape of the future of our urban areas and our environment is a governmental responsibility as well as a private one. The planning process advanced another notch up the ladder of recognition.

By 1936 the war clouds were gathering again, and the country once more turned its attention to military matters. In passing, we note the start of the first low-rent housing programs through the enactment of the Public Housing Act of 1937. This was to be a milestone on the road the federal government was to travel in broadening public responsibility for social needs and in setting the stage for the increased involvement of Washington in matters long thought of as local problems. This recognition of housing needs for all income levels led to an increased demand for greater advance planning.

It was during the depression period that we were given a telling object lesson regarding the difficulty of having sensible, organized planning in our political system and profit-oriented economy. In 1939, through pressure from some concerned citizens and President Roosevelt, the National Resources Planning Board (NRPB) was created. Probably one of the most logical and sensible things ever done by the federal government, its purpose was not only to examine resources availability but also to assure coordination of federal programs and develop national policies to guide future growth and development.

While the NRPB accomplished many things during its existence, including the stimulation of considerable state planning activity, its objective view of the utilization of resources and allocation of public works and monies left something to be desired from the viewpoint of Congress and the bureaucracy. As a result, under pressure from certain congressional members, the NRPB was abolished in 1943, leaving the congressional committees with free rein to continue pork-barrelling. Meanwhile the national defense theme and the military buildup became the principal concerns of the country, unfettered by any resource or environmental considerations.

Following World War II, from the standpoint of community development and urban form, all hell broke loose. With an exploding birth rate and the return of the military to civilian life, some areas began to look as if we were intent upon creating wall-to-wall urbanism. Aided and abetted by the Federal Housing Administration's (FHA) policy of easy mortgage money for new houses in suburbia, the years between 1946 and 1954 became the speculative developer's paradise. While there was a rush to push through more zoning ordinances and to revise some of the older ones, local governments could not keep up with, much less stay ahead of, the bulldozer. Municipalities and municipal service systems, as well as educational systems, were literally overrun. Building starts appeared like mushrooms; peach orchards, cornfields, and even swamps sprouted what was to become the symbol of the great American dream—the ticky-tacky house in an even more ticky-tacky subdivision. Unfortunately, as usually happens in periods of what is considered by many in our capitalistic system to be "economic development" boom times, planning ideals and zoning standards were relegated to the background, ignored entirely, or suddenly changed or amended to meet the demands of exploiters.

In New Jersey, where my planning consulting firm was headquartered from 1953 to 1971, the danger of grabbing at any development opportunity that came down the road was vividly illustrated. Here (and elsewhere) after the bulldozers and construction crews left, came the dawn of realism from overflowing septic tanks, contaminated water supplies, crises in traffic congestion, and double and triple school sessions. Communities rushed frantically to create planning boards (as they are called there), adopt subdivision ordinances, set up building codes, insert minimum dwelling size requirements in zoning ordinances, and generally apply Band-Aids to gaping wounds. The opportunity to be prepared by careful advanced planning had been lost. As I have frequently said in my speeches and lectures, they had forgotten that it was not raining when Noah built the ark. He had listened to the warning and did not wait for the deluge: Would that our local and state governments could learn this lesson!

Albuquerque, the city in which I became planning director in 1971 and city manager in 1972, is another good example of what happened nationwide during the post-war period. In 1940, Albuquerque was a sleepy, dusty town of 35,449. By 1950, it had grown to 96,815, largely as a result of the federal government discovering that it was really a state that was part of the United States and not a colony of Mexico. Just prior to and during the war, federal projects such as Los Alamos, Kirtland Air Force Base, Sandia Laboratory, and White Sands Testing Grounds were inserted into the New Mexico scenery. The resulting effects on Albuquerque were rather staggering. Left unbridled and largely undirected, growth continued at a pace sufficiently rapid to create a "city" of 201,189 with a metropolitan area of some 262,000 people by 1960. During all this time, Albuquerque had a planning commission, something that passed for a zoning ordinance, and a city commission form of government. Both commissions, however, were controlled by real estate brokers, developers and "all growth is good" self-interested evangelists.

This was much the situation when planning, and later managing, the city became my responsibility. Needless to say, my head felt like it was being banged against a stone wall many times until the conditions were changed somewhat for the better. At the next election, as a result of the beginning of an aroused, concerned citizenry, one of the three commissioners elected was much more inclined to be concerned about the future and putting some effectiveness in planning for the city, this being the first woman ever elected to the commission. She, with the help of the one other supportive commissioner, by cajoling and persuasion succeeded in obtaining new appointments to the planning commission (including the first woman there, too), strengthening the planning department, better zoning enforcement, and an increasing amount of community support for more meaningful planning. Unfortunately, this window of opportunity was doomed not to last.

The development interests and the power brokers began to realize that their "picking paradise" was becoming threatened. A rumor campaign was begun to convince the general public that the management of the city was not just dedicated to guide and control development, but rather to stop all growth—make Albuquerque a "no growth" city. They succeeded well enough to convince three of the five commissioners that this was the city manager's doing and that if they didn't get rid of him quickly, his ideas and programs might be an adverse factor for them in the next election. This they did, but over the objection of the general public. Consequently, through the demand of citizens, the commission was forced to create a charter study commission which, much to the surprise and chagrin of the incumbent city commissioners, recommended a change to a strong-mayor/council form of government, ultimately approved by the voters.

Under the new system, the city has returned to its days of "lip service planning," with growth continuing largely unguided. While the mayor is elected by an at-large vote, the city was divided into nine districts with all members of council responsible only to the voters in their own district. As a result, the potential for pork-barrelling, parochialism, and lack of a broad vision for the entire city is extremely high. Bickering between the council and the mayor, as well as the council members feuding among themselves over who can get the most for their district, certainly has not helped with a cooperative, comprehensive guiding of the growth of what could have been a really great city.

By 1980, Albuquerque's population was 332,336 and the 1990 census indicates that there are 480,577 people in the Standard Metropolitan Statistical Area (SMSA). This example is in no way unique. From my research visits to 15 cities across the country while writing *Planning America's Communities: Paradise Found? Paradise Lost?*[3] it was rather obvious that at least 10 of those cities, especially San Diego, San Antonio, New Orleans, and Corpus Christi, have had much the same experience in their attempts at making planning meaningful. We could further conclude that the primary reason for this truism is the lack of people understanding just what good planning is, what it can do for the public welfare, how to make it work. In addition, there appears to be an unwillingness to even become convinced of the need for planning, much less becoming personally involved.

So that there is no misunderstanding, I will indicate clearly that some sound planning was done during the immediate post-war period from 1946 to 1954. There were places with the foresight to establish and staff a planning process in advance of the growth and which fared reasonably well. However, those who had not, and even some who had tried to be prepared, found most of their efforts to deal with the problems proved to be futile or inadequate crisis reaction rather than positive advance planning. Some of this resulted from the specific unavailability of local level funding for planning and professional services and some came from the lack of recognition of the importance of and knowledge about effective municipal planning. For whatever reason, a dangling of financial aid led to several thousand master plan studies and added greatly to the number of organized planning programs. (The consulting firm I headed prepared more than 300 of what were called "701 Program" plans for municipalities, counties, and regions in the eastern coastal area in the period from 1954 to 1970; we were not alone in this kind of activity.)

There has been much debate about the "701 Program" and its effectiveness. Did it really result in a vast array of well-structured plans that in turn helped to make cities better places, or was it just a prime example of local-federal game-playing and waste of tax money? Can we say that the planning studies resulted in action to avoid mistakes or to correct ones already made? Were there situations in which communities entered the program and arranged to have plans prepared only because they labored under the illusion that they ought to take advantage of the "free" federal money?

Let it suffice to say that, while there was both good and bad planning done, the program accomplished at least two things. First, it served as a means of firmly defining a role of interest, even if somewhat proprietary and regulative, of the federal government in local community development. To some, this meant an encouragement of direct relations between cities and the federal system and a bypass of state jurisdiction and prerogative. To others, even if such were the case, this was a necessary and beneficial move because states had failed to act or had been unable to cope. There are those who feel that the blame for many, if not most, of our urban ills can be placed squarely at the feet of insensitive, ineffectual, unconcerned, and inept state legislatures. States, on the other hand, were quick to respond that the federal government had usurped the primary sources of revenue and that the solution lies where the money is.

Second, the Federal Housing Act of 1954 gave a new emphasis to local planning that served to create planning consciousness throughout the country. Even if the planning accomplished did not happen to be the best, the fact that it was going on caused many more to hear about it, become involved, and learn something about the problems of keeping a municipal government's house in order. Perhaps for this reason alone, the "701 Program" was worth the money and the effort.

Throughout the 1960s, Washington's attempts to encourage local action continued at a steady pace with the support of federal funding, although the rules of the game were beginning to change. A major change was the consolidation of all agencies responsible for any phase of administering federal grants relating to housing, planning, and community development into a new cabinet level department—the Department of Housing and Urban Development (HUD), created in 1965. Quickly following in 1966 came the Demonstration Cities and Metropolitan Development program (the so-called "Model Cities" program). This provided an excellent example of how so many Washington-generated programs are conceived with good intentions and lofty objectives, but with no thought given to the difficulty of uniform application in diverse communities, the effects of local implementation, and the reaction of the general public for whom the program is supposed to provide benefits. The experience we had in Albuquerque epitomized the impracticality of the above idealization.

The theory of the Model Cities program was that, instead of allowing individual social benefit and improved quality of life programs to be scattered in various sectors of a city, why not pick out one of the more neglected and needful areas, concentrate the whole gamut of local, state, and federal assistance there and try to make it truly a model neighborhood? This would inspire other neighborhoods to aspire to self improvement, foster greater appreciation for working with local government to make their areas a better place to live and work, and create a sense of hope instead of frustration. Since the program would probably last for years, other areas also could be upgraded and the entire city would be made more attractive and stable.

There can be no doubt that this was noble and admirably idealistic, but application proved that it had the exact opposite effect. First, there was disagreement and resentment over the drawing of the boundary lines of the selected areas. When the many programs and improvements were in place those across the boundaries felt they had been cheated and it broadened greatly the feeling of "them versus us" on the part of both the "ins" and the "outs." Secondly, some of the most fierce political battles one could ever witness took place concerning (a) who would comprise the required Model Cities board in the selected area; (b) which leader, patron, or politician would have the power of being board chairperson; (c) which favored individual or firm would be awarded the contract for home remodeling, infrastructure installation and any provision of services; and (d) who would get the jobs created through the program. Any attempt to resolve these problems succeeded only in increasing discontent and strife, both within the selected target area and throughout other parts of the city. At several of the model cities area meetings, at least in Albuquerque, police had to be called to prevent the breakout of a possible riot. With problems such as these, it became another utopian idea that was doomed to failure from the beginning by the lack of adequate prior program analysis, long-range thinking, and planning on the part of the bureaucrats and Congress. The Model Cities idea did not meet with favor from the Nixon administration and, soon after taking office in 1969, the then-president began to withhold the funds both appropriated and allocated for its continuance. Thus the program dried up and came to an undistinguished end.

During the period before the Nixon election and his early years in office, HUD came up with several other experimental types of programs, using their basic charge of improved housing and its availability and affordability for every American family as their primary justification. In 1968, we were going to reshape the urban pattern in this country with the New Communities Act. Federal funding was made available to private developers for the purpose of creating entirely new towns and cities that would be self-contained, modern, well-planned, and beautifully designed. The problem with this idea was that we had entrusted this major idea to a federal agency where no one had any experience in new-town building. They were not canny and artful enough to deal with major experienced developers interested in their own profits and not desirous of having to deal with federal regulations or having bureaucrats looking over their shoulders at every move. Consequently only two successful communities—Columbia, Maryland, and Reston, Virginia—have been built within what might be the definition of a "new town"—one created primarily by private funding.

Two other idealistic but unsuccessful federal programs of this era followed the same pattern as the ones above. Former car manufacturing executive George Romney, as Secretary of HUD, became convinced that a way could be found to build housing units cheaper than the market price at that time. In 1969, he created the "Operation Breakthrough" project. After requesting proposals from large architectural and planning firms for research funding, and choosing the resulting ideas deemed most feasible, HUD made federal money available to selected cities to undertake a housing project using one of the supposedly "new techniques and methodology." The result: when all cost factors were figured in, the per unit cost was more than what competent private developers would spend to build housing using long-practiced techniques and standard materials.

Next came the Urban Growth and Community Development Act of 1970, known as "New Towns-in-Town" because of a section providing federal aid for developers who would propose to acquire land and build a major mixed-use project in inner cities. The intention was to create a spark of revitalization and economic improvement for some of the declining cities. This too proved an ambitious but impractical dream, much like the others with but minor exceptions.

THE GREAT NATIONAL "SHELL GAME"

When Richard Milhous Nixon became the 37th president in 1969, the federal aid programs to state and local governments began to change rapidly. Nixon brought with him, and worked to eventually accomplish, his idea of a "New Federalism," heralded as a move to get "big government off the backs of local and state governments." With this, the emphasis shifted from "categorical" (by specific function) federal funding to the emerging philosophy of allocating money to cities and states and allowing them, under certain restrictions and guidelines, to determine their own spending priorities for specified federally approved programs. A city more seriously concerned about social programs than about streets and sewer plants could, for example, concentrate on social program areas. Based upon the "let the local people decide" theme, general revenue sharing was born, sounding as if we had reached utopia.

One of my memories as city manager in Albuquerque was the day the finance director brought the first general revenue sharing check for over $5 million into my office. He let me look at it for about five seconds, grabbed it out of my hand and said, "I have got to hurry and get this to the bank. We are losing interest on it every minute you look at it. " Yes, at that time we all thought that the millennium had arrived; little did we know the headaches that were to come in deciding how to spend the money and what was to happen to categorical funding. Shortly thereafter, after reason returned and more careful analysis was done, we discovered that, with the across-the-board cuts in categorical funding, general revenue sharing would provide the city some $18 million less in federal aid than we had received the year before. Needless to say, the finance director was not so happy after that.

In 1974, the President succeeded in getting a new Housing and Community Development Act passed. With it, all categorical funding ceased as the individual specific programs of HUD were shifted into a single block or package grant system. This meant that no longer would there be separate programs for metropolitan planning, urban renewal, neighborhood facilities, open-space land, or basic water and sewer facilities. Instead, Community Development Act funds would be provided to each city, as well as to the states, based upon a formula designed to attempt to assure "fair and equitable" distribution. Allocation would be left to local option. As Barnum reputedly said, you can fool all of the people some of the time, and some of the people all of the time.

WHERE ARE WE NOW?

When Ronald Reagan took office as President in 1981, it soon became obvious that whatever remained in the way of financial aid to states and cities from the federal coffers would soon be a thing of the past. Before the total effect of his policies and programs were brought to bear, there were still remnants of federal aid programs. Even with the cutoff of urban renewal funding in 1974, it was still possible for cities to obtain Community Development Block Grants (CDBG), Urban Development Block Grants (UDBG), and some special-purpose grants for economic development, mass transit, housing, and historic preservation. Most of the money from UDBGs went into inner-city commercial development. Several major new hotels financed by this program were built in the downtown areas of cities.

The only source of funding for planning was that which could be siphoned off from whatever CDBG funds a city might have. As a result, long-range planning once again fell into a period of decline and planning department staffs were reduced in many places. The effect of this drying-up of federal financial assistance and the Reagan policies was to reduce drastically the emphasis that had begun to be placed on comprehensive long-range planning beginning with the Section 701 era, and embolden a return to pragmatic, quick-fix planning. This picture, and the ultimate serious recession after George Bush assumed the presidency in 1989, became midwife for the birth of the national "economic development"—*all growth is good*—binge. As sure as the sun rises in the east, ensuing from this was the shunting aside of sound effective community planning and zoning as communities nationwide struggled to avoid economic crisis or even bankruptcy.

As the recession tightened its grip on our state and municipal governments, housing construction fell, mortgage obligations went unpaid and proposed major development projects went belly-up with developers simply walking away to leave mortgage and special district bond owners holding the bag. Financial institutions, especially savings and loan companies, folded like summer flowers as they rushed to declare bankruptcy. In many cases it was later discovered that one of the prime causes of this fiasco was just pure old chicanery and illegal misuse of depositors' funds. These conditions spawned a large increase in the numbers of homeless persons and those who had to find less costly, inadequate shelter. Numerous agencies were created to assist the homeless and to agitate for federal and state action for more effective handling of this serious problem. From these pressures, the number of defaulted loans and the hue and cry of those whose money, frequently their life savings, had been lost, Congress was forced into action "to do something."

Their solution was to create an autonomous agency called the Resolution Trust Corporation (RTC) and to appropriate billions of deficit-increasing dollars to take over millions of foreclosed homes, apartments, and businesses and to resell them in an attempt to recover as much of the lost money as possible. For months this agency seemed incapable of meeting the challenge, but eventually got somewhat organized and began to attempt to market the properties. Auctions were held and those financially able were in a position to gain ownership of several properties at bargain basement prices to hold until economic conditions improved, at which time they could be sold for a sizable profit. While this tactic did nothing for the homeless or those in need of better housing, many local housing authorities and private nonprofit organizations did manage to acquire many properties that were then rehabilitated and, with the aid of state housing authorities' tax-free bonds, were able to sell them to low- and moderate-income families.

Here a special word needs to be said about those state housing authorities and the vital role many of them have played in helping to provide adequate and affordable housing during this time of crisis. Such authorities had been created by most states at the time that the tax exempt Mortgage Revenue Bond (MRB) program for first-time home buyers with a low or moderate income was first approved by Congress, even before the recession. Not only have these agencies assisted local housing authorities and nonprofits in gaining needed housing units through their tax exempt bond sale ability, some actually acquired deserted or run-down structures, rehabilitated them, and made rental units available to those with very low income. They also were the originators of tax exempt bonds that encouraged private developers to build rental housing projects for elderly and low-income persons under the Section 8 Rent Supplement Program that existed prior to the Reagan and Bush years.

The Colorado Housing and Finance Authority, of which I have been a board member for 10 years, has done all of the above and, more recently, arranged several bulk purchases of foreclosed housing units now held by the Resolution Trust Corporation.

NATIONAL AFFORDABLE HOUSING ACT OF 1991

On November 28, 1990, President Bush signed the first major housing and community development bill that had been enacted in almost a decade. Known as the Cranston-Gonzalez National Affordable Housing Act (Public Law 101-625) (hereafter referred to as the act), it is, in effect, a consolidation of all remaining federal programs related to housing (except that funds flowing to public housing authorities are not affected) and community development into one act. However, in doing so, the new techniques and requirements for obtaining federal approval and financial assistance, and the complicated wording, have resulted in legislation that is very difficult to understand readily. The act authorized approximately $26.9 billion for housing and community development programs in Fiscal Year (FY) 1991 and $28.4 billion in FY 1992. An additional $644 million in FY 1992 and $657 million in FY 1993 was authorized for the McKinney Act, which provides for homeless assistance programs.

Submission and HUD approval of a Comprehensive Housing Affordability Strategy (CHAS) is a prerequisite for states and qualifying local jurisdictions receiving HOME Investment Partnership (HOME) or other funding under the act. An interim rule released by HUD in 1991 required that all CHAS plans for the following year must be submitted each year by October 31. To complete the required CHAS, states and local governments must include 14 separate elements:

- State's projected housing need for next five years.
- The nature and extent of state's homelessness.
- Significant characteristics of state's housing market.
- Cost of housing and impact of local tax policies and ordinances on housing affordability.
- Institutional capacity for carrying out strategy.
- Availability of non-federal and private resources.
- Plans for using HOME, CDBG, and McKinney funds.
- Plans for cooperating with local jurisdictions in the preparation and implementation of the strategy.
- Plans for coordinating the Low Income Housing Tax (Tax Credit) with the development of housing, including public housing, that is affordable to low- and very low-income families (applies to states only).
- The number and condition of public housing units in the jurisdiction and strategies for improving public housing operation and living conditions (applies to localities only).
- Activities to encourage public housing tenants to become more involved in management and participate in homeownership.
- Certification of furthering fair housing.
- Certification of compliance with federal anti-displacement and relocation assistance requirements.
- Estimated number of families which will obtain affordable housing through the state's investment.

This is a formidable list of requirements for certification by HUD. Nevertheless most states, urbanized counties, and large-sized localities have submitted their CHAS documents. At this writing it is too early to evaluate fully the effect of this complicated piece of legislation on the housing and community development needs of the nation.

Unfortunately, once again HUD has failed directly to require coordination with and involvement of local comprehensive plans, planning commissions, and planning staff functions, although an amended section correcting this is under consideration. However, many communities have had the common sense to recognize the relationship of the CHAS to their planning process and taken it upon themselves to see that their planners are involved from the beginning of the process. In Denver, for example, the CHAS was compiled by the city and county planning department.

Two other major features, one of which already has been mentioned, are important enough to be discussed. The first is the HOME program which will provide funds to states and certain local jurisdictions to invest in a wide variety of affordable housing activities, including rental subsidies, rehabilitation and new construction. The catch is that HOME requires a local funding match for which draft regulations were issued by HUD in March of 1991. The wording and the extent of the match requirement at that time were strongly opposed by the National Conference of State Housing Agencies (NCSHA). The reason for their opposition is that language in the legislation is unclear about what HUD can place in its requirements for this match. Will it insist on this being all cash or may a portion of it take the form of "in-kind" contributions as was the case in the urban renewal program? NCSHA is convinced that HUD has exceeded what it was allowed to do by the NAHA and is concerned that the large cash match it is trying to require will keep many states and local governments from participating. This is sure to be the case unless Washington takes a more reasonable approach than its present stand, which indicates there is little understanding of the dire financial straits in which states and local governments find themselves.

The second feature, somewhat more related to planning and community development than much of the act, is former HUD Secretary Jack Kemp's program known simply as HOPE. This will make funds available to provide assistance primarily to convert existing rental housing to owner-occupied housing. This grant program is divided into HOPE for Public and Indian Housing (HOPE I), HOPE for Multifamily Units (HOPE II), and HOPE for Single Family Homes (HOPE III). HOPE also requires a match from state, local or private funds, but will allow in-kind contributions approved by the Secretary. For HOPE I the match is 4:1 for federal (4) to nonfederal (1) and for HOPE II/HOPE III, 3:1. For FY 1992, the act authorizes $380 million for HOPE I, $280 million for HOPE II, and $195 million for HOPE III. The "kicker" is that we are back to the old federal "carrot and stick" game with none of the money from any part of the act available to you unless you have an approved CHAS and meet all other federal requirements—shades of the 1954 Federal Housing Act and the comprehensive plan approved by HUD requirement in order to get urban renewal grants.

So, in 38 years we have come full circle back to the further playing of "gamesmanship" with the federal bureaucrats. Whether this will work out any better than the 1954 act and all the other programs covered here only the future can tell. The legislation has admirable goals and objectives, but the question remains whether those responsible for it have given sufficient careful thought to its practicality and the ramifications of its application. A further question, even more important to the future of our cities and our environment, must be asked: Is this leading once again to the pragmatic project type of city problem solving? The National Affordable Housing Act, passed by Congress and administered by HUD, has negated everything related to federal policy set forth in the 1954 Housing Act in which the lawmakers insisted, in Section 701, that comprehensive city planning was essential to the urban renewal process. Instead, this act ignores the logic of comprehensive and coordinated use of the benefits of this all-inclusive federal aid program for housing and community development. It is my contention that this is a flaw in the legislation and a very serious mistake.

Be that as it may, planning is going to survive and increase in importance as we become even more populated across the country. In some places it will be effective in urban form building because of concern for the future by leaders and the general public. In others, it will be what I call "water-faucet" planning: it exists in name, but may be turned on and off depending upon whether there is an aroused citizen group complaining about the seeming lack of planning effectiveness, or developers moaning that the planning and zoning standards are too tough and they will have to take their "economic development" to some other city.

The development of planning has been such that regardless of where we live, in all probability we fall under the purview of a planning agency. What those who comprise this agency are doing with our most precious assets, land and its resources, as well as what they are doing that may have a bearing on the quality and character of where we live, work, and have our economic and social future, is something that should concern us all. Where we go from here and whether the things that are done through planning, or under the guise of good planning, will make our future cities, our communities, and our rural areas better places is largely up to us as citizens.

When I was teaching I used to tell my students that no planning will be successful unless there is a planning attitude on the part of the residents, political leaders, and the power structure within the affected area. Where this is not so, what is called planning can be an illusory gimmick used to develop a false sense of security on the part of those of us who are prone to apathy concerning local government and our community. Today, more than ever before, sensible, organized citizen concern can be heard and can be effective. Organized neighborhood groups working together have the power, if they would just use it, to determine the results of any local election where a void exists on the part of public officials concerning good planning. Long-range and comprehensive planning, not just short-run problem solving, is the general public's greatest hope for assuring that which is best for all of us as well as the community of the future, whether it be a physical, social, economic, or environmental concern. I suggest also that community planning with meaningful citizen involvement is one of the last ways available to us in trying to preserve a true democratic society.

> What scares Americans about national planning, regional planning, and planned communities is the fear that the government will bungle it and that it will cost a lot of money. The former is a matter of citizen participation and education, of careful public control. As to cost, it is far less expensive to build a good environment than a bad one.[4]

NOTES

1. Arthur B. Gallion, and Simon Eisner, *The Urban Pattern, Fourth Edition* (New York: D. Van Nostrand Company, 1980), pp. 49-52.
2. Mel Scott, *American City Planning Since 1890* (Berkeley: University of California Press, 1971), p. 33.
3. Herbert H. Smith, *Planning America's Communities: Paradise Found? Paradise Lost?* (Chicago: Planners Press, American Planning Association, 1991).
4. Wolf Von Eckardt, *Back to the Drawing Board: Planning Livable Cities* (Washington, D.C.: New Republic Books, 1978), p. 155.

CHAPTER

3

The Planning Process

When you hear the word "planning," what image is created in your mind? Do you think of architecture, buildings, sewer lines, streets, and other things relating to physical aspects of development? Perhaps the term connotes concern over environmental factors like air quality control, preservation of open space, conservation of resources, and regulation of nuclear power plants. Those of us interested in some of the social problems of society immediately conjure up ideas of housing programs, welfare improvement, equal employment opportunities, medical and senior citizen care, and a myriad of other things. If you are in industry or business, planning means research and development of new products, new plant construction, expansion of operation (within financial capabilities), meeting competition, and determination of present and future market potentials. On the other hand, to a great number of people, the term is extremely negative and brings forth nothing but images of governmental control, the intrusion of Big Brother into private lives and private rights, and a "planned economy." "After all," these latter say, "we certainly don't want any of that kind of stuff, because isn't that what they have in those communistic countries?"

Some time ago I was doing some planning work in a small Colorado town where this attitude continues to prevail. Yet I was there because they wanted advice on how to deal with a situation bordering on a crisis that resulted from allowing a hodgepodge land-use pattern to develop, the loss of one major industry, and a water system inadequate to serve their people. On top of this the Environmental Protection Agency and the State Department of Health had ordered that they do something about the open lagoons they were using as the only way of providing any sewage treatment. Trying to talk to them about the fact that planning and zoning might have helped to prevent these problems, but could do little if anything about them now, meant explaining a basic concept totally alien to their beliefs about the role of government. Even the idea that governmental guidance of land development could surely help them avoid problems like this in the future was contrary to their pioneer philosophy that "a man's land is his to do with as he pleases." On the Western Slope of Colorado, as well as in other parts of the country, there are many communities where people are still convinced that people and government working together in organized planning for a better future for all is indeed communistic and something to be avoided at all costs.

COMMON CONCEPT: THAT'S THE TICKET!

We can see from this that one of the great difficulties in applying the term "planning" to a governmental function is the lack of understanding of the proper role and an absence of a common concept as to the meaning of the word. We accept the fact that there is practically nothing that goes on in our private lives and our economy-oriented society that—if we are orderly people or shrewd investors—should not be well thought out and planned ahead. But when it comes to organizing our total environment and community development, from either a lack of information, a lack of interest, or some personal hang-up, we object to or end up in confusion over what should be done.

This is not totally the fault of us as individuals. Part of the problem lies in the history of our country and its development policies, part in a failure of the planning profession, and part in the political practices of the past as well as the "politics" of planning. Since the founding of our federation of states, we have enjoyed the privilege of a freewheeling, frontier-type expansion and growth. The idea existed that resources were inexhaustible, that land was unlimited, and it was every person's right to do as he or she damn well pleased so long as that could not be shown to be directly and overtly harmful to someone else. Governmental policies encouraged this through homesteading acts, support and subsidization of the railroad for development expansion, FHA single-family home mortgaging, and general deification of the philosophy that there is a pot of gold at the end of every rainbow for everybody. After all, aren't we the richest and most well-endowed nation in the world, founded on the principles of freedom, individual liberty, and justice for all? Why worry about the future in terms of city building, farmland protection, and environment when we have all those good things going for us?

It is this concept that, while generally sound and admirable, has had to be adjusted somewhat to changing conditions throughout our 200-year history. Many of us find this adjustment hard to make and painful to accept. There are others who have not accepted, and probably never will, the inescapable truth that the sheer survival of society, of us all, depends upon our being able to change our thinking and our approach to societal living in a reasonable way. Instead, oblivious to the facts, many people hang on unswervingly to the notion that such adjustment is against the principles of democracy and that what they consider to be private "rights" must be forever sacrosanct. For better or worse, we must begin to recognize we cannot retain a frontier mentality in an ever-expanding, socially complex 21st-century world. This is, and will continue to be, something with which we all must learn to deal and to live.

I KNOW YOU UNDERSTAND WHAT YOU THINK I SAID, BUT I AM NOT SURE YOU REALIZE THAT WHAT YOU HEARD IS NOT WHAT I MEANT

Why is it that so many in the general public still do not understand the importance of urban planning for their communities, by their government, and do not provide support for it? Why is it that they will go to a state or city where the beneficial effect of good planning can be recognized readily, admire it, and then go back home and be complacent about living in a place with no planning or what is only "lip-service" planning? Why are not professional planners more successful in building a concerned support base for meaningful urban planning within the area they work; isn't this something they should do? There are many answers that can be given for all of these questions, some pertaining to more than one. Several of the more obvious are: the frontier spirit, dislike of governmental "interference," general apathy about all community matters, the lack of support for and information on planning by all media forms, fear that any involvement would carry with it acceptance of a responsibility to do something, the way our society has become "me-istic," and retention of the archaic idea of the capitalistic system that "a man's land is his (or hers) to do with as he pleases"— including the "right" to make as much profit from it as possible, never mind the effect the land use may have on others.

Second, the question about the role of planners is a very important and a personally disturbing one. After being able to call myself a professional planner for better than four decades, I am convinced that we have failed in a number of ways. First of all, planning education in this country is almost universally lacking in impressing on planning students the importance of a "missionary" philosophy; that they must educate the public about city and urban planning, not just write academic tomes, do charts and graphs, and draw pretty pictures. Nor have the educators, the members of the American Planning Association (APA), the American Institute of Certified Planners (AICP), and others who call themselves planners ever been able to come up with and agree upon a simple, understandable definition of the term planning and a statement of its importance that is convincing to each individual, each family, each business. Most trained planners talk about such things as demography, cohorts, regression theory, computer modeling, projections, input-output studies, that become relatively meaningless and unimpressive to anyone largely concerned with property values and taxes. While the need is there for definition and clear statements putting it all together for any community or city, and is becoming more and more obvious, planners have yet to develop a common professional framework that lets the public know that the planning process is something upon which they can and should rely.

This shortcoming of the profession in not accepting the responsibility for building an understanding of just what urban planning is all about in elected officials, planning commissioners, and the people they serve has been a major error, in my opinion. One of the major reasons for the variety of conceptual ideas and some of the misconceptions about planning is the fact that no unified voices have been heard sounding the reason for good planning, explaining it in lay terms, and, without being only a harbinger of doom and gloom, pointing out the pitfalls and dangers of leaving the future to chance. Planners who do not think that a major part of their jobs is to be "the prick of conscience" to help the public understand that we can do better in city building and why planning is the way to do it is not doing his or her job to the extent it should be done. After 43 years of membership in professional planning societies, I can say it has always been my hope that, working together, we might provide that unified voice and that needed education. Alas, at my age now, I may not live long enough to see that come to pass.

Thirdly, we have politics, or lack thereof, in planning. I have chosen that phrase purposely, even though there are many who will say that what is wrong with planning now is that too much politics is involved.

But is there too much or not enough? Have we perhaps labored too long under the illusion that planning per se should be entirely free of political stigma and, as a consequence, permitted the professional politician to engage in the water faucet planning described earlier? I have little patience with those who use the shotgun approach of blaming "those planners" for failing to improve America's cities. The very nature of the process has been that those skilled in community planning recommend and policymakers (politicians?) effectuate.

In reality, the albatross that planners have permitted to be hung around their necks—the blame for a plethora of planning studies and reports that only end up on a shelf gathering dust—is misplaced. It should be loudly and ceremoniously hung around the necks of those who, from either self-interest, response to pressure, or lack of guts, have found it served their purposes best not to rock the boat with long-range or comprehensive programs and ideas. In many cases, because of such equivocators, the professional planner has become a scapegoat and, not being able to speak openly against his or her political bosses, has been hung for developing an unworkable plan. Unfortunately, this state of affairs has been fostered by a number of newspaper reporters and other writers who have found it easy and convenient, for their purposes, to lay the responsibility for all planning actions—or the failed actions of elected officials, federal agencies, architects, developers, and bankers—at the feet of "those planners," thus adding to the public's misconception of the profession. Outstanding examples of this are Jane Jacobs in her *Death and Life of Great American Cities* (1961), Robert Goodman's *After the Planners* (1972), and the general writings of Herbert J. Gans, particularly *The Levittowners* (1967).

Be that as it may, the need for community planning and the understanding of it by citizens continues to grow. It is my belief that such understanding must be based on knowledge, and although it may seem elementary, a definition of terms is always helpful. One of those given for the word "plan" in *Webster's New World Dictionary* is "a scheme or program for making, doing, or arranging something: project, design, schedule, etc." What we are talking about, therefore, in the community planning process is the community working together to develop a scheme or program for doing that which makes the most sense and is the best approach for communal living for everybody. This doesn't mean simply that the planners plan and the politicians and citizens sit back in judgment. It means that the professionals provide information, the people express desires and needs (and, in effect, plan), and those elected to serve carry out the scheme. This is a good opportunity to reiterate the statement made previously that a planning attitude must permeate the community, or at least the "movers and shakers," for any planning to succeed. The most successful planners have been those who were able not only to instill this in the minds of the people in their jurisdictions, but who also took an active role in seeing that "right-thinking" people were elected.

As this term "planning attitude" has already been used, and undoubtedly will be several times more, let me define it. For an individual or a community and its government, its essence lies in these things: a concern and caring about the future, a belief that something can be done about bettering our human-made and natural environments, and the recognition that long-range planning, with relevant implementing tools, is the only method available to achieve this. Supplementing this is an understanding of the importance of a sense of community, a sense of place being necessary to make a community better and improve the morality of our society.

DEFINITION DEFINES DIRECTION

Like everything else having to do with urban growth, the problems of cities, and what is happening to rural America, there has been a great deal written about the planning process. It may help our understanding if we look at some other attempts at definition. In the bible of planning education—lovingly referred to by students as "the Jolly Green Giant" due to its size and color, but more formally known as *Principles and Practice of Urban Planning* (1968)—the editors have, unfortunately, omitted a description of the planning function that appeared in an earlier edition of the book called *Local Planning Administration* (1959). While it may be a bit dated, I think it worth repeating here:

> The broad object of planning is to further the welfare of the people in the community by helping to create an increasingly better, more healthful, convenient, efficient and attractive community environment. The physical, as well as the social and economic community is a single organism, all features and activities of which are related and interdependent. These facts must be supplemented by the application of intelligent foresight and planned administrative and legal coordination if balance, harmony and order are to be insured. It is the task of planning to supply this foresight and this over-all coordination.

During the heyday of federal aid money for planning, one axiom became very obvious: If federal dollars come, following not far behind will be federal "guidelines," standards, restrictions, and definitions. In stating the purpose of federal planning assistance programs, the *Catalog of Federal Aids to State and Local Governments* provides the following definition:

> Comprehensive planning is defined as including, to the extent directly related to urban needs, the preparation of general physical plans for land use and the provision of public facilities (including transportation facilities), with long-range fiscal plans to accompany the long-range development plans; coordination of all related plans of the departments and subdivisions of the government concerned; intergovernmental coordination of planning activities; and the preparation of supporting regulatory and administrative measures.

A much more simple statement—and one probably more effective and meaningful than the above bureaucratese—can be found in Thomas F. Sarrinen's *Environmental Planning: Perception and Behavior* (1976):

> Planning may be considered the conscious organization of human activities to serve human needs. Better planning can be accomplished by greater integration of the separate components at each scale into a broader, more coherent framework. To be effective, planning must consider not only the physical environment but the way people perceive and utilize each segment of the environment.

Being somewhat biased, my preference is one I developed for students in my Introduction To Planning class, which is:

A systematic means of problem prevention and problem solving with people working through their government for the institution of programmed pre-action to direct and shape a desired result.

We could go on with any number of other definitions, but I believe a sufficient basis has been laid for the understanding of the process and of what planning can and should do. Although the term can be applied appropriately to any activity, the thing we as citizens should concentrate on is that it refers specifically to the application of intelligent foresight to the future of our community and its character and our environment.

NOW LET'S PUT HUMPTY DUMPTY TOGETHER

The basis for all planning activity is the proper delegation of governmental administrative responsibility and authority. This starts with enabling legislation adopted by the state, allowing county and municipal governments to organize for planning. All of us should be familiar with this legislation as the wording of the act sets the pattern for what can and cannot be done, even for home-rule cities. From this point we move to the local scene. To get started in planning, the governing body must enact an ordinance establishing an agency for planning (a planning commission or planning board, depending upon the terminology of each state act) and setting forth its prescribed functions. Once this has been done, there are the questions of appointments to the commission, the possible need for professional staff to do the work, and the structuring of the function into the local government. For more discussion of the makeup of the commission and its role, see Chapter 4.

Traditionally, the first major task assigned to the planning commission has been the preparation of a master plan for the entire area of its jurisdiction. Equally traditional has been the fact that the formulation of a plan is based upon an existing conditions inventory or a "resources analysis," the purpose of the plan being to allocate resources to best meet the needs of the total community. In recent years, there have been those who have faulted this approach in support of a more grass-roots type of procedure. The preference of the grass-roots advocates has been toward first determining goals and objectives through greater citizen involvement by neighborhoods and citizen action groups. Objectives, they state, should be based upon the desires of the people and the available resources.

At first glance this may seem to be a very difficult task. However, when one thinks of how instinctively each of us applies the setting of goals and objectives for our own lives, applying the process to a community appears to be rather simple. First, we should develop a clear picture of the meaning of these two words in the city planning process. The word *goal* should be perceived as the end or the final results to be achieved as a result of the planning. A goal may be a general statement such as: to improve the character and the economic health of our central business district by 50 percent over what it is now. The *objectives* then become the detailing of the functions and methodology needed to reach the desired goal.

It should be the responsibility of the planning commission and its staff to schedule widely publicized public meetings in several areas of the community to gather opinions—and, it is hoped, support—from as much of the general public as possible as a base for developing goals and objectives. In working with neighborhood organizations and civic groups, I have found that the method for obtaining this base can be broken down into a three-step process. The start is to get the people assembled to respond to the following questions: just what is our town or city now; what do we like or dislike about it; what would we want to see preserved or enhanced; what do we want to keep, but improve; and what do we want to see discouraged or even eliminated? Every effort should be made to obtain a consensus of opinion on the answers to these questions. Finally, people discuss how these goals and objectives can be brought to fruition and how the necessary action from the elected governing body can best be accomplished.

The planning commission then either appoints a number of broadly representative citizen committees to review the answers to the questions given by the various groups and collate them under topics such as economy and municipal services. The members of the commission can also do this themselves. The use of the committees is preferable as it gets more people involved and a range of viewpoints expressed. It also assures a cadre of supporters when the governing body either adopts the plan, or, in those states where the planning commission is empowered to officially adopt the master plan, a resolution of support for it. Either way, it is of utmost importance that the elected officials be on record as fully supporting the plan and the planning process. To further signify this, a statement should be prepared and passed indicating the policies the governing body will follow to implement the plan in dealing with both the public and private sectors. This statement should be widely publicized and specifically called to the immediate attention of all department or bureau heads, with instructions that they and their entire staff will be expected to perform their functions within the intent of the policy statements.

There are planning educators and writers who disagree with this type of approach to the development of a comprehensive plan, looking upon it as "the wish list" technique with little likelihood of being implemented. From my research visits to the cities included in my 1991 book, a large majority of them would have had much better success with their planning efforts had they followed the procedure outlined here. It is interesting to note that the three cities rated as achieving the most from their planning process have utilized the grass-roots citizen involvement system in formulating their plans. From my experience as both a planning director and a city manager in a city dominated and controlled by real estate speculators, developers, and commercial exploiters and their assembled clique, I am convinced that the only way planning can be made meaningful under such conditions is through an aroused citizenry demanding effective planning and, if this does not happen, throwing the elected rascals out.

John Friedmann is one of those who has been most outspoken against the traditional style of planning. In his book *Retracking America* (1973), he points out what he considers to be the faults of "allocative" planning, which he defines as "the distribution of limited resources among a number of competing users." He proposes that the process be changed to "innovative planning," which he says "is largely a self-executing activity; the formulation and carrying out of plans constitute, in this case, a single operation." In general it seems that Friedmann's thesis is that planning, to be effective, must involve more participation of competing interest groups in policy determination and that this may require institutional change rather than just central reallocation of resources. One of his reasons for concern over allocative practices is that complex modern society is dominated by special interest groups that have sufficient power to frustrate the intentions of any plan that threatens their interest. As he puts it, "allocative planning serves primarily the interests of those who are already strong."

Whether Friedmann's proposition is the correct one or not, there has been and continues to be a diversity of opinion and a goodly amount of discussion on what the proper planning function is and how it should be carried out. There is little debate remaining, at least among the more informed people in any area where urbanization has occurred or is occurring, over whether there is a vital role for governmental planning in ensuring the public benefit and protecting the public interest. With the growth of neighborhood organizations of increasing numbers of people concerned about the future of their area and their town or city, and their increasing political strength, there is hope that an even greater demand for government action in planning and zoning will emerge. The danger lies in whether the concern of these groups can continue to include the broader picture of the total city or whether they will mistakenly turn inward and become only self-interested islands ignoring everything but "what affects *my* neighborhood."

The debate will, and should, continue over how and by whom planning should be done. One thing seems certain, however: There will be increased citizen involvement in determining goals and objectives, the formulation of official plans to achieve these objectives, and the means utilized for effectuation. In today's society, the role of the planning function and the work of the planning commission must be recognized as having vastly increased in scope. Planning should now encompass a myriad of concerns not in existence, or not recognized, in the past. These include housing for the homeless and lower income families, disposal of hazardous waste materials, equitable developer impact fees, and revitalizing or maintaining the vitality of inner-city business districts. In addition, many innovative techniques are being utilized in planning and zoning that are broadening the traditional scope of coverage for the planning process and governmental action. Terms such as linkage, environmentally sensitive land protection, intensity growth management controls, and concurrence all indicate the extension of planning into new areas for protecting the public welfare. Some of these will be discussed in more detail in later chapters.

Along with all of this, the establishment of priorities for funding long-range planning programs as compared with pragmatic projects will become even more of a major issue as the financial crunch on local governments continues to increase. In large urban areas the competition between centralized planning and neighborhood self-determination undoubtedly will continue to grow. Whether a communitywide comprehensive plan should be assembled from a collection of neighborhood or micro-unit plans, or the broader view taken first and neighborhood planning adjusted as part of the whole, remains a matter of contention. For any community just organizing a planning program this is one of the first policy decisions to be made. Even if planning has long existed, this is a dilemma that should be freely and openly discussed if the development of a plan is to be successful.

A ROSE BY ANY OTHER NAME

For our purposes in this book, regardless of the divergent opinions as to procedure, it is reasonable to assume that whatever *form* we find more appropriate, it will nonetheless utilize the same *tools* for planning. Again, although these have undergone and will undergo changes, a view of the future does not indicate that, in our form of governmental system, we will be able to abandon the traditional methods of land-use controls, environmental protection, urban form shaping, and financing of projects and programs. In other words, while the approach to and the format of a master plan may change, there will still be the need for a basic frame of reference to give us a sense of direction. Call it what you will, under our system of law and under statutes that state legislatures will be willing to adopt, a form of "master plan" that will continue to be advisory and recommendatory in nature will be fundamental and the touchstone in the planning process. Whether this is a "policies plan" or a "physical plan" (see Chapter 5—The Master Plan) is up to each community to determine. In either case, it is important that we as citizens be informed and know just what is meant when someone tells us that something is being done because "it is in accordance with the master plan."

A second tool is zoning (see Chapter 6). Even though zoning came into general acceptance before organized planning, it is well established now that, to be properly and effectively done, such land-use controls as zoning should be based upon a well-thought-out comprehensive plan. Whether this occurs in actuality or not, zoning has become an extremely powerful instrument of government. There are few other adopted laws of local government that affect our private lives and our economic well-being more. In meetings with my students, I frequently asked them the question, "If you had the desire to make yourself into a dictator or totalitarian monarch in the United States, absolute control over what two things would make this the easiest to accomplish?" They usually have little trouble with one of these—offering "the minds of the people" as an excellent possibility. They have put forth a variety of ideas for the second, and they sometimes express shock when I propose the theory that complete control of the use of land is another excellent choice. Careful analysis will tell you that this is the fundamental base of all economics and that, next to mind manipulation, the most effective weapon for human behavior control is control of individual economic opportunity—the control of the pocketbook. This is why I have difficulty understanding the lack of general concern and interest on the part of the public about zoning.

The power to control land use is one of the most important powers allocated to government. Used properly, it can be one of the greatest assets in improving our community's character, our environment, and our way of life. Used improperly, it can be a means of political retribution, service to special vested interests, personal economic enrichment, and the attainment of more power. Unfortunately, I have seen it used for all of these purposes in several communities. A flagrant case involved a city where the dominant force on the planning commission was a very influential real estate broker who headed one of the city's largest firms. It was amazing how all zoning changes in which he, his firm, or his closest pals were involved slipped through so easily while those proposed by or benefiting competing real estate brokers invariably were found to be "contrary to the public interest" and usually rejected. Quite naturally, the commissioner's volume of business did not suffer from this.

How the power to control land use is used depends upon how much we as citizens know about it and how involved we are in making sure that any action taken does result in a benefit to the "public health, safety, and general welfare"—the charge established in all zoning legislation. Zoning in whatever form, whether it includes such modern techniques as planned unit developments, growth management programs, or transfer of development rights, will still be a major mechanism for shaping urban and suburban form and the use of land in rural areas. As such, it only makes sense for each person to understand fully not only the principles and theories of zoning but also the methods of administration and enforcement employed. Of even greater importance is for all of us to remember, understand, and become converts to the precept of a planning attitude together with the existence of a public "right" as well as a private "right" and the necessity of balance between these two, as was pointed out in Chapter 1.

In planning circles, it has become habitual to explain to anyone who will listen that the only major city in the United States that does not have a zoning ordinance is Houston, Texas. In fact, the citizens of Houston have twice voted down the very idea. Some years ago, in a speech given at a national planning conference, I heard the then-mayor of Houston defend his city's "lack of modern land-use controls" by saying that, in his visits to other cities where zoning existed, he failed to find they were any better. They still had hodge-podge development, transportation arteries lined with cheap commercial establishments, and just as much environmental pollution as did his city. While the mayor was basically correct, he could have been saying, in effect, "Our slums are no worse than your slums, and we haven't even let it bother us." Actually, this was not the thrust of his remarks, for he went on to point out that much of the same type of land-use controls and development guidance had been achieved in Houston by the use of deed restrictions or private land covenants and, even more importantly, through effective subdivision controls—the third basic tool of planning. It should be noted that many of these deed restriction contracts were to apply for a stated period of time and were instituted many years ago. The expiration date has passed, or is about to, on several. To reinstitute a set of deed restrictions is very difficult because the approval and signature of every property owner must be obtained.

Once again the possibility of a zoning ordinance for Houston has appeared on the horizon. After a push by a group of citizens in favor of the idea, the city council in 1991—an election year—voted unanimously to have a zoning ordinance prepared. As the first step, they renamed the planning commission the planning and zoning commission. This was followed by hiring some 40-plus new people for the zoning division of the planning and development department and retaining a group of consultants to help in the preparation of an ordinance. Two volunteer groups were formed to assist the commission—one with the ordinance text, the other with zoning maps showing district delineation. Commission members were assigned to work with each of the groups. The target date for presentation of an ordinance to council was set for July 1992.

Although city council, as in all cities, has the authority to adopt the ordinance, council twice previously (1948 and 1962) chose to let the voters decide after holding its public hearings. As mentioned earlier, both times the proposal for zoning was resoundingly defeated. However, in 1962, approximately 50 percent of the land inside the city limits was vacant; now only about 20 percent is vacant. In Texas all things are big, and that 20 percent represents about 100 square miles. There are, as always, some very interesting political complications. The council is elected for two-year terms with elections in odd-numbered years. In November 1991, the woman mayor of the last 10 years was voted out and a dynamic attorney/developer elected. To further complicate the zoning problem, voters in the last election approved term limitations that might mean a turnover in the 1993 election of 13 out of 15 council seats. Then again, the entire council and the mayor could remain exactly the same. It seems that, in typical Texas political style, the term limitation statute contains a loophole allowing anyone facing an end of term to seek reelection if he or she can obtain a stated percentage of signatures from constituents supporting continued candidacy.

In the meantime, progress toward the preparation of a proposed zoning ordinance and the accompanying zoning maps proceeded in an attempt to meet the council's July 1992 deadline. The planning and zoning commission's staff and consultants held public meetings, then assembled their recommendations, which were turned over to a zoning strategies committee of 40 to 50 members appointed by the mayor and approved by council.

After starting their review and holding several public meetings, that committee recognized that it would not be able to meet the deadline and asked council for an extension. Council extended the date to January 1, 1993, and passed an Interim Neighborhood Protection Ordinance containing regulations regarding land use, building placement, relation to existing use, and major project proposal review in predominantly residential areas. This interim ordinance was to stay in effect until July 1, 1993 or upon adoption of a comprehensive zoning ordinance, whichever came first.

The zoning strategies committee continued its work, held additional public meetings, and referred its recommended zoning ordinance and maps to the planning and zoning commission in late 1992. The commission staff presented the recommended Houston Zoning Ordinance to the council on January 11, 1993. Several more public comment meetings were held, and the ordinance was placed on the council agenda with the intent of completing the final reading by May 1, 1993. Some Houstonians felt that date was overly optimistic.

Meanwhile, the interim neighborhood protection ordinance has been most effective in seeing that proposed major developments fit in with existing characteristics. The interim regulations are intended to protect residential uses adjacent to vacant lots where development is proposed. The proposed use must be compatible with and complementary to the adjacent lot or lots. In this way, Houstonians have been introduced to the regulation of land use through a form of zoning. They have also learned what is going on in their neighborhoods while learning how zoning-type regulations are applied by the city. The existence and enforcement of the interim ordinance has put the development community on notice that this council means business and is serious about zoning.

As is to be expected in Houston, petitions are now being circulated, once again seeking a general referendum on the question of zoning in the city. But a two-year time limit must be observed between referendum votes. Even if the petitioners are successful in collecting sufficient signatures, they would miss placing the question on the regular November election ballot by two days. Either a special election would have to be called, or the matter would be held for the next regular election. If the council adopts the proposed ordinance before such a referendum can be placed on the ballot, an interesting legal question arises. It is the opinion of the Houston city attorney that Texas law prohibits the repeal of an entire, legally adopted zoning ordinance by a referendum vote. A poll conducted by the zoning strategies committee showed that 70 percent of those contacted still favor zoning for the city. So goes the continuing saga of land-use controls through zoning in Houston.

In theory, the use of governmental police power to establish standards for the subdivision of land supplements zoning and does not relate to land use, building placement, parking requirements, and other elements found in zoning ordinances. Subdivision controls, as Houston has seen, can be a most effective and important means of aiding in the planning process. It is important to understand that, while planning and the master plan are considered advisory, the implementing strength lies in the two uses of the police power of government—zoning and subdivision controls—to restrict each of us for the public good. Both of these must be correlated closely with the master planning process and used only in a way that carries out the objectives of that process. (For further discussion, see Chapter 7—The Regulation of Land Subdivision.)

The fourth tool of planning about which we should talk in some depth is the capital improvements program (see Chapter 8 for additional details). As vital as this is to the establishment of community character, the operation of effective government, and the tax demands on each and every one of us, it never ceases to amaze me how little is known about it and how little it concerns most of us. Yet every community has a capital expenditure program, whether planned or not, and it accounts for a large part of the local taxes we pay. It is the largest single item, other than schools, deriving its financial support from the real estate property tax—that tidy sum we pay with each mortgage payment on our homes or whatever other real estate we own. Put simply, capital improvement expenditures are the way that all public improvements, whether they be school facilities, parks, sewers, water lines, libraries, museums, streets, or what have you, are provided, repaired, improved, or enlarged. These are the source of the amenities of a community, the things that make it attractive to developers, industrialists, businesspersons, and ordinary homeowners. Together with the efficiency of administration, a progressive attitude, and meaningful and effective social programs, capital facilities provide the trunk of the tree of intangible aspects that make the difference between a good community and one that just is. They are the spinal cord upon which can be built a healthy community body. Here again, without citizen awareness and involvement, the use and distribution of these funds can be misdirected and made into a powerful, but dangerous, political force.

IT'S YOU AND ME TOGETHER, BABY

The most effective tool of the planning process is citizen involvement—you and me. (See Chapter 12 for additional discussion of this topic.) This participation should begin with the concept of the planning program, be part of its organization and structuring, and continue throughout development, administration, and effectuation of the process. In other words, it is a never-ending challenge to us as citizens, yet a must if planning is to be worth the effort. Of particular importance is the role of the individual citizen and neighborhood groups in setting the goals and objectives of the master plan or anything done under the guise of planning. Just what is it planning can and should do for us? What have we now, and what do we want in the way of a community? How can we as citizens play an active role in plan development, administration, and enforcement? These are all questions to which we should have answers before we let ourselves become confident that the planning being done is the way that planning in a democratic society should be done and that we are doing the best we can for our community.

This brings us back to the essential element—a planning attitude. If we don't see the absolute necessity of improving or we don't want to improve community life and our environment, even if it runs countergrain to political expediency, we will continue to see ineffective, meaningless usurpation of the planning process for our cities, counties, regions, and states. The basic principles of planning have to do with improving the general amenities of societal life and making our towns and regions better places in which to live. As each unit grows and develops and fits into the overall pattern of the region, so does the region prosper or wither. Without proper development for municipalities and counties in the states, the areas in which we live and work, and about which we are concerned, cannot grow and prosper. Change of some kind will undoubtedly come to all of the places where we live; some form of development is inevitable. The only question is: What kind of development shall it be?

The choice is, of course, up to the people who live in and govern each place. Change can be for better or worse, but there is no such thing as a static community. A community or region will either improve or deteriorate. The late Hugh Pomeroy, one of my old friends in the planning field, used to delight in taking this point and making a dramatic example in his stirring, evangelistic speeches. He would cite a city that had remained at about 40,000 people for three census enumerations and therefore felt that it was very stable and static. Hugh then went on to show how a careful demographic study had indicated that, while the total population figure may have remained unchanged, internally the city was in a vital, seething state of flux. Age and ethnic changes had taken place, neighborhoods had shifted, the business community had changed in location, and the overall complexion of the city and its people had altered entirely over the years.

Soundly planned areas achieve a desirable degree of stabilization. This stability of development will be seen in any community that has a pattern, that knows where it is going and how it intends to get there. In such a place, planning means a great deal to the individual property owners. They can rest assured that the residences they buy today are protected from an investment standpoint, that their neighborhoods are not going to deteriorate because of undesirable development. At the same time, the overall economic base of the community will be sound because of ample opportunity for the expansion of business and industry.

The fact is that good, well-publicized planning and the setting of high standards for assuring quality in zoning and urban design regulations have been proven as the best way to attract the right kind of economic development; that which will be a stable, long-term investment in the economic base and will enhance community character. Again, the research done in 15 cities for my 1991 book proved this point. Portland, Oregon; Charlotte, North Carolina; and Boulder, Colorado, are three outstanding examples of how meaningful planning and high standards can pay off. In a time of recession where most of the other cities visited were grasping at any proposal purporting to contribute to employment and the economy, never mind the quality, these three cities were locations so much in demand that they could pick and choose from among any number of applicants seeking approbation, selecting only the ones offering the best possible benefit to their community. It is extremely difficult to comprehend why all but a few elected governing bodies seem unwilling or incapable of understanding this truism.

Having stated what good planning can do and what its legitimate purposes are, I should point out that there are a number of things that planning cannot and should not do. Regrettably, attempts at the improper use of planning in some cases have resulted in failure and misunderstanding of its proper purposes. Planning cannot automatically solve all of the ills of the community. The mere fact that there is a planning commission or even a master plan will not alone result in the correction of past mistakes or even in the prevention of new ones. Planning, to be effective, must be supported by policy-making and an action program. Far too many communities have fallen victim to the illusion that the unveiling of a spanking new plan is the end of all necessary effort and that the mere existence of a plan means that their worries are over.

Planning cannot solve the problems of an outmoded tax structure, nor was it ever intended to. If the taxing system is weak or archaic, nothing in the planning function can fully relieve the undue burden placed upon real estate. Misunderstanding this, many have hopped on the bandwagon in the belief that planning can stop development rather than guide it. While it is true that good planning results in more orderly growth, it should never be used to attempt to build a fence around a community to keep others out. The planning process, when practiced correctly, will not have as its purpose exclusion of all others, but, instead, will illuminate the advantage of quality controlled growth for planning change. Only speculators and exploiters will chorus the cries that your planning and regulations represent your way of become a "no-growth" community.

These and many of the other everyday ills of society and our present way of life will not be solved just because we have planning. It is certain, however, that without some organized effort on the part of all of us to tackle the problems we face from growth and development and to use the collective tools available in a positive way to provide a sense of direction, life will become even more difficult and undesirable. To provide the means for us to see that this does not happen is what community planning is all about.

> The book suggests, in fact, insists, that planning based on informed choices is the answer; that the future lies in combining government decisions with a vigorous private sector, building on individual energies and aspirations, not on unbalanced drift, leaving the nation's destiny and reputation to be buffeted by economic and technological change and international upheaval.
>
> *Melvin R. Levin*

CHAPTER

4

The Planning Commission

It has been interesting over the years to observe the reaction of various individuals upon their initial appointment to a planning commission. Some feel pride and real interest in the opportunity to be of service to the community. These are people who have been and are concerned about the future of urban society. They recognize that major problems exist and that it is going to take concerted citizen involvement to effectuate planned change. They are sincere, dedicated people who, it is hoped, are prepared for the possible frustration of finding that political expediency sometimes has a way of prevailing over logical solutions. On the other hand, many planning commission appointees are very familiar with the politics of government and appointments, far more than they are with the problems of land use, pollution, capital improvement needs, and municipal financing. There have been many who have said, "It's only to be expected that I should be appointed. After all, I've made the right political connections and worked hard for the right party. Besides, I want to run for council, and this is as good a place as any to start." This is prevalent, unfortunately, in far too many of the appointments made and, regrettably, something that has held back progress toward improvement.

An even worse impediment to objective and beneficial action is the stacking of the commission with those whose economic livelihoods depend on or can be improved by growth and expansion of the kind achieved at the expense of the community and the general public. This was the situation found in the city of Albuquerque when I started there as planning director. The planning commission was composed of seven men: two residential real estate brokers, an architect involved in local development, two engineers who did 90 percent of all new subdivision work in the region, a retired army general, and a junior high school principal. (I never did figure out what political connections the last two had that led to their appointments.) I am sure I don't need to tell you what kind of far-sighted "planning" action was taken by such a group. Fortunately, as was indicated earlier, things changed for the better and the composition of the commission improved, at least during the time I was involved.

This unfortunate makeup of a planning commission, and the reason for the appointments is not all that unique. I am all for planning being made more relative to the political process, but fervently oppose the practice of appointing people to planning commissions just because they belong to the "right" political party, have been political workers, contributed campaign financing, or have done some other favor for an elected official. It is just as bad, if not worse, to appoint a person in a business or profession such that their influence, exerted on commission decisions, could offer any opportunity for personal gain. Obviously, both of these may well have been the reasons for the composition of the Albuquerque commission. What is frightening is that these deplorable criteria are used in the greater majority of appointments made by elected officials to planning commissions, zoning boards, and just about any other board or commissions of which you can think. This is the theory of "you pay your dues and you get rewarded"—and we sit back and wonder why good planning and zoning are not being practiced in our community?

In those places fortunate enough to have elected officials who have risen above this theory and made considered appointments of worthy persons, the public owes them their complete support. To those people appointed, I say do not feel uneasy if you begin to realize that you don't know everything there is to know about community planning and zoning; just be determined to be willing to learn, listen carefully, ask questions, and read as much as you possibly can. The most important charge for you is that you continue to be concerned about the future and dedicated to doing all you can to improve it for your community.

There have been many others who, like you, have a desire to do the best possible, take their responsibilities seriously, and yet find themselves faced with the quandary of how to go about learning enough to really contribute. This was best expressed in a comment made to me by a new planning commission appointee a goodly number of years ago. It went something like this: "Yesterday I was just an ordinary citizen, and I knew little or nothing about planning. Today I am a member of an official planning commission. I don't feel any different. Was there supposed to be some magic in the swearing-in, and am I now supposed to be an expert? What do I do, and how do I get started?" Thankfully, this person had an inquiring mind and was not satisfied to approach the new task being less than well-informed. In acquiring someone with that attitude, the city had picked an excellent planning commission member who would render valuable service to the community. The fact is, however, that not all new appointees are similarly imbued with the desire for knowledge.

SEEK ADVICE AND YE SHALL FIND IT

Planning commissions frequently make use of citizen advisory committees nominated by them and approved by the mayor and council. These can be established for ad hoc purposes to study and provide additional citizen input on a specific critical problem about which controversy is likely. Some planning commissions use one or more standing advisory groups, meeting with them regularly to keep them informed and supportive of the work of the commission and its staff. One of the areas in which the use of a citizens' advisory committee can be most helpful is in the preparation and ultimate adoption of a capital improvements program. As with all such auxiliary groups, this committee should be composed of representatives from all socioeconomic and geographical areas of the city. When used properly, the advisory committee for the capital improvement program should not only take part in the preparation of the program, but should also be the primary advocates for the passage of the bond proposal needed to carry out the expenditure program.

NEXT WEEK WE'VE GOT TO GET ORGANIZED

In order for anyone, planning commission member or just an interested citizen, to understand planning and the duties and responsibilities of a planning commission, it is desirable to understand the theory behind the governmental structure established to facilitate the process. Let's start by remembering that our system of government dictates that the final responsibility for policy, decision making, and action rests with those elected to office to represent us. A cardinal principle in local governmental law in the United States is that, while elected officials may delegate administrative responsibility, legislative authority (decision making) cannot be delegated. Therefore, there can be no doubt where former President Harry Truman's old saying "The buck stops here" rests as it applies to action taken or not taken in our towns. It sits squarely on the elected mayors and council members. As I have said so often, successful planning is not assured just by appointing a planning commission, no matter how capable the members of that commission may be. Success will be directly proportionate to the concern, support, and understanding of the planning process, as well as the planning attitude of the legislative body.

We have noted that administrative and advisory responsibility can be delegated. We have seen, also, that planning, early in its history, was conducted on a rather informal basis. These first efforts came from privately sponsored committees or groups of concerned professionals with little or no official status. As the nation and its urban problems grew, it became evident that effective results were dependent upon governmental assumption of planning as a legitimate concern. With the advent of planning as an organized function of government, it became necessary to devise machinery for its operation.

The pioneers in the field were strongly of the opinion that mixing planning with politics and political structure was something to be avoided. They were convinced that planning, in order to be meaningful and effective, should be as free as possible of political pressures. The theory was that the agency responsible for the planning process, while being a part of and in direct touch with government, should be to a degree apart from and lifted above routine pressures and political campaigns. The desirability of continuity and of avoiding complete turnovers of entire commissions following elections was stressed; this, too, could best be achieved if the planning function could retain some freedom from the political structure. Because planning should be a reflection of the views of the citizens, the early commissions were organized so that the majority, if not all of the members, represented the general public. Thus was born the idea of the lay advisory and recommendatory body, which has carried through to today. In this way, too, the idea was formulated for the local government agency that came to be known as the planning commission or planning board, depending on the individual state legislation.

As more communities using their home-rule powers established planning boards or commissions, it became obvious that cities were serious about planning for future growth, and state governments began to adopt enabling acts allowing all incorporated units, whether they had home rule or not, to create commissions empowered to make and adopt master plans. As noted in Chapter 2, planning and zoning had grown so rapidly in the 1920s that the U.S. Department of Commerce felt compelled to promulgate model state enabling acts for use as guidance in adopting state legislation.

Regrettably, the drafters of these model acts, either from lack of understanding that all good zoning should be based upon a well-conceived comprehensive plan, or because pressure from rapid adoption of haphazardly drafted state legislation for zoning grew much faster than planning activity, made the mistake of putting the zoning cart before the planning horse. Consequently, when the U.S. Department of Commerce issued the model Standard State Zoning Enabling Act in 1922 there was little reference to the relationship between zoning and planning, thus creating the impression that zoning stood independently on its own. This misinterpretation haunts us even today with many elected officials, parts of the general public, and even some judges firmly convinced that zoning does not need to be based upon that for which it should be an effectuating tool: well-conceived land-use planning. Fortunately, more and more state court judges are recognizing the value of a planning base and are insisting that local governments submit documentation showing the relationship to planning when their adoption of a zoning ordinance, an amendment, or even a variance is challenged in court.

This grievous error was compounded with the issuance of the 1928 model Standard State Planning Act by the Department of Commerce. Instead of clearly stating that planning was to be the foundation on which zoning should rest, the drafters simply gave that process a passing glance by suggesting that new zoning ordinances, revisions, and amendments should be referred to the planning commission for review and recommendation—if a planning commission existed. The 1928 model did accept the philosophy of the nonpolitical, citizen-dominated commission, to be created by ordinance by the mayor and council and with members to be appointed by the mayor. Members of the agency were to be appointed to serve nonconcurrent terms, thus assuring sufficient carryover of a majority of members for each succeeding year. The commission should be charged by the elected officials in the creating ordinance with its roles and responsibilities. The model suggested: preparation of planning studies, formulation and adoption of a master plan, provision of advice and recommendation on zoning and subdivision matters, recommendation of a capital improvements program, and the general provision of advice to elected officials on any other matter referred by the mayor and council.

Although it was clearly indicated that these models were to serve only as guidance, many states adopted them verbatim. Even today, when all 50 states have some form of planning legislation for their municipal units, you still will find many provisions of the 1928 prototype setting the rules for this year's planning activity. The more progressive states such as Oregon, Florida, New Jersey, California, and Washington have advanced into much broader and more future-oriented state enabling legislation. On the other hand, I could hand you a copy of the Colorado planning (or zoning) act, read from the model and, with but few exceptions, you would be able to follow me word for word. And this is what Colorado municipalities, as well as those in many other states, have to work with as we face the 21st century!

CAN YOU TRUST A POLITICIAN?

No doubt the pioneers in the field felt that they were acting with wisdom to establish the planning organization as far outside the political arena as possible. As things have turned out, and with the advantage of hindsight, I must question whether this is the way to have effective planning in today's society. Elected officials are the ones who shape a community and its policies. Whether this is good or bad, it is the political system of the United States, and getting elected to public office (especially getting reelected) requires a willingness to become involved—or immersed—in politics. As a consequence, the recommendations of a planning commission, frequently not fitting within what may be politically expedient, are often ignored, and planning departments and commissions lose favor because they are too theoretical, too impractical, and not in tune with the real world. The facts of life are that, regardless of who is on the planning commission and how great the planning proposals may be, the key to implementation rests with the members of the local governing body. They are the ones who adopt the budget (including that for planning activity), pass zoning changes, have final say on what subdivision regulations will be, approve urban renewal projects, and, in general, decide where the city is going and who will do what to get it there. This is not to take away from the excellent work that has been done and is being done by many planning commissions around the country; nor am I even hinting at their abolishment. What I am saying, however, is that I am convinced of the necessity to recognize that in our system of governance, politics is the name of the game. Planning commission members and professional staff planners who really are concerned about the future and want to help improve it have to accept this fact and learn to play that game just as well, if not better than, the professional politicians. Failure to do so will mean that our planning efforts will continue to have difficulty in influencing enforcement of governmental policies.

Surely members of planning commissions and their professional staff persons know people within their city or town who have a planning attitude, believe in good planning, and recognize the important role elected government must play to effect planned change that is the fundamental purpose of the entire planning process. Why not do more to seek them out, encourage them to be more involved, and even encourage them to run for office on a future-oriented planning platform? Unheard of, outrageous, perhaps, but the time has come for planners and those who believe in planning to start taking a few risks. Until we do make planning more politically important and politicians more aware that solid support of sound objective planning is essential to their political careers, we will continue to go through the motions of having planning that pays little more than lip service to the true meaning of the process.

Planning should be an essential part of politics, and politics has to be a part of planning. It is my contention that I was able to do far more for the cause of planning and orderly growth in the minds of the general public as a city manager, and even as an unsuccessful candidate for mayor, than I could have done ever as planning director. If you think that this means that I feel that more people trained in planning should get into politics, you bet your sweet bippy I do!

YOU'VE GOTTA START SOMEWHERE

If you live in a community that does not have a planning commission, you may wonder how they are started. The actual stimulus for organization at the local level may, and frequently does, come from several directions. Many planning commissions have come into being through the farsightedness and determination of individual mayors or elected council members. In other situations, some form of citizen instigation has resulted in action. A neighborhood organizes because of some crisis, and from this develops the kind of citizen involvement that influences the elected officials to consider an ordinance creating a commission and starting the planning process. Frequently, the spark for action comes from an organized group such as the Junior Chamber of Commerce, the League of Women Voters, or a taxpayers' association.

One example of how a stimulus, coming originally from only two persons, accomplished a major change for the better comes from a municipality in New Jersey. It was a bedroom community primarily for commuters who worked in New York and had little time to be concerned or interested in their local government, much less whether or not it had a planning program. Soon after World War II, the town found itself overrun by some of those suburban "dream home" subdivisions, aided and abetted by a governing body rife with private interests. There was no planning or planning commission; however there was something meaningless called zoning, from which a variance easily could be obtained just by a handshake—provided one of the hands contained money. Things went from bad to worse; schools were on double sessions, garbage was not collected, traffic became a serious problem, developers were not required to put in sidewalks and could skimp on other amenities. Two concerned and determined women took it upon themselves to start a crusade against what was happening (or not happening). They were soon joined by others who suddenly began to realize what all this was going to cost them to correct in the years ahead. The result was the creation of a planning commission, a new zoning ordinance, and, at the next election, a new governing body.

Organizations, groups, or even individuals can become effective forces when they become genuinely concerned about the way their communities are run and start asking questions. In a very short time, they usually become aware of the fact that planning is the practical way to cope with the problem of the general future welfare of any area and that the organization of a planning commission is a good way to start. Interested citizens, in turn, arouse others, and the groundswell soon becomes obvious to elected officials, even if they have been less than enthusiastic about the mechanism for long-range planning.

In a great many cases, regrettably, there will not be the two, 10, or 20 people to start something like this. Lacking such a stimulus, residents don't want to be bothered for fear of having to become involved, even perhaps assume some responsibility for making things better and, besides, television is such a noncommitment-requiring spectator sport. Such places are the ones where no one becomes impressed with the need for action until some particularly unfortunate occurrence takes place. This may take the form of a poorly designed and improperly planned subdivision of overwhelming proportions, a piecemeal zoning change to satisfy special interests, a use variance to allow a supermarket in an all-residential zone, or even the pollution of the water supply. This was the case with one community where, on several occasions, I had attempted to interest the local officials in planning in advance of the building boom. They would have none of it—could not even be bothered to think about a revised zoning ordinance that would do a much better job than the one to which they were paying tacit attention.

The driving force of the building boom after World War II caught up with this community just as soon as the developers learned about their lack of preparedness, and the community underwent development at an astronomical pace. Three thousand homes were built in two years, many of them on 6,000-square-foot lots with individual septic tanks. Unfortunately, the underlying soil was practically impervious hardpan, and the resulting health hazards soon became obvious. When seepage began to trickle through the subdivision and the pavement itself began to slide downhill, the community woke up. Needless to say, there was a great scurry to organize a planning commission, create a subdivision ordinance, and revise the zoning ordinance. The locking of the barn door after the horse had been stolen did little good. Through haste and pressure from the development interests, the revised zoning ordinance was of lower quality than it should have been and, for the most part, the energy and money spent on planning was wasted. No planning or zoning could have corrected the multiplicity of errors that had been allowed to occur.

The fact that there is less likelihood of such a situation arising now results from a variety of things. As has been noted, whether the numerous federal aid programs, especially Section 701 of the 1954 Federal Housing Act, resulted in any notable accomplishments or not, at least they contributed greatly to increasing the number of local planning agencies. The requirement of some sign of planning action in order to qualify for grants placed the federal government squarely in the position of midwifing the births of hundreds of new planning commissions. During the life of the aid programs almost all carried with them this message: "Do some long-range planning and get citizens involved if you want federal aid." While the gamesmanship played by local governments' staffs and/or consultants in obtaining grants may have negated to some extent the fulfillment of the intent of that message, at least the term *community planning* and the need for it to be in place was widely spread.

In addition to the federal influence, the adoption of mandated planning by a growing number of states, some even requiring state approval of local plans and implementation ordinances, most assuredly means that the mechanism for being prepared to better meet any future building boom is in place in those states. From my research in Oregon, I have become convinced that this trend, and I believe it will be a trend, should be emulated by every state for several reasons. These include: laying the foundation for being prepared for planned change, improving planning's quality and effectiveness, avoiding incompatibility of land-use controls at community boundary lines, and providing the best opportunity for advanced intercommunity coordinated development plans. Essential to the success of this idea, however, is a carefully considered and clearly understandable land-use policy statement adopted by the state itself. Failure to do so will seriously detract from mandated local planning, especially the vital coordination between incorporated municipalities and surrounding unincorporated areas.

Another factor making it advisable to maintain a successful, active planning commission is the increasing number of federal and state environmental regulations. For example, the California Environmental Quality Act requires every city to have an environmental quality agency with almost autonomous powers. In all probability, legislation establishing regulations pertaining to protection of environmentally sensitive areas will continue to increase, especially in those states with heavily populated urban areas. As this happens, planning commissions considering rezonings, site plan review, and subdivision regulations will have to be aware that there will be additional federal and state agencies scrutinizing their actions regarding such things as floodplains, wetlands, and storm runoff. (See Chapter 13 for a discussion of new federal acts with local impact.)

As a result of all this, together with the increasing understanding among concerned citizens that planning is an essential governmental function, few urban places today are without some form of planning and a planning commission. Whether this somewhat coerced action ly effective and whether sensible planning has been n enthusiasm are different questions. In fact, these are the of us should be asking ourselves now if we live where there is a planning commission. Have the commission and the elected officials really had their heart in the process, or has it been something done just to meet mandated requirements and other pressures? Has there been improvement of the environment, the quality of life, and the community character? Does the general public know what planning is being done and who is doing it, and do they understand and support it? These and many other questions need to be asked and answered positively before anyone should be satisfied with just an "Oh yes, we have planning." It is up to us to be sure that we really do have an effective process.

FIRST, SET THE STAGE

Regardless of motivation or stimulation, the first necessary step under the state enabling acts is for the governing body to pass an ordinance creating a planning commission; establishing its membership, makeup, and numbers; and outlining its responsibilities. Once a planning commission has been organized, there remains the question of where it fits into the organizational structure of the community. Normally, enabling acts indicate that most of the members are to be appointed by the mayor; the appointments may or may not be subject to the approval of the governing body, depending upon the enabling act and the incorporation charter of the municipality. In the case of the mayor-council form of government, it is usually understood that the planning commission is a part of the administrative office of the mayor. Although reporting to the council generally, it is responsible to the mayor. This, at least, is the position that the planning function should occupy. In the council-manager structure, the appointments are usually made by the council, and, while the manager works closely with the commission, it has primary responsibility to the council. The arrangement in other types of governmental structure may vary slightly, but the planning commission should be considered to be a citizen advisory arm to the policymakers and to the chief executive officer.

To aid the planning commission in its work, most communities also create a complete department of planning with a staff, just as there is a department of public works or parks and recreation. Again, depending on the city charter, the creation of this department may require a charter amendment, or it may be that the mayor and council are authorized to do this by resolution. This department might consist of only a professional planner as planning director and some administrative assistants, or it might include a large number of trained and supportive personnel, depending on the size of the community. It should be recognized that such a department invariably has a dual responsibility. The department staff must work closely with the appointed planning commission, providing them with information upon which to make recommendations and respond to their directions. They also must work cooperatively with the elected officials, the mayor and/or city manager.

This dual responsibility can place the planning director in the awkward position of having to resolve conflicting views of theoretical planning and pragmatic politics. It is a capable planning director who can avoid being damaged in this cross fire. Having been the planning director, I have to admit that I had a closer relationship with the planning department than did either the planning commission or the council when I become city manager in Albuquerque. We even went so far as to organize all department heads into a task force to meet with the planning director weekly just to talk about planning for the future city and its current needs. In the minds of some of the department heads it was unthinkable, but it worked!

As a result of moves such as this, it has been suggested by some that a separate agency for planning in the form of a commission is no longer necessary and that the function and the department should be part of the chief executive's office. The arguments for this include the proposal that effective planning is really a part of management, that coordination is better achieved in this manner, and that all planning proposals should be closely related to the municipal budget. As a consequence, many feel that a better approach would be to have all planning responsibility placed with the chief executive, with a PPBS (Planning, Programming, and Budgeting System) as the means for putting it all together. The mayor or manager would then work with council, utilizing a broader citizens' advisory group or groups to be sure of having citizen input and opinion. This approach was pushed during the days of the federal grant programs and Washington usually insisted that the chief executive not only be involved, but also be the one responsible for the effectiveness of any federally funded program. This discussion over the best approach will continue for some time, with both methods being used. By no means, however, is the day of the somewhat independent planning commission over. It is still a very good, effective approach for smaller communities and rural areas.

Regardless of whether planning is advisory or a part of management, the important thing is to be sure that the established process is meaningful and has the full support of the elected officials. This needs to be more than just tacit endorsement and certainly more than mere acquiescence under pressure to create a planning program. Although they are infrequent, I have known of situations where elected officials basically opposed to the idea of organized planning went through the motions of establishing the process with the full intent of seeing that it failed so that they could put an end to "this planning nonsense" once and for all. It happened several years ago in an eastern Pennsylvania county, where a county planning program was inaugurated and a planning director hired at the insistence of interested citizens. The planning director spent a year fighting a losing battle against complete isolation and a ridiculously low budget. He was assigned a small room in the county courthouse but was unable to obtain furniture and was not even permitted to have a telephone. After a few months of going to the corner phone booth to make calls, he moved on to greener pastures and the county planning program folded.

Happily, this story is the exception rather than the rule. Even better, it can be reported that the next election found new county officials in office, and the planning function was restored and went on to do an excellent job that continues today. This indicates the importance of informing people and the media about the planning function, what it can do for them, and why it is vital that they understand and support this function. Where planning is supported intelligently, the duties and responsibilities of the planning commission are the subject of public discussion. Of course, as its name implies, the first responsibility of the agency is to plan. It must develop thoughtful plans for the future provision of municipal services and for the development of the total community. Planning is an organized process geared to provide the best possible blueprint for the most efficient municipal action. It is not just collective thinking or spur-of-the-moment decision making. One of the delusions to which certain planning commissioners are subject is that no special preparation is necessary to understand planning: their position alone confers clairvoyance upon them. Regardless of the sincerity of individual members, and regardless of their basic familiarity with the community, "planning" that is merely collective thinking without investigation and analysis is both insufficient and ineffective.

The earlier reference to budgets and finances leads into a realistic examination of the present tightening crisis in state and local government budgets. We all are aware that the country has been in a serious recession. At the same time there is little or no federal financial assistance to local governments still available. As discussed earlier, most remaining federal programs are being consolidated into the 1990 National Affordable Housing Act with concentration on housing and very little said about planning. This means that planning commissions, local government officials, and those interested in preserving the planning process, competent planning staffs, and effective programs in their community are going to have to give serious thought to this problem. Mistakenly, some elected officials consider planning somewhat intangible and, frequently, when caught in a bare bones budget situation, jump to the conclusion that planning is one place that would be easy to cut. The only counteractions, if this attitude prevails in any community, are strong support by taxpayers and news media who believe in planning's value; or, should the supportive appeal not be present or fail, the development of greater efficiency by the planning commission and staff. A way must be found for developing plans and planning studies more quickly and more cheaply without any sacrifice in the quality of the work.

PUTTING THE AVAILABLE TOOLS TO WORK

The work of a planning commission usually takes the form of organizing a master plan or development plan or, perhaps, the revision and updating of an older one already in existence. The term "master plan" was devised to indicate comprehensiveness during the early days of planning and has been the one in most common use. It is the term that has been incorporated in most of the state enabling acts, and it has received considerable acceptance as an appropriate designation of the culmination of the planning process by the courts of this country. It must be remembered, however, that planning is advisory to the elected officials and the public. Even if a state enabling act allows official master plan adoption by the planning commission, little, if anything, will result from the worthwhile endeavor without the full support of the elected officials.

In addition to the development of the master plan, the planning process includes the more commonly understood and accepted legal document known as the zoning ordinance. Zoning is an effectuation tool of a plan or project for future community growth. As alluded to earlier, it is extremely important that zoning be kept in tune with the plan and that it reflect the latest consideration available from the planning process. The control and regulation of subdivision activity within the community is also a function of the planning process. The planning commission usually is the administrative agency authorized to review and recommend action to the governing body or, as in some local ordinances, has been given the authority to approve "minor subdivisions" that are clearly defined by the ordinance. This, too, must be closely coordinated with overall planning activity. As part of the master plan, proposals will be made for the provision of future public facilities. The projection of the cost of facilities and when they should be provided is part of the capital improvements program, which is, in turn, a part of planning. (These basic tools of planning are discussed in great detail in the following chapters.)

Because planning deals with future streets and roads as well as existing ones, some planning statutes provide that the development of an official map of the municipality shall be included within the prerogatives of the planning commission. The actual adoption of such an official map, which is binding as to street locations, streets or alley vacations, and rights-of-way, is a function of the governing body and is adopted by enacting an ordinance. Many state enabling acts also provide for the referral of any other matter to a planning commission at the discretion of elected officials or public agencies. A variety of duties have thus been assigned, including such things as suggesting revisions for building codes, surveying overlapping street names and recommending a renaming program, studying the efficiency of the garbage disposal method practiced by the municipality, determining where the next needed sanitary landfill location should be, recommending ways a recycling program should be operated, and suggesting the procedure for handling hazardous waste within the community or its passage through in trucks.

Whatever the program undertaken by a planning commission, it should have as its primary motive the careful formulation of a master plan. The commission should always remember that the program is basically one of coordinating and pulling together various ideas concerned with the development of the community. The desired comprehensiveness can be obtained only if the planning commission has at its disposal adequate information to reach intelligent decisions. Once a commission is organized and begins to familiarize itself with its role, there is usually a concern about its administration. Frequently, members have been frustrated and confused because they have been left to fend for themselves within the municipal administration. They have hesitated to assume initiative and have not been at all sure just what was expected of them. Any planning commission member should understand that, once organized, the responsibility for initiating a program and its internal administration should be accepted by the commission. This does not mean that activity contrary to the policies of the established local government should be undertaken!

The commission, however, should make certain that it does not permit itself to become just a rubber-stamp organization, simply adding legitimacy to any action taken or requested by the governing body or administrative departments. The role of the commission should be that of studying, proposing, questioning, and even criticizing where necessary. It must be remembered that the real function is to make certain that the best interests of the entire community are being protected and enhanced. That is a far cry from the situation that I ran into in one eastern city when I was called in to discuss the possibility of a consulting job. Upon arrival at the appointed place, I discovered only the mayor, the president of the council, and the city attorney present. When I asked about the planning commission and their role in the project, I was informed that they met only on call and that I really should not worry about them. I am happy to report that I was gracious enough to allow another consultant to have the pleasure of that contract.

Normally, a properly organized planning commission meets on a regularly scheduled basis and at least once a month. Many meet more frequently, and some of the best ones that I have known have one regular monthly public meeting and one or two monthly work sessions. These work sessions are primarily for the commission itself and are used to do the actual planning work. During that time, they meet with their staff and/or consultants or hear reports of subcommittees and then consider action that can and should be taken. In this way, they are able to handle routine assignments and still not lose sight of long-range objectives. An efficient commission normally has its own set of bylaws. The bylaws establish the time and place of meeting, the officers, the subcommittees, and the procedure for conducting business. A helpful model set of bylaws usually can be obtained from the state agency concerned with planning, a state league of municipalities, or such national organizations as the American Planning Association. As is the case with model forms of any kind, these suggested bylaws should not be copied verbatim but may be used as the basis for the formulation of a specific set of procedures with the advice of the municipal attorney.

The important thing is for each planning commission to know where it is going and just how it is going to get there. A definite procedure and a formal organization will go a long way toward making a smooth operation. This will also be of great help to newly appointed members as the commission changes because of expiring terms, resignation, illness, or death. Subdividers should know exactly what is expected of them and how they can get their subdivision plats processed. Any citizen or citizen group should know that they can be heard and when and how this can take place. Anyone interested in having a public hearing conducted should be able to find out quickly how it can be done and how it will be run when it is scheduled. While the commission should be careful not to overload itself with administrative detail, it should be equally careful that it does not permit itself to operate in a slipshod fashion. Most importantly of all, it must never permit itself to go about its tasks in a vacuum. Each commission member should constantly reflect on the thought that his or her client is the general public and it is to the public that they should feel responsible. No plan works without citizen participation, understanding, and support, just as the same must come from the elected officials.

GETTING ALONG WITH OTHERS TAKES PLANNING, TOO

Another vital question of concern to a successful planning program's operation is the relation of the planning commission and its staff to the governing body and other officials of the community. Because the primary role of the planning commission is as adviser to the governing body, the relationship between these two groups must, of necessity, be cooperative and extremely close. Mayors and councils or city commissioners should keep the commission informed of their problems and their progress in dealing with them. Conversely, the planning commission that does not have a close relationship with elected officials is doomed to failure. In my consulting days I had some experience with just such an example of this lack of liaison in a Delaware city. Operating under a city charter, the planning commission was totally separate from the governing body.

The planning agency had spent some four years in building a working vocabulary of planning and thoroughly understanding the problems of the community. They now were extremely enthusiastic about the development of a comprehensive master plan and an urban renewal program. Unfortunately, because no one from the governing body had been in on the discussions and the planning commission had not bothered to keep them informed, this same enthusiasm was not shared by the elected officials. The result was that there was resentment on the part of those officials against the planning commission's zeal. These officials, not having been encouraged to have a "planning attitude," felt that a master plan was just a means of wasting money and, further, that the commission was usurping some of their power. This is a perfect way to ruin the possibility of having a successful planning program.

On the other hand, the inclusion of elected officials as members of the planning commission does not always guarantee the necessary support. I once worked with a community where, along with a majority of nonofficial persons, two members of the governing body also were planning commission members. During the preparation of the comprehensive plan I met with them as each study phase of the plan was completed. A copy of the material was sent to them two weeks before the meeting. Unfortunately, you could not depend on the elected officials to attend these work sessions regularly. One or the other might come, but only once or twice were both present. When they did show up they would sit there, nod their heads in agreement, never ask questions or make any comments.

When the complete draft of the plan had been put together, a public meeting was scheduled for it to be presented to the community for discussion. The commission chairman, after some opening remarks, called upon me to outline the principal features of the plan. When this was completed the chairman opened the meeting for comments from those in attendance. At first, the comments were intelligent and helpful, but then one belligerent individual seized the floor and began a harangue against the whole idea of planning, big government trying to tell people what to do, and on, and on, finally ending with, "Besides, we don't need no outside consultant coming in here and telling us what's best for us!" Now, just what do you think the one elected official who had attended the most work study meetings did? He jumped to his feet, grabbed the microphone and said; "Oscar, I'm glad you said all those things. I sure have felt that way too and I've been against this damn thing right from the start!" You talk about the feeling of the rug being pulled right out from underneath you—this was a personification of that for me, as well as most of the planning commission. Once again, we have a strong argument for being sure that you have indoctrinated, educated and, if necessary, browbeaten some "planning attitude" into your elected officials if you want to get very far with your planning endeavors.

The proper relationship between the governing body and the planning commission is that of a corporation's board of directors with its technical advisory committee. If the proper aims of both groups are diligently pursued, the results can be extremely successful. The governing body cannot, of course, give up its policy-making role, nor can it delegate legislative authority. It can, however, make valuable use of its technical advisory arm, the planning commission.

Employees of the municipal government also should be made to feel a part of the planning program. The work of the municipal engineer, the building inspector, and the zoning officer are integral parts of planning activity. In many cases, these positions are filled by devoted public servants who have, over a long period of time, gained a tremendous insight into the problems of the community. Their special skills are invaluable in effectuating the decisions reached in the planning program. Again, the proper relationship is one of cooperation and close liaison.

What you do when this is impossible because of the individuals involved is another matter, especially if you don't have the support of the governing body. Many times, long-tenured bureaucratic department heads have built up an even greater political power base than some of the elected officials and operate in their own little independent empires. This is most likely to occur in the engineering department: most long-term engineers have a dislike of planning and planners and their power base is very strong, especially if they are the ones who recommend the awarding of contracts for construction projects for facilities and systems. A word from that type of engineer to contractors who have been awarded contracts can make raising funds for a candidate's campaign a very easy job.

During my tenure as city manager in Albuquerque, this was a problem with which I had to deal. The director of public works (an old-school engineer) had been there much longer than I had. When I started to have all department heads at a weekly overall city planning meeting, he was not about to do anything he thought would weaken his baronial fiefdom. He told me he was too busy for such things, that he had seen city managers come and go and added that he would be around long after I was gone. Sure enough, he was right; he remained on the job for several years after I left, but was replaced by someone else after a new mayor was elected. I am happy to report that after every other department head showed up at the first meeting, he did join us, attended regularly, and actually made some valuable contributions to the effort. The moral: Don't think you can buck entrenched bureaucrats if you don't have the muscle.

The commission must also be prepared to deal with other public agencies. The good member will understand that the development of a master plan or the formulation of a coordinated planning program cuts across the areas of responsibility of the school board, the urban renewal authority, the housing authority, the parking authority, the board of health, the zoning board of appeals, and many other agencies. All of these agencies are concerned with specialized functions of government. They feel, and justifiably, that their functions are important. They cannot be ignored if the planning program is to be successful. The commission must learn to assume a coordinating role tactfully and without creating a feeling of interference.

The planning commission must also recognize its responsibility to keep the public informed. The activities of the commission should be a matter of public knowledge if citizens are to reach intelligent conclusions on planning matters. Efforts should be made to get all forms of media to name one of their reporters to regularly cover planning commission meetings and to see that the information gathered is passed on to the public. Now that cable TV is widespread and usually has one or more channels reserved for public affairs, there is an excellent opportunity for members of the commission to inform the public themselves by appearing and discussing what they are doing. The best cure for rumormongering and emotional antiplanning attitudes is prevention: Get the facts on the public record first!

Depending upon the requirements of the state enabling act, the planning commission frequently is made up of five to nine persons, and membership is divided between appointed citizens and elected officials of the municipality. In most cases, the majority of the commission comprises appointed members holding no other appointed or elected office. If members' terms are staggered, some member of a newly formed commission will be appointed for a one-year term, some for three years, and some for six years. Thereafter, any person reappointed or newly appointed would be appointed for a six-year term. All of this is just an example. The length of terms should be a local decision, but I strongly recommend that the staggered term method be used for the sake of the continuity.

I have been asked many times to define the best type of person for membership on a planning commission. This is an extremely difficult assignment and one that I have constantly sought to duck. There is, of course, no one best candidate for membership. Although the individual's knowledge and experience are important considerations, they are secondary to a genuine interest in the community's problems and a concern about its future. It is much easier to answer the question by indicating the kinds of persons who should not be placed on the commission. Some of these have been referred to earlier but the two most important caveats are: Never appoint someone just because of political ties or obligations, and no appointment should be given to anyone when there is even a glimmer that they can personally benefit economically or any other way by having such a position. Also, I am strongly in favor of trying to have good representation from both sexes, all ethnic groups, and diverse economic standings. Where the planning commission is so small that this cannot easily be done, then I urge the creation of a larger citizen advisory council where all interests can be provided equitable representation. The test of probable success, more than a specialized background, is dedication, commitment, honest concern, and at least a smattering of my favorite phrase: "A planning attitude."

A planning commission and its resultant program will be no better than the raw material used in its construction. In this case, the raw material is the quality of the personnel selected.

CHAPTER

5

The Master Plan

The next chapters will discuss the four traditional basic tools of the planning process. These are the master plan, zoning, subdivision controls, and capital improvements programming. While there are those who say that these avenues available to local governments to aid in development and land management are no longer as effective as is needed, they are still the major processes recognized by state enabling acts. They are the legal foundation upon which all other approaches and techniques must be based, whether we are talking about growth management, performance zoning, planned unit developments, transfer of development rights, or any of the other modern, flexible approaches to land-use regulation. All elements of planning, even most of the social concerns, are anchored upon or affected by the way in which land is used. Community character is set, general economic well-being is built, cultural and social amenities are provided, and ease and convenience of circulation are determined—all by what occurs on the building blocks of land parcels fitted together like a jigsaw puzzle to make the total environment of any urban area. Fundamental to the ability of the general populace or the community to do anything about this urban environment, to shape it in accordance with principles and thought-out objectives is some idea of a blueprint for growth—the master plan. It may be called a development plan, a comprehensive plan, a general plan, or any of several other terms that have come into popular usage in recent years; but if it is to be official and legal by state statutes and acceptable by the courts as a basis to defend against a legal challenge of enacted land controls, it is still the master plan.

UNDERSTANDING IS NOT ALWAYS EASY

Even though the term planning and the process have been around for many years, there are many people who have no idea of what it is, what its purpose and objectives are, what it looks like, or, if meaningful, what far-reaching effects it has on individual and community lives. There are probably very few cities of any size that do not have, or have not had prepared, something called a master plan. Yet a random survey of any 100 people on any main street, asking them whether their community has such a plan and whether they are familiar with it, would produce some extremely disappointing results. This comes back to one of the primary problems of planning in this country. We have had to face the necessity of developing something that can be used by government to direct the private use of land before we have done the job we should have done in educating people about this necessity and the process. When we find those who know about planning, we still find that they lack knowledge about a master plan and what it can and should do. Many times when I hear a person attempt to offer an impression of a master plan, I am reminded of the story of the blind men and the elephant: It seems that the understanding of the term depends upon the particular part of the animal being touched.

To help in knowing what to look for, and so that we will all have a better chance to get in touch with the same piece of the "elephant," I have frequently suggested a number of things one should expect to find. First of all there should be printed material giving a reasonable, concise summary of the plan and the process of its formulation. Included should be goals and objectives of the overall plan and each of its parts. These parts should cover such things as population and demography, land use, traffic and circulation, parks and open space, housing, utilities and services, drainage, social programs, urban design standards, and general cultural characteristics—both present and future. In the definition of future needs, specific ways should be indicated for carrying out the proposals and seeing that they become reality. There should be a clear discussion of what, why, where, and when with regard to everything advocated for the future community. There should also be evidence of the amount of involvement of the public, the local administration, and the elected officials in the preparation as well as in the effectuation to date. (I would add that if the master plan doesn't do this, perhaps we need to think about getting involved and helping to see that it does.)

To better understand what the master plan is, or should be, perhaps we should start with an exploration of the desirable objectives and purpose. Simply stated, they are the same as that of the planning process—to shape a better community and to avoid costly and undesirable mistakes detrimental to the well-being of the public interest. The master plan is the tangible expression of how this is to be done. It should depict in words and graphically all that anyone would need to know to understand what studies have been made, what problems need to be solved, and steps that need to be taken to accomplish the objectives. As to the latter, the foundation of the plan's proposals and objectives should be goals established through citizen involvement. When this has been formalized, the next step, one that is so very important, should be the adoption of an administrative policy statement by the governing body indicating its support and commitment to the planning process, setting forth specific steps to be taken to achieve the desired goals, and a directive that all municipal departments and agencies are to cooperate fully with the plan's development and its effectuation. In other words, a good master plan should be the means whereby the people, working with the planning commission, its professional staff and the elected officials, have said, "This is what we know our community is today—the good and the bad—and this is what we want to see it become in five or 10 years."

DEFINITIONS REVISITED

There has been much written about master plans with many definitions given. What I have said to this point is only an attempt at a general concept summary. Actually, just what the master plan is and should or can do depends largely upon the state legislature and the wording used in the enabling act it passes. Even though there is a great deal of similarity from state to state, specific items covered do vary according to each state's interests and traditions. Anyone interested in knowing more about the legal status of a plan, and what an adopted plan should contain, can obtain a copy of a state planning enabling act and carefully read its provisions. These state acts are very good sources of information, and, in most cases, a lot of good thought has gone into their preparation. Reference will be made to three of these acts for further explanation of the purpose and objectives of a master plan and the kinds of things that should be included, but, even more importantly, to show how the philosophy behind planning and the process has changed in the last several decades.

The first example is an older act, since revised and updated, that was passed in New Jersey in 1953. Those involved with its formulation wanted to have the most modern and best definition and statement of purpose possible. For the state of the art at that time, they did achieve this. The definition read:

> . . . a master plan for the physical development of the municipality shall comprise land use, circulation and a report presenting the objectives, assumptions, standards and principles which are embodied in the various interlocking portions of the master plan. The master plan shall be a composite of the one or more mapped and written proposals recommending the physical development of the municipality which the planning board shall have adopted either as a whole or severally after public hearing. Such master plan may include proposals for various stages in the future development of the municipality.

To provide additional clarification of the scope and purpose, after listing a number of individual areas of concern that could be included in the plan studies, the legislation then stated:

> In the preparation of the master plan, the planning board shall give due consideration to the probable ability of the municipality to carry out, over a period of years, the various public or quasi-public projects embraced in the plan without the imposition of unreasonable financial burdens. In such preparation, the planning board shall cause to be made careful and comprehensive surveys and studies of present conditions and the prospects for future growth of the municipality. The master plan shall be made with the general purpose of guiding and accomplishing a coordinated, adjusted and harmonious development of the municipality. . .

This certainly gave a good idea of just what a master plan was all about and for many years provided a sense of direction for New Jersey municipalities. A careful reading, however, and some thorough application to the scope of community concerns today, clearly indicates that the scope must be much broader. It is to be noted that in 1953 the emphasis was still almost exclusively on the physical aspects of development. Very little was said specifically about social concerns and problems, environmental considerations, or citizen and community involvement.

In fairness, it must be pointed out that New Jersey now has one of the most progressive mandatory planning enabling acts in the country. Each municipality and county must have prepared and adopted a master plan meeting the standards and requirement of the legislation. Every six years after adoption these plans must be comprehensively reviewed and updated. Zoning enaction and amendments must conform to the current plan. In addition, as a result of a leadership role taken by the New Jersey Supreme Court in both planning and housing issues, the state has a far-reaching "fair share" housing policy that requires all municipalities to be able to show that their land-use regulations provide for meeting their fair share of the regionally established needs for low- and moderate-income housing. If a community is challenged in court for failing to provide its fair share and the court finds this to be the case, the supreme court's rules strongly suggest that the trial court appoint a "special master," usually a professional planner, to work with the local government in developing revisions to meet the fair share requirements. The special master then will testify before the trial court at a rehearing of the case in 90 days as to whether the amendments allow the municipality to meet the requirement.

There is every indication that a trend (it has been referred to as a "quiet evolution" by some) may be developing among states for adoption of legislation mandating planning and land-use controls and setting forth specific policies that must be followed and the elements to be included in the comprehensive plan. This conclusion is supported by the fact that, in addition to New Jersey, a stronger state role in directing local governments in planning and land-use controls exists in Florida, Oregon, Vermont, California, and Washington. The governments in these states have recognized the need for a coordinated and somewhat standardized planning process on a statewide basis. In addition, legislators have become aware of some subtle (and some not so subtle) changes in public attitudes about such things as environmental values, protecting historic resources, affordable housing, balancing economic development with protecting the environment, and so on. What these states have done, and probably others will be doing, is to reassert a stronger role for state government in preserving the quality of life and the development of urban form within their state. From what I have observed about the effectiveness of planning in states that espouse the idea of "local control" for planning and zoning, this "quiet evolution" may be an idea whose time has come—if not long overdue.

THE INGREDIENTS DETERMINE THE QUALITY OF THE PRODUCT

There can be no question that local and county planners must depend on the wording of the state enabling act for what they can and cannot do. It then follows that if any legislation is to be passed that provides the kind of guidance and direction needed to ensure effective planning at the state, region, county, or municipal level, it must be a priority for those elected representatives comprising state government. Unless an understanding exists regarding the importance of planning for the future, a planning attitude, and a willingness to resist opposition from special interest groups, no state can ever expect to have the kind of enabling framework needed by its jurisdictions to cope successfully with the development of urban form in the complex, largely unconcerned society in which we live. Any state government that does not recognize that, in today's world, it has the ultimate responsibility of providing policy guidance for the use of every square mile of land in the state, regardless of whether the local units of government actually develop the plans, is guilty of neglect of duty and misfeasance.

CAN GROWTH MANAGEMENT BE MANAGED?

The Oregon Approach

By way of comparison to the 1953 New Jersey planning enabling act defining just what a master plan is and should contain, we turn now to Oregon's as it currently reads:

> **ORS 197.015, Definitions:**
> (5) "Comprehensive plan" means a generalized coordinated land use map and policy statement of the governing body of a local government that interrelates all functional and natural systems and activities relating to the use of lands, including, but not limited to, sewer and water systems, transportation systems, educational facilities, recreational facilities, and natural resources and air and water quality management programs. "Comprehensive" means all-inclusive, both in terms of the geographic area covered and functional and natural activities and systems occurring in the area covered by the plan. "General nature" means a summary of policies and proposals in broad categories and does not necessarily indicate specific locations of any area, activity or use. A plan is "coordinated" when the needs of all levels of governments, semi-public and private agencies and the citizen of Oregon have been considered and accommodated as much as possible. "Land" includes water, both surface and subsurface, and the air.[1]

That covers a lot of ground (as well as water and air), giving local governments ample policy direction, yet remaining rather general and leaving them some flexibility. By the way, blame the drafting lawyers for the long sentences and the legalese, not me.

Anyone who has read my book *Planning America's Communities,*[2] knows that I am a big fan of Oregon's state and local planning process and the way it is practiced. In fact, after my study of the planning efforts in 15 cities across the country, Portland was rated as having the most obvious planning attitude and the most meaningful planning effectuation of all cities studied. In addition, it is my opinion that Oregon has the most comprehensive and the best statewide planning program and enabling legislation of the 50 states. This all started with the passage of Senate Bill 100 and the signing of it into law by the governor in 1973. Prior to that time, the role of the state in land-use planning done by local communities was comparatively minuscule; under then-existing enabling acts, local governments did the actual planning and zoning largely at their discretion. Some jurisdictions had very effective plans and land-use ordinances; some had none at all. Incidentally, the Oregon Land Conservation and Development Commission (LCDC) has published a summary of the state's planning laws entitled *Oregon's Statewide Planning Program,* from which much of this information has been taken.[3]

With Senate Bill 100, the state required all of Oregon's 242 cities and 36 counties to adopt comprehensive plans and land-use regulations. It specified planning concerns that had to be addressed, set statewide standards that local plans and ordinances had to meet, and established a review process to ensure that those standards were met. The state asserted greater responsibility in an area that traditionally had been a local concern, but the state also gave over some of its traditional powers to local governments. It promised that state agencies would work with local governments to develop coordinated comprehensive plans and that certain state agency programs would conform to local plans after their approval by the LCDC. This agency, created by Senate Bill 100, is composed of seven laypersons appointed by the governor and confirmed by the state senate. Members receive no salary. It is the policy-making body that sets the standards for Oregon's statewide planning program.

Two other state agencies play an important role in municipal and county planning and land-use controls. The first is the Department of Land Conservation and Development (DLCD), which administers Oregon's statewide planning program and provides professional staff support to the lay commission that oversees the program, the LCDC.

This is not an uncommon arrangement in Oregon; almost all of the state's major programs use it. The DLCD has a central staff in Salem and field representatives in five other cities. The second agency, the Land Use Board of Appeals (LUBA) is unique in that it is essentially a state court that rules on matters involving appeals concerning land-use regulations. Established in 1979, it is a three-member panel that operates as an independent tribunal. An appeal of a municipality's or county's zoning change, for example, would go first to LUBA, then to the state court of appeals, and finally to the state's supreme court.

This extensive program for land-use planning in Oregon has the following primary objectives: the conservation of farm land, forest land, coastal resources, and other important natural resources; the encouragement of efficient development; coordination of the planning activities of local governments and state and federal agencies; the enhancement of the state's economy; and the reduction of costs to the public that result from poorly planned development. To accomplish these objectives, the state has established 19 statewide planning goals; interestingly, the first one is citizen involvement and the second is land-use planning. The others cover everything you could possibly consider to affect the growth and development of the state. The last one is ocean resources.

All of this has not been done by the elected leadership in Oregon without some strong objection from vested and special interest groups. Consequently, Oregon voters have had to show their support of this farsighted legislation at the polling booth three times as the result of the initiative petition and referendum process. In 1977, the vote was 57 percent for preserving the program. The vote in 1978 was 61 percent for and 39 percent against. In 1982, it again received the approval of the voters by 55 percent to 45 percent. Another attempt to destroy the act was made in 1984, but by this time Oregonians had had it and petition advocates could not get enough signatures to put the question on the ballot. As there has been no further attempt, perhaps those seeking to kill this comprehensive measure have learned that the people of Oregon love their great and beautiful state and its cities and they want to keep the quality of life that exists there.

Florida's Growth Management Approach

Two years after Oregon's passage of Senate Bill 100, Florida adopted its Local Government Comprehensive Planning Act of 1975 (Chapter 75-257, Laws of Florida.) This mandated that each unit of local government must create a planning agency before July1, 1976 and that, by July 1, 1979, each jurisdiction must have prepared and adopted "a comprehensive plan of the type and in the manner set out in the act." Local government was defined as "any county or municipality or any special district or local government entity established pursuant to law which exercises regulatory authority over and grants development permits for land development." If any local government unit failed to meet either of these mandates, the state Department of Community Affairs (DCA) was given the authority to prepare a plan for that unit. As a result of this act, planning activity flourished in Florida; however, growth continued at a rapid pace and the need for protection of land, resources, water, and waterfront development increased further.

Consequently, in 1985 Florida technically repealed the 1975 act and adopted what is cited as the Local Government Comprehensive Planning and Land Development Act, which most refer to as the Growth Management Act of 1985.[4] A careful study reveals that the 1975 legislation was carried over almost intact into the 1985 act with only a few minor changes and the addition of substantial procedural and substantive requirements. The overall result was to strengthen the controls of the state authority as well as its power to make binding rules for the local governments. DCA did this with 73 pages of detailed requirements and standards which became Chapter 9J-5 of the Florida Administrative Code, known as Minimum Criteria for Review of Local Government Comprehensive Plans and of Compliance. Although the provisions contained in Chapter 9J-5 are not part of legislation, it is the policy in Florida to allow administration departments to prepare and adopt standards and guidelines concerning their operation and the carrying out of the administrative policy authority provided to them in a legislative act. This is much like the operation of the federal bureaucracy when Congress passes a broad authorizing act for a federal department. The Housing and Urban Development Department is a shining example of this.

Some of the important provisions of the 1985 planning legislation are worth examining in greater detail, although it would be impractical, and, perhaps, not particularly enlightening to try to cover all of them here. A general understanding of what the state is trying to do can be obtained from including two of the eight provisions contained in the section on intent and purpose:

> (1) In conformity with and in furtherance of the purpose of the Florida Environmental Land and Water Management Act of 1972, Chapter 380,

> Florida Statutes, it is the purpose of this act to utilize and strengthen the existing role, processes, and powers of local governments in Florida in the establishment and implementation of comprehensive planning programs to guide and control future development.
>
> (2) It is the intent of this act that its adoption is necessary so that Florida local governments can preserve and enhance present advantages; encourage the most appropriate use of land, water, and resources consistent with the public interest; overcome present handicaps; and deal effectively with future problems that may result from the use and development of land within their jurisdictions. Through the process of comprehensive planning, it is intended that Florida units of local government can preserve, promote, protect and improve the public health, safety, comfort, good order, appearance, convenience, law enforcement and fire prevention, and general welfare; prevent the overcrowding of land and avoid undue concentration of population; facilitate the adequate and efficient provision of transportation, water, sewerage, schools, parks, recreational facilities, housing and other requirements and services; conserve, develop, utilize, and protect natural resources within their jurisdictions.

It is the intent that adopted comprehensive plans shall have the legal status set out in this act and that no public or private development shall be permitted except in conformity with comprehensive plans, or elements or portions thereof, prepared and adopted in conformity with this act.

As a state-mandated local planning process developed and grew, along with it has come required state review and approval, followed by specific citing of the "elements" expected to be included within the comprehensive plan. Elements are topics such as land use, transportation, utilities, and housing conditions that must be included in the plan in order to gain state acceptance. An important change in Florida's 1985 act was the provision for regional planning agencies designated by the state to exercise responsibilities under the law in a particular region of the state. These regional agencies perform the first review of any local government's proposed comprehensive plan or a plan amendment before it is passed on to the state planning agency for its review and action. Florida's legislation provides an elaborate list of subjects that must be considered in the formulation of a comprehensive plan, set forth in seven major element headings, most of which contain numerous descriptive subheadings. These are divided into mandatory and optional categories. The first six are required for all plans while the first two in the optional list are considered mandatory for communities with a population exceeding 50,000. Any locality may choose to include all of the categories designated as optional. If you would like to find out everything about what a thorough comprehensive plan should contain, but were always afraid to ask, get a copy of Florida's County and Municipal Planning and Land Development Regulation legislation and peruse its 43 pages carefully.

Florida's legislation provides a rather complete assemblage of the elements to be considered for a comprehensive plan and, so the reader will have some idea of the detail included, both the mandatory and the optional elements are shown below. These provide an excellent means of understanding just what a master plan is and the ingredients that go into it. In most cases the entire section will not be provided, but only the portion necessary to show the thrust of the intent of each section:

> (1) The comprehensive plan shall consist of materials in such descriptive form, written or graphics, as may be appropriate to the prescription of principles, guidelines, and standards for the orderly and balanced future economic, social, physical, environmental and fiscal development of the area.
>
> (2) Coordination of the several elements of the local comprehensive plan shall be a major objective of the planning process. . . .
>
> (3) (a) The comprehensive plan shall contain a capital improvements element designed to consider the need for the location of public facilities in order to encourage the efficient utilization of such facilities. . . .
>
> (4) (a) Coordination of the local comprehensive plan with the comprehensive plans of adjacent municipalities, the county, adjacent counties or the region; with adopted rules pertaining to designated areas of critical state concern; and with the state comprehensive plan shall be a major concern of local comprehensive planning process. . . .
>
> (5) The comprehensive plan and its elements shall contain policy recommendations for the implementation of the plan and its elements.
>
> (6) In addition to the general requirements of subsections (1) through (5) of this section, the comprehensive plan shall include the following elements:
>
>> (a) A future land use plan element designating proposed future general distribution, location, and extent of the uses of land for residential uses, commercial uses, industry, agriculture, recreation, conservation, education, public buildings and grounds, other public facilities and other categories of the public and private uses of land. . . .

(b) A traffic circulation element consisting of the types, locations and extent of existing and proposed major thoroughfares and transportation routes, including bicycle and pedestrian ways.

(c) A general sanitary sewer, solid waste, drainage, potable water, and natural groundwater aquifer recharge element correlated to principles and guidelines for future land use. . . .

(d) A conservation element for the conservation, use and protection of natural resources in the area. . . .

(e) A recreation and open space element indicating a comprehensive system of public and private sites for recreation. . . .

(f) A housing element consisting of standards, plans and principles to be followed in the provision of housing for existing residents and the anticipated population growth of the area. . . .

(g) (for local governments coming under the Coastal Zone Management Act) . . . The coastal zone management element shall set forth the policies that shall guide the local government's decisions and program implementation with respect to the following objectives . . . (there are 10 set forth.)

At this point the mandatory required elements for all local government units end; however, for those communities of 50,000 or more people, (7)(a) and (7)(b) below are mandatory. Any local government desiring to do so may include all of the listed optional elements.

(7) The comprehensive plan may include the following additional elements or portions or phases thereof:

(a) As a part of the circulation element of paragraph (6)(b) or as a separate element, a mass-transit element showing proposed methods for the moving of people, rights-of-way, terminals, related facilities and fiscal consideration for the accomplishment of the element.

(b) As a part of the circulation element of (6)(b) or as a separate element, plans for port, aviation and related facilities coordinated with the general circulation and transportation element.

(c) As a part of the circulation element of paragraph (6)(b) and in coordination with paragraph (6)(e), where applicable, a plan element for the circulation of recreational traffic, including bicycle facilities, exercise trails, riding facilities, and such other matters as may be related to the improvement and safety of movement of all types of recreational traffic.

(d) As a part of the circulation element of paragraph (6)(b) or as a separate element, a plan element for the development of off-street parking facilities for motor vehicles and the fiscal considerations for the accomplishment of the element.

(e) A public buildings and related facilities element showing locations and arrangements of civic and community centers, public schools, hospitals, libraries, police and fire stations, and other public buildings. . . .

(f) A recommended community design element which may consist of design recommendations for land subdivision, neighborhood development and redevelopment, design of open space locations and similar matters. . . .

(g) A general area redevelopment element consisting of plans and programs for the redevelopment of slums and blighted locations and for community redevelopment. . . .

(h) A safety element for the protection of resident and property of the area from fire, hurricane or manmade or natural catastrophe. . . .

(i) An historical and scenic preservation element setting out plans and programs for those structures or lands in the area having historical, archaeological, architectural, scenic or similar significance.

(j) An economic element setting forth principles and guidelines for the commercial and industrial development, if any, and the employment and manpower utilization in the area. . . .

(k) Such other elements as may be peculiar to, and necessary for, the area concerned and as are added to the comprehensive plan by the governing body upon the recommendation of the local planning agency.

(8) All elements of the comprehensive plan, whether mandatory or optional, shall be based upon data appropriate to the element involved. Surveys and studies utilized in the preparation of the comprehensive plan shall not be deemed as part of the comprehensive plan unless adopted as a part of it. Copies of such studies, surveys, and supporting documents shall be made available to public inspection, and copies of such plans shall be made available to the public upon the payment of reasonable charges for reproduction.

In addition to what has been covered, there are several mandated provisions indicating the intent of the state legislature to see that all local governments have plans and make those plans meaningful, and that there is coordination of planning throughout the state. For example, two new terms, Development Order and Development Permit have been made a part of the planning function. The definitions within the act are as follows:

> (6) "Development Order" means any order granting, denying or granting with conditions an application for a development permit.
>
> (7) "Development Permit" includes any building permit, zoning permit, subdivision approval, rezoning, certification, special exception, variance or any other official action of local government having the effect of permitting the development of land.

It therefore appears unlikely that you are going to get the necessary development order and development permit in Florida unless the requirements are set forth in an adopted comprehensive plan and the land development regulations are met.

In spite of what was said earlier about many state planning enabling acts not requiring the approval of the governing body and allowing a master plan to be adopted officially by a resolution of the planning agency, Florida concludes that this is not the modern way to ensure the active involvement of the elected governing body. Consequently, under subsection (15)(a), where the requirement for two public hearings is found, the method of adoption is spelled out:

> (a) The procedure for transmittal of a complete proposed comprehensive plan or plan amendment pursuant to subsection (3) and for adoption of a comprehensive plan or plan amendment pursuant to subsection (7) shall be by affirmative vote of not less than a majority of the total membership of the governing body in the manner prescribed by this subsection. The adoption of a comprehensive plan or plan amendment shall be by ordinance. . . . (Who said legislative lawyers didn't know how to draft a simple statement like the last one?)

It is probable that as more states move into legislative revision and update of their planning enabling acts by inserting mandatory provisions, the approach of requiring adoption of plans and amendments by governing bodies will meet with favor. Some may argue that doing so will make planning more political than it should be, while others will say that it is about time we hung the responsibility for either a good or bad planning program around the necks upon which it belongs—the members of the governing body. That way we will know where to place the blame, or praise.

Washington State's Approach

Like several other states, Washington's legislation requires the establishment of urban growth boundaries, but only by counties and cities at a specified population level; other counties and incorporated areas are not required to do so. Thus, only 16 of the 39 counties in the state are mandated to develop comprehensive plans and follow the other provisions in the state act. Other counties may do so voluntarily and, to date, 10 more have chosen to comply with the legislation.

The act requires every affected community to develop a comprehensive plan by 1993. A plan for protecting designated resources in critical areas was to be completed by 1991. However, due to the scarcity of funds for accomplishing the required work and the difficulties encountered in meeting the original deadline, an extension was granted and some jurisdictions have yet to complete their critical areas plan. In addition, the act requires local governments to link urban growth areas, capital facilities plans, and level-of-service standards. In contrast to the Florida and Oregon legislation, the Washington act allows impact fees to be imposed only for roads, parks, fire stations, and schools. Indications are that the act has been highly contentious, is progressing rather slowly, and is facing numerous challenges from cities, counties, and private development interests. The major problem seems to be the feeling that the legislation is an edict from the top down, with an attendant lack of broad-based understanding and support from the general public, especially in lesser developed cities and counties. Remember the caveat that state-mandated regulations are going to be successful only where there is a prevalent statewide "planning attitude" or else a major crisis occurs or things have gotten so bad that a groundswell of resentment gives birth to a call for corrective action from the general public. On a smaller scale, the same holds true for stringent growth management controls at the local government level.

NOW THAT WE KNOW ALL THIS, HOW DO WE DO IT?

Once there is general acceptance of the components of a master plan, the next question usually asked by most planning commission members is, "How do we get one?" There is nothing to prevent a community from preparing a master plan with the talent of the local commission. This has been done in some cases, usually where there are a number of extremely devoted and civic-minded members. The do-it-yourself master plan is, however, extremely difficult to achieve. The probability that any member will have sufficient time to gather the essential information and material is very small. Beyond that, preparation of a competent plan requires a high degree of technical knowledge that is not usually found among citizen appointees. While it is true that members can broaden the scope of their technical information base, the time available for study is limited. The best method of obtaining a master plan becomes a matter of securing competent professional help. The technical personnel can be made available either on a permanent staff basis or from a planning consulting firm. The permanent staff is usually employed by the city and is responsible to the planning commission. If a consulting service is used, the consultant is also engaged by the city and works directly with the commission. (For a more complete discussion, see Chapter 9—The Care and Feeding of Planning Professionals.)

Still another way for a local government to secure professional help and technical assistance is found through state, regional, or county planning agencies. Almost all states have an organization charged with state planning activity and may have arranged for their staff to actually perform some of the services needed to develop local plans. Even more involved in assisting local planning are regional and county organizations. In some areas, communities can contract to have the professional staffs of such groups undertake studies or prepare a complete master plan. Some people have resisted and resented the efforts of these agencies, feeling that this is just another attempt of "big government" to take over and run local affairs. Though there may be some justification for this feeling, it must be remembered that successful planning at the local level requires cooperation among all affected governments and coordination of activity and development policies among local, county, regional, and state agencies.

Even with all of this discussion about the purpose of a master plan, what it is, and how it is put together, we still need to say something about form and format. What does it look like? Actually, plans come in a wide variety of forms. Usually, regardless of the approach taken, there will be a printed summary for public distribution. This will, or should, include written text, statistical tables, charts, graphs, and graphic depiction of the community and the proposals. There is always a master plan report or reports explaining the studies undertaken, the findings, conclusions, and recommendations. Also, there should be a clear discussion of how citizens were involved in the plan formulation. Did suggestions come from neighborhoods, were citizen organizations contacted and did they participate, and was there a concerted and structured effort made to develop the goals and objectives of the plan through this involvement? Regardless of how derived, these should be the basis of any plan proposals. The final product can be put together in any number of physical forms, shapes, and sizes. There are big ones, fat ones, color-printed ones, little ones, and summary ones. Due to the cost of printing and distribution, it may be difficult for all of the background material to be included in whatever product is made available generally. Those who are genuinely interested should know where all of the documents can be studied, and easy access to them should be provided.

During my consulting days, in an effort to get information about plans and their proposals into the hands of as many people as possible, I encouraged communities to print plan summaries in newspaper tabloid form. These could be folded into convenient mailing pieces, run through the tax assessor's office for addressing, and sent to everyone on the tax rolls. Of course, other copies were distributed to apartment renters and kept available for people to pick up. On a few occasions, local newspapers were cooperative enough to print such tabloids and distribute them free of charge. In several places, a brief citizen questionnaire was utilized to solicit reaction and further input.

TRADITIONAL VERSUS INNOVATION

At this point, some comments seem in order regarding the long-term debate over the relative merits of the form and format of a master plan. This discussion centers around the question of whether or not the traditional master plan, with its physical depiction of present conditions, resources, and proposed changes directed toward long-range propositions, really meets today's needs. Those who say otherwise support the idea of a "policies" plan that concentrates on examining present conditions and problems, establishes policies to deal with these, and then recommends specific techniques and priorities for changes and improvements. The policies plan may be presented in text form but will have supporting graphics, charts, and tables, which may or may not be included in the plan summary made available to the public. Many will present the master plan in separate sections, with one devoted to policy questions, one to the physical capital needs and improvements, one to social programs, and one to suggested and recommended effectuation ordinance adoption or amendments. (Samples of the policies section from the master plan of Denver, Colorado, are given in the Appendix.)

Supporters of this approach believe that people are much more interested in today than in the future and further, that it is more important to deal with the pragmatic immediate problems of community life than to have fancy colored pictures of idealistic schemes for future land use and facilities projected anywhere from five to 25 years in the future. On the other hand, those who defend the traditional master plan are equally convinced that planning that is not long-range and does not project a future vision gives little sense of direction and falls short of providing needed inspiration. For what it's worth, my own belief is that the best answer lies somewhere between the two extremes. Planning, to be comprehensive, should be long-range, but there also should be a divisional time frame relating to immediate goal achievement by policy changes. The best plans in the future will be those that take long-range capital expenditures for physical facilities and improvements necessary for social, cultural, environmental, and economic betterment and separate them from a well-stated set of immediate and mid-range policy statements that establish current priorities.

WHAT TO DO UNTIL THE BABY ARRIVES

Another question that arises frequently concerns the time required to develop a master plan, since it usually takes from 12 to 24 months to complete a thorough master planning project. In the meantime, the problems of the community go on and commission members grow concerned about what to do until the master plan is completed. It seems to me that the first and probably best bit of advice is to be cautious, but do not panic. Development and growth cannot be stopped. Decisions will have to be made that in many cases will have an effect on the master plan; therefore, care should be exercised to make certain that sufficient consideration is given to each proposal and that each member is conscious of the meaning of the pending master plan. While the plan is being prepared, there are many other things that can be done: independent investigation of planning principles in general and the reading of publications regarding master plans and planning would be extremely valuable.

In addition, the planning commission member who is conscientious should become even more familiar with the community and its characteristics. While he or she may have lived there a number of years, the individual probably will be surprised by the many tangible and intangible characteristics that have gone unobserved until looked at through planning eyes. Trips into various parts of the municipality both alone and with other members will be extremely helpful. At the same time, it should be stressed that it is of vital importance for the commission members to be completely familiar with the work that is going on regarding the master plan. Discussions, meetings, visits to the planning office, and reading of memoranda and reports are important.

NOW, LET'S MAKE IT LEGAL

Once a plan has been prepared, it should be adopted and given some official status. The procedure for doing this varies from state to state, and, again, the enabling act should be consulted. Following the idea that master plans should be advisory and therefore not legislated as such, most of the legislative acts say that the planning commission may adopt all or a part of the master plan by resolution and that amendments to the plan may be made the same way. Before this can be done, there must be a public hearing. As an illustration of the adoption procedure, note the following section from Colorado's rather outdated enabling act:

> **31-23-208. PROCEDURE OF COMMISSION.** The commission may adopt the plan as a whole by a single resolution or may by successive resolutions adopt successive parts of the plan (said parts corresponding with major geographical sections or divisions of the municipality or with functional subdivisions of the subject matter of the plan), and may adopt any amendment or extension thereof or addition thereto. Before the adoption of the plan or any such part, amendment, extension or addition, the commission shall hold at least one public hearing thereon, notice of the time and place of which shall be given by one publication in a newspaper of general circulation in the municipality and in the official newspaper of the county affected. The adoption of the plan, any part, amendment, extension or addition shall be by resolution of the commission carried by the affirmative votes of not less than two-thirds of the entire membership of the commission. The resolution shall refer expressly to the maps and descriptive and other matter intended by the commission to form the whole or part of the plan, and the action taken shall be recorded on the map and plan and descriptive matter by the identifying signature of the chairman or secretary of the commission. An attested copy of the plan or part thereof shall be certified to each governmental body of the territory affected and after the approval by each body shall be filed with the county clerk and recorder of each county wherein the territory is located.

HOW LEGAL CAN A PLAN GET?

For a more current and descriptive procedure giving legal status to an adopted comprehensive plan, we turn again to Florida's legislation. This section establishing the legal aspects of a plan provides an excellent comparison with the much older attempt, still existing in its statutes, from Colorado. Examination of the difference between the two states' provisions also illustrates Colorado's assignment of plan adoption to the planning commission, with no reference to governing body action, as opposed to Florida's requirement of action by elected officials. That state's legislature concluded that mere planning commission adoption is not the modern way to ensure the active involvement of the elected governing body.

Earlier, I quoted Florida's general intent statement regarding the legality of comprehensive plans and land development regulations. There are four major actions, with several subsections spelling out the extent to which Florida has established the legal effects of an adopted comprehensive plan. A number of these venture into territory not common to most state planning enabling acts. Also, a full section is devoted to explaining how a development order and developments must be consistent (one of the legislative drafters' favorite words) with the comprehensive plan. The uniqueness of many of the requirements and conditions merits a summary of the importance of these provisions in expanding the authoritativeness of the planning process. The entire sections and subsections are not included in some of the following:

> **163.3194. LEGAL STATUS OF THE COMPREHENSIVE PLAN**
> (1)(a) After a comprehensive plan, or element or portion thereof, has been adopted in conformity with this act, all development undertaken by, and all actions taken in regard to development orders by, government agencies in regard to land covered by such plan or element shall be consistent with such plan or element as adopted.
>
> > (b) All land development regulations enacted or amended shall be consistent with the adopted comprehensive plan, or element or portion thereof, and any land development regulations existing at the time of adoption which are not consistent with the adopted comprehensive plan or element or portion thereof shall be amended so as to be consistent. . . .
>
> (2) After a comprehensive plan for the area, or element or portion thereof, is adopted by the governing body, no land development regulation, land development code, or amendment thereto shall be adopted by the governing body until such regulation, code or amendment has been referred

either to the local planning agency or to a separate land development regulation commission created pursuant to local ordinance, or to both, for review and recommendation as to the relationship of such proposal to the adopted comprehensive plan, or element or portion thereof. . . .

(3)(a) A development order or land development regulation shall be consistent with the comprehensive plan if the land uses, densities or intensities and other aspects of development permitted by such order or regulation are compatible with and further the objectives, policies, land uses and densities or intensities in the comprehensive plan and if it meets all other criteria enumerated by the local government.

(b) A development approved or undertaken by a local government shall be consistent with the comprehensive plan if the land uses, densities or intensities, capacity or size, timing and other aspects of the development are compatible with and further the objectives, policies, land uses, and densities or intensities in the comprehensive plan and if it meets all other criteria enumerated by the local government.

(4)(a) A court, in reviewing local governmental action or development regulations under this act, may consider, among other things, the reasonableness of the comprehensive plan, or element or elements thereof, relating to the issue justifiably raised or the appropriateness and completeness of the comprehensive plan, or element or elements thereof, in relation to the governmental action or development regulation under consideration. The court may consider the relationship of the comprehensive plan, or element or elements thereof, to the governmental action taken or the development regulation involved in litigation, but private property shall not be taken without due process of law and the payment of just compensation.

(b) It is the intent of this act that the comprehensive plan set general guidelines and principles concerning its purposes and contents and that this act shall be construed broadly to accomplish its stated purposes and objectives.

With this wording regarding the legality of an adopted comprehensive plan, Florida seems to have left no stone unturned in seeking to assure that there is no question about the intent of the legislature. Some of our other states where legislation is either silent on the subject of the legal status of a comprehensive or master plan, or which have only unclear, disputable wording, such as Colorado, would do well to consider borrowing some of the wording from Florida's act. Nevertheless, as is the case with all legislation, no matter how careful and specific the drafting of a measure is, there always will be something found in it to which individuals or groups will object, declare unclear and confusing, and legally questionable. Such has been the case in Florida and, interestingly, a goodly number of the attacks against the legislation have been founded on two very common words: consistent and concurrent.

To attempt to avoid misunderstanding over the first of these two, consistent (or consistency), the legislature has included a section defining the term "consistency." I am not sure whether, as difficult as it is for the English language to engender a commonality of understanding, that the language used in the definition doesn't muddy the water more rather than clearing it up. Here is just a sample: ". . . for the purpose of determining whether local comprehensive plans are consistent with the state comprehensive plan and the appropriate regional policy plan, a local plan shall be consistent with such plans if the local plan is 'compatible with' and 'furthers' such plans." The section then goes on to define the term "compatible with" and the word "furthers" in much the same manner as used in defining consistency. It is easy to see why lawyers have been eager to accept clients who have a disagreement with a ruling based upon the lack of consistency, or not being consistent with either local plans, regional plans, or the state plan. There have been just such cases against both the 1975 and the 1985 legislation; however, no definitive decisions have been issued.

CONCURRENT CONTROVERSY

The word from the Florida act that has caught the attention of lawyers, developers, land owners and planners all over the country, as well as stirring up controversy and legal battles within that state is "concurrent," usually referred to as the matter of "concurrency." The basis for the disputatious aura surrounding this seemingly harmless word, as well as "consistent" above, arises from the legislature seeking to state clearly their intent regarding provisions of the Minimum Criteria for Review of Local Government Comprehensive Plans and the Determination of Compliance of the Department of Community Affairs (DCA). Both of these are part of chapter 9J-5 of the Florida Administration Code (FAC), which the legislature wanted to strengthen by adding specific statements of legislative intent. With a provision in the 1985 legislation, the DCA was ordered to adopt the amendments necessary "to conform with the requirements of this legislative intent by October 1, 1986." These statements of intent, including the one on "consistent," as well as "concurrent," and all the others thus became part of the review process for local comprehensive plans.

Why did this provision pertaining to concurrency become as controversial as it has in Florida? The answer is that it was placed in a section of the act, included in part below, requiring that facilities and services needed to serve new developments be in place *concurrent* with the impacts of such development or be guaranteed by an enforceable development agreement. Needless to say, such a provision was not received by those in the real estate field and the development industry with joy and a loving embrace. Such a provision would naturally arouse national interest. Those involved with land development would be concerned with such a provision being adopted in other states, while local governments and their planners possibly would be thinking, "Hey, this is not a bad idea. Maybe it would help us in dealing with our problems." Whether this kind of speculation continues or not, the word "concurrence" has been bandied about enough that it conjures up an image of a new technique; however, while some people understand what it means, a great many, although having heard about it, do not. Therefore, even though there has been an abundance of attention given to Florida's "Growth Management Act," we add one final quote so that readers of this book may, at least, see where all this started.

163.3177, Section (10)

> (h) It is the intent of the Legislature that public facilities and services needed to support development shall be available concurrent with the impacts of such development. In meeting this intent, public facility and service availability shall be deemed sufficient if the public facilities and services for a development are phased, or the development is phased, so that the public and those related services which are deemed necessary by the local government to operate the facilities necessitated by that development are available concurrent with the impacts of the development. The public facilities and services, unless already available, are to be consistent with the capital improvements element of the local comprehensive plan as required by paragraph (3)(a) or guaranteed in an enforceable development agreement. This shall include development agreements pursuant to this chapter or in an agreement or development order issued pursuant to chapter 380. Nothing herein shall be construed to require a local government to address services in its capital improvements plan or to limit a local government's ability to address any service in its capital improvements plan that it deems necessary.

A reading of the above goes a long way in explaining why there is some confusion and consternation about this requirement of "concurrent." It is clear that this is an attempt to allow local governments to link controlling development to the availability of, or the guarantee of, essential facilities and services. This is a most commendable objective. Several questions, however, arise from the lack of clarity of the language in this particular section. Does the wording of the statute grant the authority to require that all or part of the costs of any facilities and services not currently available be borne by developers? How is the extent of the impact of a development determined and by whom? If an impact study determines that the latest planned development is just the one that will require a series of major improvements, such as larger pipe size in either water or sewer service mains not on the property, can the development be turned down if such a capital expenditure has not been anticipated in the municipality's capital improvements program? These and many other questions are yet to be fully answered, but undoubtedly the courts will do so in the future.

THERE ARE PLANS AND THEN THERE ARE PLANS THAT WORK

With an enabling act such as this, it is clear that the master or comprehensive plan does have the opportunity to be a meaningful and effective document. The legal status is helpful, but the important point is how the plan is supported and used by citizens, planning commission and governing body. No decision relating to community growth, redevelopment, social improvement, or budgeting should be made without consultation with the plan and an examination of the effect the decision will have on the plan's objectives as they relate to the total community. This is not to say that the plan will be infallible or that it is rigidly cast in concrete. It does say that the plan's purpose should be to bring into focus sufficient information and data so that the best possible objective value judgment can be made. Only if used in this way by mayors, councilpersons, directors of public works departments, developers, and interested citizens can master plans and planning be something more than attractive reports and interesting exercises. The development of an understanding of this by the governing body and the public is the responsibility of the planning commission.

So we see that all planning commission members should recognize that their work is really only getting off and running when the plan has been prepared. The completion of the plan is by no means the completion of the planning program. The plan must be publicized, explained, examined and revised where necessary. It must also be kept current and not hung on the wall in the form of a beautiful colored picture, delightful to see but bearing no resemblance to the actual community unfolding outside the municipal building. It must be used in order to be effective. If it is not going to be used, it will, of course, have no effect upon the community and will be simply an academic exercise with a small degree of value in return for the investment of time and money put into it. To assure that this latter doesn't become the result in their community, the planning commission should accept the responsibility of becoming the watchdog for protecting the future effectiveness of the comprehensive plan, insisting that it be used in decision making, keeping the general public informed and involved, and diligently working to see that all of the plan's adopted recommendations are taken seriously and reach fruition. Remember, the future of your community is at stake.

NOTES

1. Oregon State Legislature, (Oregon Revised Statutes, Chapter 97, 197.005-197.860), 1985.

2. Herbert H. Smith, *Planning America's Communities: Paradise Found? Paradise Lost?* (Chicago, Planners Press, American Planning Association), 1991.

3. Oregon Land Conservation and Development Commission, (Oregon's Statewide Planning Program), 1986.

4. Florida State Legislature, (Florida Revised Statutes, Part II, 163.3161-163.3243), 1985.

CHAPTER

6

The Relationship of Zoning to Planning

Over the past several decades, zoning has become a much used word in the vocabulary of the average citizen. This does not mean, however, that we have achieved a consensus of meaning on the word or that the average citizen has learned to distinguish between good and bad zoning. Nor does it mean that everyone is in favor of zoning. It does mean that the course of events has led to a legal tool to help control the phenomenal growth and development that has taken place in this country. This tool is the zoning ordinance.

As more and more communities adopt new zoning ordinances and revise old ones, the responsible citizen becomes curious to learn more about the subject. Because effective zoning is dependent upon the support of informed concerned citizens, it is important to have a good understanding not only of the term but of all the ramifications of this essential element of the democratic process.

HOW IT ALL GOT STARTED

In thumbing back through the pages of time, it would probably be difficult to identify the precise point at which zoning started. It is known that the beginnings of zoning were quite different from the modern, sometimes overly involved, ordinances of today. It is also well established that the first zoning attempts were primarily for the purpose of preventing so-called objectionable uses from occurring in residential neighborhoods. The first recorded court cases are California cases dealing with a brickyard and a hand laundry that were declared to be undesirable neighbors for homes.

As the 20th century got under way, additional experiments in the regulation of the use of structures began to appear in various parts of the country. Also, persons interested in civic improvements, architects, engineers, landscape architects, and lawyers advanced the idea that the American city was a disgrace and needed drastic improvement that could come only from some form of governmental regulation. Attraction to this field resulted in several lawyers becoming specialists in this form of legal regulation, foremost among them Edward M. Bassett. Many credit Mr. Bassett with being the father of zoning as we know it today.

These two additional ideas (the use of buildings and civic improvement) appeared in the first comprehensive zoning ordinance in this country, an ordinance for the city of New York, in 1916. Here, for the first time in our history, a major city enacted a law regulating the use of land and buildings, the density of population and the height and bulk of structures. Several other major zoning ordinances quickly followed in other cities, many requiring litigation and court tests. Courts' reactions to these ordinances varied, but the fundamentals of legal acceptance of zoning were established by the Supreme Court of the United States in 1926 when it refused to intervene in a case in which a state court had upheld a zoning regulation. (*Village of Euclid v. Ambler Realty Co.*)[1] This case still stands as the legal foundation for the right of government, the community as a whole, to restrict with reasonable regulations what happens on every piece of privately owned land under the jurisdiction of any governmental unit's zoning ordinance. After this far-reaching, memorable decision, zoning flourished, but it should always be kept in mind that there continues to be judicial examination of the reasonableness of the techniques and procedures involved.

Since those early days we have seen a great many changes in society, and experienced numerous history-making events. We have been through a great depression, federal pump-priming of a recovery, a world war and three armed conflicts, and a population and building explosion. Community and city planning has developed as a function and a responsibility of government and we seem to have begun to understand effective zoning must be based upon a well-conceived, comprehensive (master) plan. Experts in fields of sociology, economics, and geography all have repeatedly called our attention to the existing and projected population growth and the spread of urban development. Experience has shown us that, in such times as these, exploitation, self-interest, greed, and a lack of foresight are always highly evident.

The result has been the regrettable morass we know as "urban sprawl," in all probability, the worst inheritance, next to the astronomical national deficit and overall debt, left to our children. With this horizontal sprawl has come loss of open space, decreasing land suitable for cultivation and crops, traffic congestion, and freeways turned elongated parking lots during morning and evening rush hours. Also, it is my sincere belief that a loss almost as important to future generations and to our society in general is the loss of a sense of community, a sense of place. It is very evident that we have not learned much about how to correct the sprawl problem as we continue to see it relentlessly rolling onward. Nor have we even learned that the result of lackadaisical spreading of our urban areas is the most inefficient, expensive, unattractive, and undesirable way to build our urban environment. I hope we have at least learned enough to know that people, left to their own devices without self-regulation, will almost inevitably destroy the desirable features of environments, and that zoning is a necessary regulation to give order and direction to the development and redevelopment of our cities.

IF YOU'RE GOING TO DO IT, YOU OUGHT TO KNOW WHY

While many aspects of zoning are subject to a variety of interpretations, the basic concept is the exercise of the governmental power to legally regulate the use of land and the structures thereon in such a way as to protect public health, safety, and general welfare. In other words, zoning is the enactment of a law by public authority that controls and regulates private property. A more complete description of the zoning process has been given in *Local Planning Administration* (1959) as follows:

> Zoning consists of dividing the community into districts or zones and regulating within such districts the use of land and the use, heights and area of buildings for the purpose of conserving and promoting the health, safety, morals, convenience and general welfare of the people of the community. Zoning is the instrument for giving effect to that part of the comprehensive city plan or master plan which is concerned with the private uses of and the private developments on privately owned land—as distinguished from that part which is concerned with public uses and facilities. The zoning map or zoning plan along with the regulations

> pertaining thereto are thus a part of the master plan—in essence the comprehensive use plan of the community—while the enactment of the zoning ordinance and its administration are the legislative and administrative acts or processes for giving effect to or carrying out this part of the comprehensive plan.

From this it can be seen that zoning is of extreme importance to existing and future development of a community. Because it does restrict private property utilization, many people resist zoning. It could even be asked why it has spread so rapidly and been so widely accepted in the face of this opposition. Former New Jersey Supreme Court Justice Harry Heher explained that and added to our understanding of the basic definition of the process when he said in a public address in 1956:

> Zoning is the modern response to the individual and collective needs of community life, the living together of unrelated, interdependent people, a society growing more complex as it expands. Although a concept of comparatively recent origin, zoning has its roots in basic societal necessities and pressures that from the very beginning of social life demand the accommodations of individual interests to the common good and welfare. . . .

Before any community can zone, it must have the authority to do so granted to it by the state legislature. In each of the state enabling acts, most of which are based upon the standard enabling acts prepared by the U.S. Department of Commerce in the 1920s, a statement of purposes of zoning is set forth. The ones included most commonly are:

1. To lessen congestion in the streets.
2. To secure safety from fire, panic, and other dangers.
3. To promote health, morals, or general welfare.
4. To provide adequate light and air.
5. To prevent overcrowding of land and buildings.
6. To avoid undue concentration of population.

While the language may vary and embellishments may be added from state to state, these are the fundamentals usually set forth as the objectives for zoning in any enabling act.

There are, however other purposes that have become commonly accepted as desirable goals for zoning. For example, it is well known that zoning is the means of achieving a logical pattern of land-use developments. Without zoning, land-use development will be haphazard and hodgepodge. Through zoning, land utilization can be guided in such a way that it will make sense both economically and from a physical-design standpoint. This objective is achieved by dividing the zoning process into the formation of a zoning map and zoning ordinance text. The map sets forth zones or districts within which certain uses are permitted to occur and certain others are not. The text explains the uses permitted and defines the minimum standards for each zone and the use therein. In this way, similar and related uses can be kept together and dissimilar and unrelated uses can be separated so that they will not cause an adverse effect upon each other.

IS ZONING UN-AMERICAN?

There are still those who, through lack of understanding or for some personal motivation, oppose zoning as an undue infringement upon private rights. There is no question that they have the "right" to believe as they do and to oppose zoning, and there will be those who continue to do so in spite of the legal interpretations upholding zoning. The real question is whether their expressed motivation of "undue infringement" is their real one, or whether it is a veiled cover of the fear that some perceived personal economic gain will be reduced or threatened. In spite of the reasons given by those who still fight zoning, it or some similar form of land-use regulation is here to stay. If we are going have any success in shaping a better urban form, if we are going to prevent repeating some of the disastrous mistakes we have made in land development in the past, as a community we must restrict and regulate the private use of land.

The community right to zone has been well established by the courts of this country since the 1926 decision in the *Ambler* case. What must be understood is that the idea of a private right to own land does not extend to the point that a landowner can do just whatever he or she may choose on or with land they own if surrounding property owners will have their property values, their health, or their quality of life damaged. Anytime something happening on one parcel of land projects a damaging or adverse effect, in any form, beyond its property boundaries, the fundamental rights of other landowners and the community as a whole to enforce reasonable governmental regulations and restrictions transcend that of the private right of ownership of land. This is the rudiment upon which zoning stands and that must be accepted in order to understand and support the idea of public controls over private land and its development.

Fortunately, the numbers of those who accept the legitimacy of zoning well-founded in sound planning principles are rapidly increasing. This point needs even wider discussion and public attention, for some of the most justified criticism comes from improper action taken under the name of zoning. I was once asked to take the negative side in a debate on the question, "Is zoning an unconstitutional infringement of private rights?" in a Pennsylvania community in rural Bucks County. My worthy opponent for the evening was a well-meaning individual whose viewpoint could easily be justified as a result of his experience. He had previously lived in a community in which zoning had been subjected to a great deal of political abuse. The only zoning he knew was certainly objectionable, and, as a result, to him the entire principle was wrong. When I see a situation like this, I am reminded that the failure of individuals is often used to justify discarding the system. The world would have been in sad shape if we had decided to give up the use of ships just because the Titanic sank.

The secret to overcoming this is to better the system, correct mistakes, and accomplish the more universal education of our people in order to permit them to judge quality. Fundamental to this is an understanding of the role of planning in zoning. While zoning predates planning in most communities, it has become increasingly evident that this is similar to not providing a solid foundation for a building. Zoning based upon a well-documented land-use plan makes sense. Zoning based upon arbitrary opinion, the pressures of vested interests, and the pet schemes of individuals does not make sense.

It is the role of planning and the function of the planning commission to provide a means to avoid the danger of an undue and improper discretionary approach to zoning. Whether the matter under consideration is a new zoning ordinance, an amendment, or a variance to stated requirements, the work of the planning agency should provide the foundation for the wisest possible decision. If the planning function has been followed properly, information is readily available to evaluate the question of the benefit to the total community and the general public welfare in every zoning question. If zoning is the legal means of regulating private property to achieve orderly land-use relationships—and there is no doubt that it is—how can any new zoning ordinance even be considered unless it is founded upon the precepts of planning and supported by adequate study? I can attest to the desirability of this from the times I have appeared in court as an expert witness. Presenting information to show that careful planning studies were the foundation upon which the zoning ordinance about which I testified was the prime reason we won the case. All lawyers involved with land-use law, especially municipal and county attorneys, should notice a trend: Judges, even in conservative states, are asking to be shown that a foundation for a challenged zoning provision is provided by a comprehensive plan and specific studies made prior to its adoption. It is also true that more judges are becoming interested in having someone with planning training and experience, such as a member of the American Institute of Certified Planners, appear as an expert witness to add to the interpretive testimony.

EVEN ZONING NEEDS PLANNING

As more recognition is given to the principle that all zoning should be based upon long-range comprehensive planning, many states have revised their enabling acts to require that this process be followed. Many zoning enabling acts require the planning body to act as the commission responsible for drafting a new zoning ordinance. If not actually stated, there is a strong implication in most acts that the planning commission should perform this function. In those states in which a separate zoning commission is permitted, close coordination with the existing planning commission is essential; and, even in the absence of a planning commission, the principles of comprehensive planning should still be applied to the formulation of the ordinance.

My own opinion is there should never be a separate commission for zoning, and all planning commissions should be designated as planning and zoning commissions. If anyone doubts the advisability of this, I suggest that they examine the damage resulting from divided planning and zoning functions in San Antonio, Texas. In fact, I would go so far as to recommend the practice already in place in a number of local governments: the combining of the functions of planning, zoning, and land subdivision regulation into one consolidated ordinance called the land development ordinance (or code). It is then only logical to assign administrative responsibility to one agency—the planning and zoning commission.

When a planning agency is assigned to perform this function, it has at least three responsibilities. First, it should conduct studies to determine the most appropriate zoning districts and regulations based on good planning. These studies should generally follow the outline presented in the preceding chapter on the master plan, particularly with regard to the elements of land use, population, transportation, and economics.

Second, the planning commission immediately should start to involve and enlist the support of the general public. This can be done in a number of ways. The most important is personal contact with organized neighborhood groups, civic organizations, business groups, and representative professionals, especially lawyers (being sure to bring the municipal attorney in at the very beginning of the process). The sooner you get these people involved the better you will be able to begin to get a handle on their likes and dislikes and what kind of support and opposition you can expect. Try to work closely with those identified as likely opponents to the whole idea, and begin to encourage participation from those who seem to be supportive or, at the very least, willing to learn. You should not expect, and you will not get, the involvement of a majority of the community in organized meetings and I would note that such meetings are a fertile field for anti-zoning rumor-spreading by the "aginners." To help overcome this, the commission should prepare some straightforward, understandable brochures or pamphlets and send or distribute them to every residence, soliciting the participation, involvement, and support of those living there.

While all this is being done, the commission, the staff, and perhaps consultants are busy with framing-up the draft: preparing the map and soliciting ideas about what should be covered and how it should be presented in the text. The cooperative work with the public continues and possibly a fairly large citizen advisory committee has been organized comprising representatives from the various formal groups with whom the commission has been working. Eventually, after meetings, discussion groups, and small group brainstorming, what appears to be the most satisfactory ordinance draft and preliminary map has been assembled. The time has arrived when one or more official public hearing(s) must be held by the commission. The purpose of this is to provide an opportunity for the public, which has been officially notified by media announcements and a legal notice, to express their opinions, and to hear and record these opinions for the purpose of referring to them as work continues on the final product. Remember, a good commission never waits until the officially required hearing to make certain that the public understands the work and views of the commission, and that the commissioners, in turn, understand the views of the public.

Finally, having worked closely with the elected officials during the work of developing what will be proposed, the commission submits to the elected officials its recommendations for the ordinance and map or maps. It is the responsibility of the governing body to make final determinations after conducting at least one public hearing on what is proposed and then enact the recommendations, if appropriate, into law. If the governing body does not agree with what has been recommended, it may change or revise the ordinance and map, suggest restudy and send it back to the commission with recommendations, or reject entirely what has been submitted. When the latter action is taken, it usually requires a two-thirds vote of the entire governing body instead of a simple majority. If, however, the proper coordination and liaison has existed between the commission and the governing body, little difficulty should be experienced. To make certain that the recommendations are understood, the commission should provide sufficient data indicating the reasons for its conclusions. It is also wise for the elected officials and commission to meet together several times prior to the introduction of the ordinance to jointly explore and discuss the reasons behind the proposed ordinance.

These same principles should apply in the comprehensive revision of an existing zoning ordinance. Because many ordinances were adopted prior to planning, the need for a general redrafting frequently exists. Even the best zoning ordinance needs to be subjected to reexamination and revision approximately every five years so that it remains reflective of changing conditions. Here, again, the planning commission is the appropriate review agency.

AN APPEALING APPROACH

Once an ordinance is adopted, a zoning board of appeals must be created. Some say that the board of appeals, inasmuch as it deals more directly with zoning, should be the agency that redrafts the ordinance. While the knowledge and experience of the members of the board of appeals should certainly be used, it is not appropriate for that body to redraft the zoning ordinance. This would be comparable to asking the courts to draft the legislation they are required to sit in judgment on at a later date. It is the responsibility of the planning commission, however, to make certain that the knowledge of the members of the board of appeals is interwoven in the ordinance revision. At the same time, it is the responsibility of the members of the board of appeals to recognize their role in zoning and to cooperate in every way possible.

Far too many zoning boards have failed to accept the relationship of zoning to planning, and some even resent the fact that the planning commission has anything to do with zoning. The classic example of this occurred some years ago in a major New Jersey city. An old zoning ordinance was being revised: under New Jersey law, a function of the planning agency. Members of the zoning board took offense that they were not asked to do the job and announced that they would boycott any meetings called to discuss the revision. Not satisfied with this, they even organized opposition to the suggested revision. They were joined by the building inspector, a political hack, and succeeded in blocking the passage of the revision for three years, by which time all progressive changes had been withdrawn from it. It is interesting to note that, in this city, the members of the zoning board were paid a salary, and appointment was considered a political patronage proposition subject to all kinds of organization pressure, which resulted in a basic oversight of the question of individual qualifications for membership. This may help to explain the action in this case, as well as the fact that in one year in the same city, 110 requests for variance from the ordinance requirements were received and 100 were granted.

Proper action by any board of adjustment is dependent upon a thorough understanding of the planning principles involved and the comprehensiveness of the zoning process. The zoning board has the authority to grant or recommend exceptions and variances where necessary in order to avoid hardships that would result from the strict enforcement of the ordinance. Granting indiscriminate variances or special favors can eat the heart out of good zoning quicker than any other action. A variance can result in changes in characteristics that will destroy the appropriateness of good zoning requirements. Poor zoning board action and governing body support of such action is, in my opinion, the greatest cause of the beginning of blight and the creation of slum conditions that we have today.

An example of just such a situation occurred in a New Jersey community for which I worked to prepare a comprehensive plan and the recommended framework for a new zoning ordinance. These studies indicated that one of the most obvious needs of the community was for an attractive, substantial commercial area. At the same time, the desirable characteristics of open space and other suburban amenities needed to be preserved. A special highway commercial area was devised with rather elaborate standards for lot coverage, setbacks, parking, and landscaping. During the adoption of the zoning ordinance, an individual with special interests challenged the ordinance in court. After a most extended and expensive litigation, the ordinance and its principles were upheld in their entirety as a part of a comprehensive plan.

The community then looked forward to a brighter future with desirable commercial ratables. Alas and alack, the zoning board, which evidently thought that all of the advance preparation was simply an academic exercise, failed to keep this in mind. Within one month after the final settlement of the case, a large store decided to locate in the area. The developers, of course, wanted to squeeze the most out of the land that they possibly could. Consequently, they applied to the zoning board for a variance, pleading hardship, although economic hardship is not a legitimate consideration. Within 15 minutes, the board granted them variances from seven of the basic requirements, any one of which alone would have destroyed the meaning of the ordinance. Fortunately, there is a happy ending to this story. The planning commission immediately protested, gained the support of the governing body and the people of the community, and had the variance revoked. Regrettably, there are many similar occurrences each day that are not reversed and therefore go their merry way undermining good zoning and planning.

WHAT MAKES IT TICK?

Now that the important task of getting a zoning ordinance in place has been completed, no matter how perfect it may be, do not sit back and think that it will be cast in stone and remain unchanged for years. Conditions change within a community and there are always unforeseen economic shifts locally, statewide, and nationally that can necessitate a revision of zoning policy. New building and development techniques may be postulated, and even something placed in the ordinance that seemed so perfect at the time it was proposed may be found not to be working just right to accomplish the desired results. The function of zoning in controlling the private use of land makes it a potentially political animal, and as elected officials change, so may the pressures of political influence. This is something to be guarded against and certainly not encouraged, but in the real world the possibility must be accepted as a reality. Any of these factors can result in amendments being proposed to the ordinance by the mayor and council, neighborhood groups, interested individuals, and always, special interest groups. In fact, if the planning commission recognizes that something could be improved and made more effective, it is only logical, and is their responsibility, to prepare an amendment and recommend it to the governing body for adoption.

When an amendment is proposed, the zoning ordinance usually requires that it must be submitted to the planning commission for review and recommendation to the governing body before it can be adopted by that body. Just as in the case with any ordinance referred to the planning commission, one or more public hearings are required before the commission's recommendation is forwarded to the governing body. In the case of a suggested amending ordinance, the role of the planning commission is of utmost importance. This is emphasized by most zoning enabling acts requiring a vote greater than a simple majority of the members of the governing body to override a planning commission recommendation. It is the commission's job to determine the effect of the proposed zoning change on the comprehensive plan and to be extremely protective of that plan. That agency should be in the best position to make a determination of such effect and to clearly state the reasons for the commission's conclusion and recommendations. If the planning body finds that the proposal would benefit the overall planning process, but the body is not completely in agreement with any part of the comprehensive plan, it should propose an amendment to the plan to continue the compatibility between both documents.

Improper amendments, as well as ill-founded zoning variances, can weaken or destroy good zoning and, in the long run, can destroy the prospects for good planning effectuation. In reviewing an amendment, the planning commission should be certain to give careful attention to the following:

1. The effect of the proposed amendments on the comprehensive planning of the entire municipality.

2. The changes in community characteristics that may take place because of the projected change.

3. The relative effectiveness or ineffectiveness of the present wording of the ordinance, and whether a justification for change exists because of either special reasons or a change in conditions.

4. Whether the amendment is designed to correct an improper situation or would result merely in the granting of special privileges.

If these factors are carefully considered and sufficient data are available for evaluation, a sound recommendation will result. In some cases, it may be necessary to make special studies and surveys to obtain enough information to answer the questions. Where this is true, the commission should not hesitate to investigate, making certain that professional technical assistance is used wherever possible. In the case of a major amendment, a good technique for ensuring that the above points are thoroughly explored is to require an environmental impact assessment of the project proposed.

The final factor to be considered in the relationship of planning and zoning is that of enforcement and administration. To some, it may seem that, inasmuch as these are not the responsibility of the planning commission and not directly connected with planning as such, they are of questionable importance and not worthy of mention. To me, nothing could be further from the truth. I have seen many good zoning ordinances and the corresponding planning schemes ruined by lax enforcement and uninformed, inept administration. Because enforcement and administration are day-to-day affairs, they can have far-reaching effects on the preservation of sound principles. Thus, the planning agency should be well aware of their importance, informed of their prosecution, and insistent upon their efficiency. In most communities the basic job of enforcement falls upon the zoning officer, who in many cases is also the building inspector. This public official can, by the performance of his or her duties, seriously affect the success or failure of the zoning ordinance. An ill-informed official with little understanding of the principles of zoning cannot be expected to be alert to the importance of his or her opinions or be expected to apprise the planning commission of current problems in zoning. In today's complicated urban structure, part-time enforcement is not enough.

Even full-time enforcement by an uninformed or disinterested individual can be not only inadequate but also destructive. I experienced this in one municipality in which the building inspector, again, was given the responsibility to act as zoning officer. As it turned out, he was opposed to the whole idea of zoning. He said nothing publicly about his feeling, but granted permits in conflict with the ordinance. The planning commission was lax in follow-up, and it was not until a year passed and a great deal of harm had been done to the intent of the ordinance that his peccadillos were discovered and halted.

In recent years, in addition to the zoning officer who is responsible for issuing permits, many communities have created the office of zoning examiner or zoning hearing officer to speed up the process of resolving some of the more routine zoning questions and to relieve the board of adjustment of some of its work load. This officer has been given the authority to act on conditional uses and special exceptions that are spelled out in detail in the ordinance along with administrative standards. This official also may be authorized to rule on requests for variance from the lot or area requirements when there are exceptional physical features involved that would make strict compliance with the ordinance impossible. While the use of a hearing officer can be helpful administratively, here, too, it is of utmost importance that the holder of the office be well versed in the planning process and that any action taken not be detrimental to the intent and purpose of the master plan.

FOLLOW THE YELLOW BRICK ROAD

Over the years there have been constant attempts to develop new ideas in land-use control and growth management, all of which must be founded on the principles of zoning or at least the theory of governmental police power. Some of these were around, though still in the experimental stage, before the writing of the second edition of this book and have by now become familiar to many involved in both planning and zoning. As planning commission makeups change and more people become interested in planning and zoning, these are worthy of being mentioned again:

- *Cluster or density zoning,* which allows deviation from rigid fixed lot sizes by permitting lot square footage reduction based upon an overall density factor, resulting in creating open space, less street mileage, and shorter utility lines.
- *Performance zoning,* which evaluates a development plan on density, open space provided, impervious surfaces created, and the overall impact of the development on the area.
- *Transfer of Development Rights (TDR)* whereby each parcel in a district is assigned a number of development rights based upon long-range planning considerations, including density projections. Such rights are transferable between properties in that district or other districts similarly classified.
- *Planned Unit Development (PUD)* zoning whereby, in essence, a "master plan" of integrated development of a large parcel or parcels of land can supersede the zoning standards, even to the point of allowing mixed uses that would not normally apply based upon the zoning map. The planning commission should play a large part in the processing and approval of PUDs, with particular attention paid to the compatibility with or the effect on the comprehensive plan.
- *Floating Zone or Overlay Map Zoning* is a method of allowing optional development in selected areas for which more restrictive zoning provisions have been adopted. This form of zoning recognizes that at some time in the future, it may be appropriate to allow a controlled, well-planned, more intensive use—such as a townhouse

project—rather than single-family dwellings not automatically allowed by the zone regulations. A special permit application can be submitted by a developer to seek approval under the provision in the overlay zone map that permits such an intensive use, provided that numerous controls and conditions are met. Again, this is a procedure calling for careful planning commission review and action.

All of these have contributed greatly to providing additional flexibility and design freedom to the conventional zoning concept. With this flexibility, however, has come an even greater need for correlation with comprehensive planning. The planned unit development technique, for example, is really the application of planning principles in order to achieve a more cohesive and imaginative development pattern than could result from traditional zoning. In most cases, communities using this and the floating zone technique in their zoning require all such applications to be submitted to the planning commission and approved by them before any other processing can take place.

With the drying up of federal financial aid for local governments, tightening state budgets, and the continuing anti-tax increase sentiment, communities are looking more and more for techniques to pass a large portion or at least some of the cost of servicing new developments on to the developers. Naturally, these attempts have met with major objections from the development community. The old standard arguments have been bandied about, such as: "These fees are really nothing but a development tax. They will raise the price of housing and be passed on to the consumers. This, in turn, will reduce construction, discourage buyers, make housing even more unaffordable for middle and lower income people." Another argument is that such fees are simply an expression of a no-growth attitude, which will be disastrous to economic development and the general economy.

In many cases where a growth management initiative has been placed on the ballot, whether it includes the proposal of development fees or not, the development industry has rallied together, raised hundreds of thousands, in some cases millions, of dollars, and mounted a publicity campaign to sell the voters their arguments and defeat the issue. In some communities these tactics have been successful, not just once, but several times. Such has been the case in the "growth machine" city of San Diego, California, where both propositions pertaining to comprehensive plan revisions and growth management controls appeared on the ballot and were defeated by voters duped by the development industry-fabricated arguments. As an example, in

1988 four separate proposals limiting growth and providing growth management controls were placed on the ballot—one by the county, one by the city, and two from citizen initiatives. All four were defeated after the development community had spent $2 million exerting pressure in their counterattack.

However, similar attempts have not been successful in other cities in California or across the country. One of the more striking examples is that of Los Angeles. Proposition U, to reduce the floor area ratio (FAR) of allowable commercial development on three-quarters of the city's commercially zoned land from 3:1 to 1.5:1, passed in 1986 with 69 percent of voters favoring it. According to an article in *Urban Land,* growth control efforts through tighter zoning controls and other land-use measures are gaining citizen acceptance and support and are increasing around the country. Most of this acceptance has occurred in California, where 28 such measures passed in 1986, bringing the total to 69 between 1971 and 1987. This same article reported that a 1986 survey found that 128 local jurisdictions across the country had adopted some type of growth management controls, with California accounting for more than half. Of these, 24 restricted population growth, 66 limited residential development, and 38 restrained commercial or industrial development.[2] Whether the development industry likes it or not, it would appear that growth management, more restrictive zoning, and development cost sharing are ideas whose times have come.

Fortunately, some in the development community have begun to accept this fact of life and are adjusting to it. Others are being warned by real estate writers and development policy researchers that the case for growth has waned in persuasiveness and that they need to be aware of the increasing popularity of citizen anti-growth movements. One such article is quoted below:

> These ideas—which to some appear radical and even offensive—seem to be subtly permeating the ethos of development policy and filtering into the language of regulatory provisions. Seldom mentioned in open political discourse, versions of these concepts are being widely applied by practicing planners and other professionals who craft public policies and write regulations. Everyone with a stake in real estate development should understand the potential power of these ideas.
>
> Three concepts that are gaining considerable attention are the view that proponents of urban growth are practicing a capitalistic power play unacceptable in today's world; the notion that economic gains made through land

> speculation and development should be recovered for social uses; and the proposal that long-term sustainability of the living environment demands major changes—and probable reductions—in urban development.[3]

This realistic analysis, together with the increasing financial problems of local governments, set the stage for examining a few of the more recent techniques being applied from the public side, both through zoning and other land-use controls. Some of these have been mentioned in passing, some commented on in detail, but all are listed for easy reference.

- *Adequate Public Facilities (APF)* has become a common principle in local governments' growth-control methods in areas of rapid development. The thesis is that public facilities and services must be in place in adequate supply or be guaranteed before a major development can be approved. This is covered in detail in the Florida and Oregon legislation included in Chapter 5 and shows how state legislators have granted authority, in fact have mandated it, for local governments' application.
- *Linkage* is another rapidly growing method of applying impact fees to other community problems not necessarily directly related to the site of a development. It is called linkage because the perceived problem facing the city reflects some crisis situation away from the property on which the fee is assessed, although the property's development may contribute to expanding the problem. Some examples are San Francisco's requirement for access to its rapid transit system by new downtown construction, and Sacramento's requirement of a $12,000 low-income housing fee for every new job created by development. This latter was recently upheld by California's Ninth Circuit Court in the case of *Commercial Builders v. City of Sacramento.*
- *Nexus* is a relatively recent term used by courts in evaluating the legality of a restrictive provision in a zoning ordinance where the question of a "taking" (confiscation of a property's value rather than regulation) has been raised. Courts are placing special emphasis on local regulatory action being supported by documentation that shows a "close" connection between the regulation and the governmental interest purported to be furthered by the regulation. The most quoted case illustrating the care with which regulations establishing exactions and impact fees must be enacted is *Nollan v. California Coastal Commission*, 483 U.S. 825 (1987).
- *Regulatory Discretion* is a new but growing planning and zoning concept that provides the opportunity for developing difficult prop-

erties with environmentally sensitive areas instead of severely restricting development. Extra protection for sensitive features such as rock outcroppings, steep slopes, floodplain areas, wetlands, and ponds is provided by detailed guidance and very specific procedural instructions to applicants and approval agencies. White Plains, New York, has developed such a system and, with the requirement of the California Environmental Protection Act that every incorporated jurisdiction have an environmental quality agency, a similar approach has become a necessity for that state.

• *Concurrency* and *Consistency* are the controversial terms found in the Florida Growth Management Act of 1985, thoroughly discussed in Chapter 5.

• *Impact Fees* are now in widespread use for residential, commercial, and industrial land development as a means of combating the financial crunch on local governments. Several states have passed enabling act amendments granting authority to jurisdictions to impose reasonable fees on developments to allow the sharing of costs for public facilities and services as well as, in some cases, community social needs. Impact fees have been referred to in several of the above techniques and in the discussion on the Florida act.

As time goes on and our communities continue to grow and face additional problems from development—or don't grow and must find means to stabilize and redevelop—still more new techniques and practices will be introduced. The one thing of which we can be sure is that government has and will continue to have a great deal to say about how land is used. In order to understand this, it might be well to remember the basic stimulants that have led and will continue to lead to the furtherance of zoning. A prime stimulant is that of necessity. As communities are spread upon the countryside, we have encountered the necessity of regulating one of our most precious assets, our land. We cannot face the future of becoming more urbanized without recognizing that there will be an increasing stimulant for governmental regulation on the utilization of private property. While this certainly poses a potential danger, it also offers possible salvation for our future communities. The question of *which* it shall be is largely in the hands of the citizen. If we understand zoning and recognize the importance of being a vital part of it, the end result will be beneficial and desirable. If we fail to take an interest in or to become concerned, the necessity for regulation will continue and the gap will be filled by a higher level of government with an increasing loss of freedom of choice on the part of the individual. This is of such vital importance that it should be repeated over and over.

It also should be repeated that zoning is a tool of planning and will be as strong and effective as its planning base. This is true not only in the case of the original zoning ordinance but also in revisions, amendments and variances. Any zoning change can affect the planning of a community, and close cooperation must be maintained between planning and those responsible for zoning.

> There is one simple idea about zoning that I would like to implant in the minds of council members everywhere. Whenever they are faced with a request to rezone property, they should hold this thought: When we zoned this city, we did the best job we knew how. We believed that we were as fair and accurate in drawing the boundaries and designating the use districts as it was possible to be. Anyone who wants to change this zoning map has to prove that we were wrong. If he (or she) does not prove it to our satisfaction, we do not have to apologize in any way for turning him (or her) down.[4]

NOTES

1. Village of Euclid v. Ambler Realty Co., 272 U.S. 365 (1926).

2. Douglas R. Porter, "Incipient Ideologies of Growth and Development," *Urban Land* (June 1991), p. 34.

3. Ibid, p. 34

4. Marjorie S. Berger, ed., *Dennis O'Harrow: Plan Talk and Plain Talk* (Chicago: Planners Press, American Planning Association, 1981), p. 27.

CHAPTER

7

The Regulation of Land Subdivision

Some years ago, as a planning consultant on the East Coast, one of my job requirements was to spend many hours behind the wheel of a car, traveling hundreds of miles throughout the urbanizing countryside attending meetings and working clients' communities. In going from place to place, I found myself continually struck by the effects of urban sprawl as it devoured the landscape. There were two aspects that particularly stand out in my mind. The first is what I call the rape of the roadside—the mute testimony to man's greed and shortsightedness that lines so many miles of spoiled highway frontage. That, however, is another story to be told in much greater detail at another time. The second is the way in which the subdivision of land into building lots and parcels has played leapfrog over the countryside, seemingly caring little where it makes the next leap. In many cases, there is little rhyme or reason to the areas developed. Residential communities, shopping areas, and industrial tracts are all carved out of the first field available that offers the least line of resistance. Any resemblance to a pattern or plan for general development appears to be coincidental rather than intentional. All that is required to engender a subdivision is a nearby concentration of population.

As development scatters over an area, seeking the cheapest and most easily developed land, it brings with it a great many problems. Each house must somehow have a water supply, a means of sewage, garbage, and trash disposal, and there must be schools and protection against fire and other dangers. Stores and industry likewise sometimes create more problems than advantages in traffic generation, parking and servicing. Streets and roads, many times with little thought given to their layout and design, add miles that must be maintained, resurfaced, plowed, and drained. Frequently there is little relationship between subdivisions, and streets dead-end into yet untrampled fields or hillsides. What lies on the other side of the hill or across the field is given little thought.

THE PIECES SHOULD FIT TOGETHER

The unbridled tendency of development to follow the line of least resistance, like the devastating movement of a swarm of locusts but without the same continuity, is one of the most notorious sources of planning and development problems today. Far too little attention is given to the importance of orderly relationships between areas of growth. Nor is the total solution found in requiring the installation of utilities and services in individual subdivisions. I once had some experience with a semi-rural community of some 30 square miles that had 11 separate and disjointed residential subdivisions, each with more than 300 homes. In their wisdom, the town officials thought that they would avoid a major headache by requiring the installation of package sewage treatment plants. While they did avoid the problem of overflowing septic tanks, they completely overlooked a number of perhaps even more complicating factors. For example, there was no common design control of the systems. As a result, as the area filled in and a public sewer system became desirable, an entirely new system was required because not one of the individual systems had been designed so that it could be tied to any other. Each of the 11 systems had its own disposal unit. As the developers pulled out, the municipality found itself responsible for the maintenance of each unit, which required trained technicians. In the long run, the costs of correction were staggering; in essence, the residents of the community provided a subsidy for the exploiting developers. This is to say nothing of the expense of providing schools, school buses, street maintenance, and all of the other services to this disjointed municipality.

In observing this and the literally thousands of similar situations across the nation, I wonder if we truly realize the importance of our control of land subdivision. While frequently given little attention, it is one of the most important facets of community planning and development. As a field of 10 or 100 acres is carved up, a piece of the future community is molded. Each lot, each building, each street is like a building block that will determine the characteristics, the problems, and the potential of tomorrow's community. In an era of unprecedented growth, this is the way we are building the cities of tomorrow. Even in our older areas, the subdivision of large lots, estates, and golf courses can seriously affect the master plan of the city and the patterns of development. Subdivision, defined as the division of land into lots, tracts, or parcels for the sale and development thereof, is the means by which we are fitting together the pieces of the jigsaw puzzle that will be the future community.

BEWARE OF THE "SHADOW GOVERNMENTS"

The above example of the disjointed service systems provides an excellent illustration of a widespread, troublesome phenomenon that occurred all across the country during the healthy economy of the building boom years. This was the popularity of using the special district technique in some states and the laxity of state and local governments in ensuring adequate controls and regulations governing these districts. There are many kinds of special districts, some very successful, some essential to get around legislated debt limits of governmental units, and others just another way to encourage disjointed, leapfrog development and help the developers make more money while later leaving the local government and homebuyers to wrestle with the problems. Creating special districts for a single-purpose function such as toll roads, rapid transit systems, fire protection, parks and recreation facilities and maintenance, soil conservation and many other uses usually considered to be state and local responsibilities became the easy way for established governments to avoid taking on sometimes controversial projects and getting blamed for the requisite general tax increase.

With the housing building boom that started in the 1950s, developers and their lawyers began to realize the opportunity offered by special districts for providing independent utility systems and installing the required streets, landscaping, and drainage facilities either required by subdivision regulations or the developer's recognition of the absolute need for these amenities when marketing homes. Using special districts could also allow developers to acquire land not immediately adjacent to established urban areas and thus not have to wait for the extension of local government public services or annexation. In other words, special districts became a primary cause of leapfrog development and its attendant urban sprawl. Accordingly, development interests convinced several state legislatures to enact enabling legislation allowing this organization of "shadow governments"—special districts.

These "shadow governments," especially those organized as metropolitan districts, can be created to provide almost every service that regular organized government can give except for police protection. Each district is allowed to finance its infrastructure cost through the sale of tax-exempt bonds underwritten only by the hope that enough lots and housing units will be sold to allow future residents to pay the principal and interest through surcharges levied on their properties on top of their county real estate tax. This worked well during the boom days and such districts multiplied like rabbits from the late 1950s to the early 1980s. Then conditions changed drastically with the beginning of the nationwide recession. Partially built districts with only a few lots sold and even fewer homes constructed soon discovered they had no way to pay the bond holders, many of whom were retired elderly people who had jumped to take advantage of the high tax-exempt interest the district bonds offered. The developers simply took refuge in bankruptcy, leaving the handful of homeowners holding the bag.

In Colorado alone, according to a 1987 report issued by the Colorado Public Expenditure Council, there were 1,856 governmental entities: 63 counties, 286 incorporated cities and town, 176 school districts, and 1,331 special districts, each with taxing authority. Of the total property tax revenue collected by all local governmental units in 1988, 10.24 percent came from special districts, a substantial increase of 6.21 percent over the 4.03 percent going to these entities in 1970. Very few people recognize that the steadily increasing bite of a special district's taxing potential can have a serious adverse effect on representative governments in any taxing area, in other words, any incorporated municipality or county. Such was the case in Douglas County, Colorado, when bond rating houses reduced the rating grade for all public issue bonds due to the unusually large bite taken by special districts out of the total taxable assessment in the county. It should be pointed out that, fortunately, not all states allow the formation of "developer" districts. The states that do and are known to be having trouble, in addition to Colorado, are Arizona, California, Florida, and Texas. It is worth checking to see if they are allowed in your state.

To provide some illustration of just how bad the default on special district bonds in Colorado has been, on December 30, 1991 an article in the *Rocky Mountain News* in Denver carried the headline, "Districts'

Losses Cost Investors." This article pointed out that thousands of Colorado investors are facing losses totaling tens of millions of dollars as they begin accepting the cut-rate offers tendered by the state's metropolitan districts attempting to emerge from bankruptcy. Desperate to receive any portion of their money back, the bondholders—many of them senior citizens who had hoped to build a financial nest egg for retirement—are now taking 45 cents to 70 cents on the dollar for their original investment. Many have given up entirely on waiting for the struggling housing projects to rebound and have begun paying the large interest rates on the bonds that homeowners found forced upon them. As of the end of 1991, 16 special districts representing an investment of $191.3 million in Colorado alone had filed for bankruptcy protection.

The problem is most severe in Colorado as a result of inadequate enabling legislation passed several years ago by the state legislature under heavy pressure from development special interests. The causes of this serious problem have been succinctly outlined by *The Public Capital Quarterly*:

> In some districts, a lack of oversight, potential conflicts of interest, and weak financial controls may exacerbate the problem. In Colorado, the districts are actually governed by landowners and developers. The district often purchases land, easements or rights of way from these same or related landowners and/or contracts with them to construct all or part of the infrastructure. No one outside the district offers any real oversight of district activities.[1]

This discussion has been included here for several reasons. The first is that these happenings indicate the need for paying careful attention to land subdivision requirements and annexation policies in all communities, whether or not special districts are allowed in your state. Zoning and stringent land development requirements are important tools in controlling leapfrog platting and growth of urban sprawl. This is especially true if you have an intergovernmental agreement with the surrounding county for extraterritorial subdivision control. In Charlotte/Mecklenburg County, North Carolina, there is only one planning agency for both jurisdictions. That agency studies changes and recommends approval or denial to the governing bodies affected. A similar type of cooperative effort exists in Colorado with the city of Boulder and Boulder County as well in Fort Collins and Larimer County.

Secondly, we can recognize the importance of a good planning process establishing a well-defined urban growth area outside of presently urbanized limits in cooperation with any surrounding unincorporated area. Development should be keyed to the availability of public facilities and services, both in the present and for future expansion as provided for in a carefully devised capital improvements program. Finally, we come back to the example in which separate utility systems that did not mesh with the requirements of the public system had to be absorbed and improved by the state health department. Tight controls over growth areas, whether within or out of an incorporated area, can save millions of dollars when annexation occurs or when health and environmental agencies mandate correction of errors made in permitting the installation of inadequate sewer and water facilities. All of the area yet to be developed represents other pieces of the jigsaw puzzle that ultimately will be the design of urban form and determine the efficiency with which all new growth operates.

IF THIS IS GOING TO FLY: KNOW THE CONTROLS

The control and regulation of the subdivision of land is usually accomplished by the enactment of a subdivision ordinance or the adoption of a resolution setting forth standards. In most instances, while final approval may be in the hands of the governing body, the administration of subdivision regulations is the responsibility of the planning commission. The commission may simply act as a review agency, checking the subdivision against the regulations, examining its relationship to the master plan, and passing on recommendations to the governing body for action. In some states, the planning commission may be authorized not only to review but actually to approve or disapprove subdivision plats. In many states with large unincorporated areas, subdivision control may be vested in county planning boards, a situation that is becoming more prevalent as urban growth spills outside of the corporate boundaries of cities and towns. Some states, such as Pennsylvania, have even gone so far as to permit county planning agencies to impose regulations on an incorporated area when the city itself has failed to act after a stated period of time.

Conversely, an increasing number of state enabling acts grant cities what is known as "extraterritorial" authority to regulate land development on their fringes. Thus, a city may extend its subdivision control a specified distance, usually three or five miles, from any point of its corporate boundary. The purpose is to assure the municipality the opportunity to stage its utility services in land that it probably will annex in the future and to avoid the intensification of development of the open countryside to the point that later public services would be difficult, if not impossible, to provide. The proper and careful use of this extraterritorial authority is a most important tool to a city, particularly one that forms the single central core for a surrounding unincorporated territory of a rural or semi-rural nature. This again illustrates the importance of recognizing that land subdivision regulations and controls are a vital part of the planning process.

Subdivision guidance and control can make or break a master plan, particularly in an open community. The need for municipal services will be directly related to the subdivision activity in the community. The master plan should include a careful study of all open areas and anticipate their ultimate development in identifying the most appropriate use of land. Effecting the land-use plan then becomes a joint venture between zoning and subdivision control. In areas where expansion is yet to occur, the master plan can anticipate the need for school sites, major streets, parks, playgrounds, and drainage right-of-way. Many states permit either the reservation or acquisition of these areas as the land is subdivided. Some enabling acts even provide that a fee may be required in lieu of land dedication to ensure that adequate recreation facilities are provided within the community. Certain developers, recognizing the value of their investment, are not only providing school sites but are also building the schools. When the Levitt Corporation built its third Levittown, now known as Willingboro, New Jersey, not only was school land provided, but the first high school, junior high, and several elementary schools were constructed by the developer.

Advice and assistance on how to develop a good set of subdivision regulations are available from a number of sources. The first step, of course, is to obtain a copy of the state enabling act granting the authority to local governments to adopt land development controls. A careful study of the act will provide the fundamentals of what the ordinance should cover as well as an understanding of what can or cannot be included. Where there is a well-functioning state planning agency, it can provide not only the enabling act and advice, but in all probability will have a sample model ordinance. Again, the word "model" should be carefully noted. As stated before, no model ordinance can be drafted to fit perfectly the particular conditions, intentions, or policy of every community. In addition, assistance frequently can be obtained from statewide municipal leagues, regional planning agencies, or national organizations such as the American Planning Association.

CONCRETE CONSOLIDATION CONSIDERATION

For some time now there has been a trend toward consolidation of land development controls into one package. The idea of growth management, not just individual restrictive regulations, has received a great deal of attention and gathered popularity as a means of interjecting more of the planning process into the review of both zoning and subdivision proposals. Usually this is put in place by combining zoning and subdivision controls into one piece of legislation. Considerations of new concerns such as environmental factors, adequate facilities, affordable housing, growth limitation, cost/benefit analysis, and measurement of the total impact of the proposed project are included among the items to be considered during the review process.

For those interested in consolidating development regulations, there is one publication that, while very legalistic and somewhat complicated, sets forth a quite complete suggested model. It was prepared by a committee of 19 lawyers, land development experts, and zoning experts for the American Law Institute (ALI). It was officially adopted by the institute in 1975 and published in 1976. The title is *A Model Land Development Code* and, even though it has been 17 years since it was first published, it contains some very helpful ideas and innovative suggestions. Each section has the appropriate legal language with explanatory notes following. The purpose of proposing total consolidation of all state and local government regulation pertaining in any way to land development was to encourage regulatory preparers at the state and local levels to:

> . . . venture into the matter of standardization and simplification of procedures so as to reduce the complexities that arise when a project for land use appears to have some elements of "preservation," some elements of "reconstruction," and some elements of completely new uses and construction.[2]

A careful examination of the most recent growth management acts in both Oregon and Florida discloses a rather close similarity to the suggestions made by this ALI publication.

CONTROLS MAKE DOLLARS AND SENSE

Proper anticipation of development and preparation for it through master planning and subdivision control can save the community thousands of dollars. My firm worked in any number of communities where the fact that a new major street had been proposed in advance resulted in the dedication of the needed right-of-way in accordance with the master plan as subdivision took place on each side. On the other hand, some communities have attempted to go through the motions of subdivision control without a master plan (a practice permitted in some states), or seemingly forgot that they had a plan and treated subdivision as a separate, independent operation. In either case, the effectiveness of subdivision control has been seriously limited. Without reference to a well-prepared plan, the approval of subdivision plats becomes nothing more than an exercise in collective thinking, limited in scope, discretionary in requirements, and totally devoid of comprehensive considerations.

Illustrative of this is the case of the community that failed to take into account an overall plan of streets and roads in its subdivision control. A large triangular area of several hundred acres of the community was eventually developed into five separate subdivisions. Not only was no provision made for a much-needed collector street in the area, but the growth generated far more traffic than the existing streets in the area could handle. In this case, the former mistake could not be corrected at all due to the placement of the houses, and the error was an extremely expensive one to correct. Worse, the new homes were built so close to the existing inadequate roadway that its ultimate widening destroyed their desirable characteristics and led to the spread of cheapening and ratable-destroying uses.

Subdivision regulations should clearly establish the rules under which the development of land will be permitted. Careful thought should be given to the preparation of such regulations, and they should be phrased in as clear and concise terms as possible. An understandable procedure for application, processing, and approval should be provided.

IF THE PIECES FIT TOGETHER, IT WILL WORK

A good subdivision ordinance usually contains a set of definitions, procedures for filing applications, descriptions of the methods of processing, approval procedures, design standards, and provisions for general administration. The definitions section sets forth what is meant by subdivision and may exempt a minor subdivision of a limited number of lots from the full approval process. The procedural section sets the time of filing, states the required forms and materials, and outlines the steps that must be taken. The design section deals with the necessity of installing streets, curbs, gutters, sidewalks, street signs, and trees and establishes minimum standards for each. The administration section provides for appeals from decisions, establishes final approval authority, and outlines the manner of conducting public hearings if they are required. Of utmost importance to subdivision control is the provision of a carefully drafted set of application forms for use both by the applicant and, as a checklist, by the planning commission. Usually a performance bond or guarantee is required of the subdivider to insure the installation of required utilities and facilities.

Regardless of the quality of the ordinance, the success of subdivision control and regulation will be dependent upon the care with which the ordinance is administered. A planning commission cannot take this assignment too lightly. Each subdivision plat should be carefully reviewed by the entire commission. Members should personally view the area under question. This should be done on a special trip, even if they drive by the area every day; it will appear different to them if they look at it with the map of the projected subdivision before them. In addition, each application should be carefully checked for form and adequate information. The effect on the master plan should be examined and discussed. The zoning requirements for the area should be checked to be sure they are being met. Other community agencies should be informed and consulted, particularly the school board, the board of health, and the engineering department.

The commission should not hesitate to suggest improvements in the subdivision design. In many cases, careful review can result in an improved design that will save money for both the developer and the municipality. My firm worked out a system in some of our client communities in which each subdivision plat was referred to us for review and, if desirable, redesign. A fee was assessed by the municipality against the developer for this service so that it was not a cost to the community. Not only were the communities saved thousands of dollars by the reduction of street lengths and resultant maintenance costs, but the developers on numerous occasions stated their gratitude for improvements in the design and character of the area.

Just as with zoning, recent trends in subdivision control techniques have been geared toward providing greater flexibility of design and the means of interrelating diverse, but compatible, development. As zoning tools such as planned unit development and cluster development have come more into use, a broadening of opportunities to shape community form through subdivision review and approval has taken place. To do so requires a very close coordination between the provisions of the zoning and subdivision ordinances. It is becoming increasingly obvious that the division of land that shapes the urban form and its use must be closely correlated, and each must be based firmly upon the total comprehensive planning process.

A word should be said about the importance of subdivision controls as applied in land development of other than single-family residential areas. Frequently industrial, commercial, and multifamily uses necessitate the subdivision or resubdivision of land to achieve the desired site. This is especially true in the use of the planned unit development concept (see Glossary, Page 231) and in the assembly of parcels for redevelopment in some older areas. A good set of subdivision regulations requiring extensive design and site plan review can ensure an attractive and efficient result. Such things as traffic circulation, ingress and egress controls, landscaping, and open-space development can be part of the overall approval package and can make the difference between an outstanding project and another drab scar on the horizon. Many subdivision ordinances require this type of design review before approval can be granted.

Of equal importance is understanding the value of dedication of land and easements through subdivision review. Several years ago, the courts looked rather unfavorably on requiring any outright dedication of land from a developer, whether for parks, schools, or any other public purpose. This attitude has changed decidedly as the problems of municipal financing have increased. Dedications of land for parks, passive open space, schools, bike trails, and safe access for children over and under major traffic arteries are now commonplace. As the energy crunch continues, the availability of public lands for bicycles, walking, and even mopeds will remain a major concern. Often this can be tied to other vital aspects of development controls as well—stream right-of-way protection, flood control, and drainage. A wooded trail along a drainage easement that allows safe pedestrian and non-automotive vehicle movement can be a priceless asset to both the community and the subdivision.

What all this adds up to is that subdivision control is an indispensable tool of community planning. This is true whether you think of the need for guiding the future development of your community as a "growth management plan" or still utilize the separate but related functions of zoning and subdivision controls. Just as zoning shapes and maintains the community character, subdivision controls shape the development pattern of individual areas and, consequently, the whole community. Subdividing patterns will determine the adequacy and efficiency of future streets, utilities, schools, police and fire protection, and garbage collection, as well as the economic benefit or liability of any particular subdivision to the overall governmental unit. Good subdivision planning and controls are the ways we can permit development while making certain that, when development occurs, it will fit into the overall scheme of the master plan with the least damage and the maximum benefit to the community.

NOTES

1. "Special Districts In Trouble," *The Public's Capital Quarterly* (Spring 1991), p. 8.

2. The American Law Institute, *A Model Land Development Code* (1976), p. xv.

CHAPTER

8

The Capital Improvements Program

Americans are cost-conscious and, in most cases, conservative about expenditures in everything but government. More and more of our total income is taken to run the business of government, with each succeeding year seeing a continuation of rising budgets and expanding operations. Now we are looking at an increase in the national deficit of some $300 to $400 billion dollars a year with the total debt racing past $4 trillion and no indication of any immediate change for the better. Somehow we seem to have become conditioned to expect huge amounts of public funds to be expended and to believe that little if anything can be done about it. While it may be necessary to accept the idea that little can be done about the continual rise of funds required to provide the demanded services, a great deal can be done about seeing that the money allocated for public improvements is well spent. By enacting Proposition 13 in 1978, California voters severely restricted their state's governmental spending by limiting the tax that can be placed on real estate. Perhaps I am wrong to say "little can be done about the continual rise of funds," but I am not sure that Proposition 13 was the right approach. We can do a great deal to assure the public that its money is buying the most needed project and that the results will make good sense. On a municipal level, this can be accomplished through the use of the capital improvements program.

PROGRAMMING PUBLIC FUNDS PAYS OFF

Every day in this country, literally millions of dollars are expended in connection with public improvements, and by public improvements I mean any service or facility provided by a government and paid for with public funds. The construction and maintenance of water systems, sewer systems, streets, sidewalks, municipal buildings, parks, and fire stations are among the items considered in the capital improvements program. Schools, while usually considered separately, are a vital part of the community's capital expenditure program, particularly during a time of growth and expansion. All of these facilities and services are being planned, built, and maintained by our municipal governments and school districts each hour of the day.

The provision of these services and facilities is essential to our way of life. In fact, the real justification for municipal government lies in its ability to provide protection, services, and facilities better and more economically than we ourselves can accomplish as individuals. Yet probably 75 to 90 percent of the funds spent for public facilities are used on projects that have not been subjected to a careful analysis that justifies their need and makes certain they are an integral part of a comprehensive long-range plan. Instead, they are approached on a piecemeal basis as the need arises and the pressure becomes great enough to force action. Time has shown us that our politicians much prefer to wait to respond to a crisis as opposed to planning ahead; in a crisis they know they can gain public support, while to anticipate problems and call public attention to them almost always will be controversial and politically damaging. This is a major built-in obstacle to successful long-range planning.

One of the most important purposes of planning is to anticipate the needs of people for public improvements and to provide a sensible program for meeting those needs. This is the function of the capital improvements program phase of master planning. The program is usually supplemented by the development of a capital improvements budget. The program itself is a summary of the needs of the community in terms of public improvements, the estimated costs of these improvements, and the development of logical priorities for their provision. The needs are determined by the master plan and the work of the planning commission in analyzing land-use and population trends, economic pressures, and general development potential in terms of the financial capacity of the governmental unit to provide the service. The priority of need can be determined only after a careful study of the master plan and a detailed analysis of the opinions of various municipal departments about their needs. Each improvement should be justified in relation to all others. The more a project is needed by the total population, rather than by just one or two groups, the higher its rating should be on the priority list. The cost of the total program must be related to the economic base of the community and what it can afford at a given time.

DON'T GET CARRIED AWAY ON THE "RATABLE BANDWAGON"

As general obligation bonds usually are issued to provide the funds for capital improvements, and as most of the money to repay these bonds comes from the ad valorem or real estate property tax, all proposals must be carefully scrutinized as to how they will affect and relate to the tax assessment base. All states control municipal borrowing, either by establishing a bonded indebtedness limit or by state approval of municipal budgets. Thus, a city may not indiscriminately borrow money or exceed the amount set by the state, except in the case of an emergency that threatens health and safety. The debt ceiling and amounts that have been borrowed and not repaid must be taken into account in preparing the budget for any future capital expenditures. As net taxable valuation rises through economic growth, and as past obligations are paid off, the municipality's borrowing capacity increases. This system has been one of the major causes of governmental units closing their eyes to sound planning principles and jumping on the "ratable bandwagon," allowing poor development that promises to increase the tax base.

Such shortsighted, costly, mistake-prone practices greatly increase during times of heavy economic recession and have been intensified during recent years by the federal government's withdrawal from almost all of its financial aid and grant programs. When these two conditions prevail, a chain-reaction follows in which tightening state budgets place the burden of maintaining infrastructure and essential public services squarely on the shoulders of the public finance "orphan" level of government—local counties and municipalities. Thus they feel their only hope for survival is to go for the short-range, quick fixes represented by speculative economic development, which later prove to be mistakes costing more than any derived benefit. One needs only to look at some of the suburban shopping centers and strip commercial developments, either with more vacant stores than active ones or totally in bankruptcy, to substantiate this postulation. When viewed correctly, all of this makes the process of careful capital improvements programming even more essential for any community that really cares about its future.

The development of a capital improvements program, if it is to be successful, must be a cooperative endeavor. Each and every operating department of the municipality or county must be willing to understand and support the program. In large measure, the basic capital needs are determined by the information compiled from individual departments. This is usually done by sending forms and questionnaires to each department head. The department head indicates the department's capabilities, its shortcomings, anticipated needs for new services, and necessary replacements for old facilities, with cost estimates where appropriate. When this information is returned to the planning commission, it is carefully studied and evaluated in terms of the overall community. A complete list of the needs for efficient service over a five- or six-year period, with approximate costs, is then prepared as the program of capital improvements and recommended priorities are assigned each item. A capital improvements section of the community budget is then adopted by the governing body for the first year to take care of the financing of that portion of the projected improvements that the community can then afford.

Many states require by statute that local governments prepare and adopt a capital budget. This is frequently overlooked, particularly in smaller cities. It is, however, part of the planning function to insist that careful capital improvements programming and budgeting are worked out and that they have the support of the people. Where the capital improvements program is practiced, it is found to be an extremely valuable tool. City managers have long been advocates of the idea of capital budgeting. Many of them feel not only that it is the desired way of properly programming an improvement but also that it is the best way of avoiding undue pressure from vested interest groups for pet projects.

CAPITAL PROGRAMMING PORTENDS PEOPLE PARTICIPATION

When I served as city manager of Albuquerque, I found the capital improvements program to be one of our most important undertakings. Each year it was approached with concern that the needs outweighed the available finances and a desire to make certain that each dollar brought the most service to the total population. It is equally true that some of the most controversial discussions with department heads and pressure groups in the city took place over the final decisions made. Many cities have found a well-prepared program extremely useful, and such places as Cincinnati (long noted for its advance planning), Dallas, Phoenix, and Hartford have used capital budgeting as a most successful way of anticipating new expenditures and bond issues well in advance of emergency needs. By so doing, a city administration can prepare studies and illustrate the necessity for each project to the people.

This cannot be overemphasized. Without the understanding and support of the taxpayers and voters, no capital improvements planning will reach fruition. In Albuquerque, each time we were successful in a bond issue, much of the credit could be given to a representative, aggressive citizen committee organized to study, support, and publicize the needs of the city. Philadelphia and other places have used the media—especially radio spot announcements—to inform citizens of the proposal details and to explain just why each is needed. Places that continue to have successful bond issue votes in spite of the rising resistance to increased governmental spending have all pursued effective public information programs.

LARGE OR SMALL CITIES, THE IDEA WORKS

It should not be assumed that the value of such a program is limited to the larger cities. No community should operate without a carefully thought out capital improvements program. The smaller city or village may be worrying only about the provision of a few new sidewalks or the paving of a few streets, but wise programming, based upon the master plan, can be extremely beneficial. Just take the example of the community that has an effective planning commission and approaches its growth problems seriously. The citizens may suspect that they will soon reach a point of growth at which their present waterworks will be inadequate, but they aren't quite sure when that point will be reached. They begin a master plan study that shows regional pressures and past trends indicating a potential for 3,000 more people within the next five years. The land-use map and traffic studies show not only that this growth is likely but also that there is an area of the community ripe for new subdivision. The services needed to provide adequately for the new people can then be calculated. It is recognized that the water plant needs rebuilding and that new service lines are a must if the area is to prosper. Through careful study and cooperation with the water department, the planning board schedules the items in the capital improvements program and the financing is provided in the budget at an early date.

Through the same process of future planning and thoroughly developed, people-supported capital improvements programming, any community can anticipate the need for underground service lines installation and see that they are completed before a new street or sidewalk is paved, thereby saving itself substantial unnecessary costs down the road. This same practical economic principle can be applied to obtaining easements for utility lines or maintenance access in advance of development instead of later having to deal with individual property owners.

Compare this situation with that of the community that couldn't be bothered with all the fuss. They just left things to chance. If a street light burned out, it was replaced. After all, it is easier to spend folks' money if there is an emergency, and there is really less pressure than if you explain to them a need in advance. It also merits noting that it is easier to pass out political favors if there is not too much on paper about what ought to be done. This community proceeded on its merry way, meeting emergencies as they arose, and even then on a stop-gap or piecemeal basis. Of course, they never really improved; in fact, they even went downhill and were always over their heads in debt. They also found that some of the better industries passed them by, but after all, they weren't wasting any money on this planning foolishness. In case this strikes you as funny, think about it carefully. It could be your community. I have seen a good many places just like it.

Capital works programming can succeed and can be a valuable effectuating tool of sound planning. It is frequently resented and resisted. Sometimes, because of petty jealousy, an individual department head who feels that cooperative capital works programming will interfere with his or her own empire building will attempt to discredit or delay it. Sometimes elected politicians will try to discredit the procedure, knowing that their porkbarrel method of dispensing services as favors may be interfered with. Regardless of the reason for objection, the well-versed planning commission member and interested citizen will realize that sound capital improvements programming and capital budgeting are the keys to long-range economic stability within the framework of the master plan.

CHAPTER

9

The Care and Feeding of Planning Professionals

Whether you are a member of a planning commission, a citizen group leader, or simply a person interested in what's going to happen to your town, it is desirable for you to know a little about who is going to be parceling out planning advice in your community. This means, or should mean, the planning professional, the person who delves into data collection and research, comes up with analyses, and makes recommendations to the planning commission and the policymakers. Just what kind of people are these and how do they come by the title of professional planner? Doesn't everybody plan? Aren't my ideas of what our community should be 10 years from now just as good as anyone else's? The answer to the last question is probably "yes"—if we all had the kind of training that teaches us to examine thoroughly and think comprehensively in terms of total societal concepts, and if we could really think objectively instead of personally about where we live.

The planning professional should be a generalist who has knowledge of sociology, ecology, economics, geology, engineering, law and public administration, and at least some understanding of physical design. The effective planner must also have an understanding of people and how to deal with them and have the patience to accept frustration. Above all else, while retaining professional principles, the planner must become a skilled student of politics but not a politician. This is the kind of awesome charge those of us in planning education must face every day: to provide this kind of background and knowledge in the brief period of our relationship with students.

AND THE LORD SAID, "LET THERE BE PLANNERS"

The function and the profession of planning have expanded rapidly over the past several decades. Future prospects appear to indicate an even further expansion of both government and citizen-activated community planning. This planning will no longer be confined to land use, public facilities, and physical growth but will include dealing with social problems, programs for community services, citizen organization, and other "software" matters. All of these will affect our lives in one way or another and, while planners are not decision makers, the work they do will influence the decisions that will be made. For that reason, the citizen should know who the planners are, the training and experience they have had, and the nature of their role in shaping policy.

The first planners in this country were persons who, in a position of leadership, had vision and foresight. Paterson, New Jersey, for example, points with pride to the fact that Alexander Hamilton provided it with its first plan for development. Thomas Jefferson had an intense interest in architecture and city planning. The founders of Washington, D.C. went so far as to engage a specialist, Major Pierre L'Enfant, to lay out the circles and radials now famous in that city, if not effective in today's traffic. Many of our existing cities can thank their early pioneers for the few spots of green and open areas that remain, such as the park squares in Philadelphia. While some professionals in allied fields began to appear on the planning scene in the late 19th and early 20th centuries, it was not until the public works program of the depression years that the specialized practice of the profession emerged.

With the planning and programming of public works for relief purposes came the realization that they should be related to comprehensive planning. As a result, state planning boards were formed and enabling legislation for local planning was passed. Architects, engineers, and landscape architects became involved in land planning. It was soon recognized that physical planning alone was not enough, and economists and sociologists were brought into the field to perform essential research. As the merits of the idea of comprehensive—that is, physical, social, economic, and environmental—planning became obvious and the demand for planning increased, it was only logical that a separate profession should evolve and educational institutions should initiate specialized training.

The number of institutions so doing has grown phenomenally in recent years. When I departed from an architectural background and ventured into planning in 1947, I found no more than five such programs and all at the graduate level. The total student enrollment could not possibly have exceeded 100. At present, planning, or some related area of specialization, is taught in organized schools or departments at some 100 colleges and universities, at both the undergraduate and graduate levels. More schools embark on such programs every year.

LOOK, MA, I'M A PROFESSIONAL

Today, a well-schooled planner is given courses in planning principles and concepts, methods and techniques of research and analysis, social problems, citizen activation, housing, environmental concerns, law, public administration, economics and governmental finance, and physical design. The student may be basically schooled in a physical science or in a social science and may begin specialization at the graduate level or may enter one of several undergraduate planning schools right out of high school. While there are those who insist that persons skilled in one of several allied fields, such as architecture or engineering, are qualified professional planners, it is becoming more and more generally accepted that comprehensive land-use planning is a separate process requiring, for maximum competence, special training as well as specialized experience.

As the planning profession evolved and grew in numbers, some of those interested in furthering professionalism of the field came together in 1917 to form the American City Planning Institute, which later became the American Institute of Planners (AIP). Created primarily to service practicing professional planners, AIP adopted membership requirements that precluded elected officials, planning commissioners, and others interested in the planning process from becoming members unless they were also planners. In recognition of the need for a service organization for those involved or just interested in planning and zoning matters, the American Society of Planning Officials (ASPO) was established in 1934 with the purpose of conducting research and promoting planning in general. Both organizations grew rapidly over the years, especially after World War II. While cooperation existed between AIP and ASPO, some members of each began to advocate their consolidation into one group. After a considerable period of discussion, and in spite of strong opposition from many members of both groups, the two organizations merged in 1978 to form the American Planning Association (APA).

APA, which continues to provide assistance and service for the general public, became the parent organization from which was created the American Institute of Certified Planners (AICP). Members of AICP must also be members of APA. Of 28,000 APA members, some 6,500 are AICP members. AICP is now the organization limited to practicing professional planners, who must pass a qualifying examination to join. The examination cannot be taken until an applicant has had a minimum of four years of experience in planning; however, if that person has a bachelor's or master's degree in planning from an accredited planning school, the experience requirements are reduced by one and two years, respectively. The authority to create a planning school accreditation board was obtained jointly by APA, AICP, and the Association of Collegiate Schools of Planning (ACSP) in the early 1980s. Since the start of the planning school accreditation process, there have been 62 planning programs granted accreditation status; each of these is subject to a review every five years by the Planning Accreditation Board (PAB).

The matter of whether professional planners should come under a state licensing or registration act has been the subject of considerable debate over the years. Many AICP members strongly support this idea, primarily because, without it, anyone can claim to be a qualified planner. Just as many, if not more, members argue against any form of licensing or registration, claiming that becoming an AICP member and being certified by that organization is sufficient. At present, only two states, New Jersey and Michigan, have laws setting requirements for planners. In New Jersey, those practicing planning must obtain a license to do so, after passing an examination. However, during the early years of the law, political pressure from professions such as architecture, engineering, and landscape architecture resulted in the granting of planning licenses to members of those professions without an examination and merely by paying the fee. Fortunately, the legislation has been amended to require each person seeking a license to take and pass an exam. Michigan, on the other hand, has a law that requires anyone calling himself or herself a planner to have passed a qualifying exam and be registered. Several states, such as Kentucky, have instituted some measure of proof of qualifications through the appropriate state department, which issues certificates with designations such as "planner-in-charge" or "approved planner." In the meantime, sign painters in 48 of the 50 states stay busy painting the word "planner" or "planning" on the office doors of members of other professions.

A planning commission embarking on its job very quickly finds that professional services in some form are not only desirable but are usually essential. The typical commission is composed of persons who, though interested and perhaps partially skilled in planning, lack a complete knowledge of planning techniques. In addition, members are, in many cases, active civic leaders with their own professions to practice. The amount of time most can devote to the development of plans for the community is limited. Few, if any, technical surveys and studies can be accomplished by two- or three-hour meetings once or twice a month. It thus becomes obvious that if planning is to be meaningful, someone skilled in its practice and with time to devote to its prosecution must be found. This means the employment of a professional planner. Professional services can be obtained on one of two bases—either by employing a full-time resident staff or by hiring a consulting firm. Whether your community uses the staff or the consultant approach, or if there is a staff and consultants sometimes hired for special projects, it is important that the individuals' qualifications be well-verified and made known to the general public. A prospective staff person or a consultant who is a member of AICP has been recognized as qualified at least in the basic planning fundamentals. This information together with a thorough check on previous employment or consulting contract performance is the best way to determine whether any planner can be of professional help to your community.

HELP WANTED: FULL OR PART-TIME

A local government technical staff is employed by the city and responsible to the planning commission (or responsible to the chief administrative officer but working with the commission). The administrative organization of staff planners varies, of course, from one municipality to another. The staff may consist of one trained planner, as in the case of small cities, or may number several planners, researchers, graphic artists, and office staff, as in the larger cities and large-scale planning operations. Many of the larger cities have an annual planning budget of several hundred thousand dollars and a planning staff that varies between 75 and 100 persons. Unfortunately, in periods of economic recession there is a tendency for elected officials in some of the large cities, and even some small towns, to look upon planning as something intangible and a logical place to save money by cutting back the department's budget allocation. This is a most unwise approach, however, because good practical planning is most needed in hard times and can make an even greater contribution to the future of a community than in boom times. Coordination, practical examination of needs, and cost/benefit analyses become extremely valuable to local governments when things are not all rosy. This is when current, thorough comprehensive plans and zoning ordinances, carefully administered and enforced, can save a community from making major mistakes by jumping at everything that may be painted as an economic stimulant, but later will become a serious liability, both financially and for the qualify of life. The budgets for planning and zoning should be the very last thing any thinking group of elected officials would consider appropriate for budget reduction. Such action only adds to the problem instead of becoming part of the solution.

Nevertheless, I found just such conditions while doing research site visits to the 15 cities studied for my 1991 book. As many as seven of these cities were struck with budget shortfall problems and had severely reduced the budgets of their planning departments. To cite just a few examples, Corpus Christi, Texas, mandated that its planning staff prepare a revised comprehensive plan by a specified date, yet the budget for the department had been continually reduced in deference to the economic conditions afflicting the city. After a serious shortfall, the planning agency staff in San Antonio had been almost decimated. The remaining small group was able to act only as a routine housekeeping force, even though the city's future demanded the strongest possible planning and zoning functions. My visit to New Orleans elicited the shocking information that its planning department budget had been cut almost every year in recent times. Their comprehensive plan had not been updated and revised due to lack of funding for more than 15 years.

Even California, usually the "boom" state, has not escaped. In addition to the overall discouraging economic conditions, one cannot help but wonder about the role played by the infamous Proposition 13 in making things even worse for the state, especially state and local government functions. As a result, governmental agencies have necessarily experienced reduction of personnel and support services; unfortunately, particularly planning departments. Whenever times get tough, shortsighted politicians invariably look to the planning budget as an easy place to cut because they are convinced that this will raise the least howl from the public. San Diego offers a good example of this even though the city continues to be one of the fastest growing in the county with the concomitant problems of boom town expansion. The need for an ample budget and sufficient qualified planning staff would never be greater than during the growth period that existed at the time of my visit there and continues to a large extent today, in spite of the nationwide economic downslide.

PROFESSIONAL PERSONNEL PREFERRED

The majority of local planning offices are the small, one- or two-person operations, usually consisting of a planning director, an assistant, and a secretary. In these small staff offices, the selection of personnel is extremely important. The planner must have a well-rounded background. He or she may be working on a technical study of traffic circulation one minute and be expected to deal with a complicated zoning problem the next. The individual must be skilled in technical matters, be a public relations expert and an administrator, and at the same time be able to deal with political intrigue and changes in the power structure of the community. The success or failure of planning as a process can be dependent upon the planner's ability and personality.

It is of utmost importance to the program to make sure that the personnel obtained are the best for the job. Many planning programs, off to a flying start amid local enthusiasm, have been set back or completely killed by selection of the wrong personnel. I well remember an illustration of this in a New York community. There, after years of effort, a planning program was initiated with great fanfare and public expectation. For over a year, the program developed nicely: a master plan and a downtown rebuilding scheme were formulated with the assistance of consultants. The community, wanting to ensure continuity, decided to engage a staff planner. The salary scale was comparatively low, to keep it in line with established governmental salaries, and the community was a challenging one for any planner. After advertising, some six or eight applicants were interviewed and several were offered the job, only to turn it down. Finally, for fear that a long delay would result in the loss of the appropriated funds, the decision was made to accept an applicant with less than the desired ability and experience. As a result, within six months, the community's planning and urban renewal program was in a state of complete confusion. There developed a serious question of whether planning as a function was to be abandoned, yet the community now needed planning even more than before. While a staff operation can be effective and desirable, the importance of careful selection and the paying of a salary sufficient to attract top-flight personnel cannot be overstressed.

The second way to obtain professional planning services is to engage a consulting organization in the planning field. Consultants are available for advice on programs and review of activity or to provide actual staff services. In many communities, a combination of staff and consulting services is utilized. Here the consultant provides review of the staff work and lends experience and know-how, or undertakes special technical studies, including the development of the master plan, to supplement the work of the staff. Again, the selection of an individual or firm is extremely important.

THERE IS SOME GOOD AND SOME BAD IN ALL OF US

There are advantages and disadvantages in both methods of providing services. The success of any planning operation will, in large measure, be dependent upon the individuals involved, and it is well to be aware of all significant factors. The staff planning office offers the opportunity for the planning function to have a direct relationship with the local administration. The planner becomes a part of this administration. A planner living in the community has the advantage of intimate familiarity with the area and its problems. He or she can see the pressure spots and evaluate the matters most demanding of attention. A staff program also provides continuity and puts planning on a day-to-day basis. The planning commission has technical advice immediately available, and a direct contact with the people of the area can be maintained.

The disadvantages of staff operation frequently stem from the very things that appear to offer advantages. The local planner often gets overrun with day-to-day housekeeping chores and has little time left for real planning. The planner is sometimes too readily available to all the pressure groups and runs the danger of becoming emotionally involved, either on a friendship or interest basis. Objectivity can be lost by familiarity. In addition, it is far easier for a local staff employee to be subjected to political pressure and to weaken, understandably, when job security is at stake. At the same time, it is difficult to find personnel who have the broad experience required to ground the planning operation on sound principles. Infrequent is the one planner who has sufficient skills in all required technical fields, public speaking, public relations, and political organization to provide all that is needed for a successful local program.

The consulting system, on the other hand, has the advantage of overcoming many of these objections. A well-qualified firm can offer broad training and experience. Members of the firm usually are schooled in varying disciplines and have worked in many different communities. They can draw from this experience, saving time and, in many cases, avoiding damaging mistakes. Consultants are free to work without interference from local pressure or vested interests. Being independent of the community, they can be more objective, and, at the same time, their opinions can carry more weight. Consulting services can be obtained by communities that feel they cannot yet afford the budget required for a staff operation. In many cases, two or more communities within an area can combine and, using the same consultant, obtain staff services for the expenditure of far less money than required for individual staffs or even a combined staff.

The most frequently mentioned disadvantage of the consulting system is the danger of one-shot, package planning. This certainly should be avoided; if the program is carefully undertaken, it can be. In addition, the consultant may be unable to become as familiar with the community as a staff planner. He or she can prepare technically competent studies that overlook matters of immediate local concern. The work can also be made meaningless by the failure of the planning agency to become an integral part of the project. There is, too, the difficulty of keeping the planning commission and the public well informed as each part of the program unfolds.

Having been on both sides of the fence (public staff planner and private consultant), I cannot help but have mixed emotions, which I believe allow me to see the advantages and disadvantages of each method rather objectively. As a former president of the American Society of Consulting Planners, I can strongly endorse the multifaceted expertise of the private practitioner. As a former planning director, I can say with assurance that the continuity of staff planning is vital and beneficial. My conclusion bears out the idea that even if you have a good staff, there are times when a consulting firm can be invaluable.

The desired program for any given community is, of course, the program that best serves the community's needs and suits its characteristics. Whether this is staff alone, consultant alone, or a combination of the two, there will be advantages and there will be pitfalls. Good planning commission members recognize this, as they realize the importance of the individual characteristics of planning personnel. The key to success of any planning program is the care with which the personnel, whether it be staff or consulting firm, is selected. Good commission members also recognize that no professional can solve all of the problems alone. They must have the understanding and support of the local people—local policy and ultimate effectuation will always be the responsibility of the planning commission and elected officials. In most cases, the results of the planning program will be determined by the combined abilities of the professional planner, lay members of the planning agency and the elected officials.

THE DAY OF JUDGMENT MUST COME FOR ALL

As there are going to be more planning commissions and more planning professionals involved with all of us in the future, it is reasonable to reflect on a few guidelines that might be helpful to citizens in evaluating and dealing with both. Some are questions to which answers should be known; others are caveats about which we need to be aware. They include, but are not necessarily limited to, the following:

1. Who is considered to be the client? Is it the mayor, the council, the political structure, the developers, or the people in general?

2. Are the professionals and the commission members keenly aware of the importance of citizen involvement and citizen opinion? Do they welcome participation and comments from citizen organizations and individuals?

3. Can the commission members or the professional be counted on to be objective, impartial, and reasonable? Is there any strong personal motivation, such as real estate investment or furtherance of other business interest, that may cloud thinking and create a conflict?

4. What is the professional's background in education and experience? How did the individual fare in any other communities in which he or she worked? What kind of formal training has the person in planning? Is he or she a member of AICP?

5. Are the commission members and the professionals socially aware? How do they deal with minority problems, the question of adequate housing, and the need for increasing economic opportunities for all? Can they work with people of all ethnic and economic groups in a fair and considerate way?

6. What is the administrative structure for planning? Are the professionals given a realistic opportunity for the expression of ideas and the offering of advice, or are they expected to be "rubber stamps" for politically expedient action? Do the mayor or chief executive and council members have a planning attitude and insist that the planning department receive the necessary cooperation from other departments and agencies?

7. Is the planning director truly a professional with the administrative capabilities to run an efficient department or is that official strictly a political appointee who must be very careful not to "rock the boat?"

8. Are the staff members competent? Are they permitted free expression of ideas and opinions and encouraged to further their own education and knowledge as well as develop new concepts and techniques?

9. Is there turnover of personnel and have highly regarded professionals left for other more satisfying and better-paying positions? Is meritorious service rewarded by advancement and assignment of additional responsibility?

10. What was the last proposal of a major consequence to emanate from the planning professional or the department? How was its presentation handled, and what was the result in action or lack thereof?

11. Does the public in general know of the work of the planning department? What is their opinion of it? Have the professionals gained the respect of the citizens, the planning commission and the governing body, or are they just there so we can say there is a planning function?

12. Most important of all—do the elected officials fully realize that they are the only ones who can make policy and that "the buck stops" right in their chairs?

WE'RE ALL IN THIS TOGETHER

A satisfactory answer to all of these questions is needed if there is to be a meaningful planning process. Planning is a function of collective society working together to better the environment; the professional is only the catalyst. No professionals who feel that they are planning *for* people instead of *with* people are going to be very effective; nor are they professionals in the true sense of the word. At the same time, all of us should remember that the planner is a human being, too, with feelings and pride. Regardless of how we may disagree with their ideas, each is also entitled to the same kind of courteous treatment, objective consideration, and fair play as we expect they will provide us. We should keep in mind that we are all in this together: only by working together as those who share common concerns can we expect to make things better. The job of your professional planner is to help you, me, and others to make this possible.

CHAPTER

10

Planning and the School Board

One of the most perplexing mysteries in modern society is our persistence in the separation of community planning and school planning. Not only are they undertaken completely separately, but in most places they compete for the same diminishing tax dollar. Planning for community development and planning for schools have so much in common that merely to say so seems redundant. It is not even the chicken and the egg question of which came first: the interrelation is so great that they should be planned for in concert—collectively and cooperatively. It is only in this way that the school system can adequately serve its jurisdiction and that the community or communities involved can relate their growth policies to the educational system. Even more importantly, this is the only way that both community needs and school needs can share equitably in the division of the tax dollar.

AS THE TWIG IS BENT, SO SHALL IT GROW

The provision of adequate school buildings on well-located sites is one of the most important community responsibilities. Each area must provide the needed facilities and personnel to school the youngsters who live there and who are yet to come. The school board has little to say about the rate of growth of any area, yet it is obligated by law to provide an adequate public education system. With the rising costs of construction, and operation after construction, we find that larger and larger percentages of the local tax dollar are going into school coffers. In some cases, 75 to 85 percent of the total tax funds necessary for local public purposes are used for schools. The anticipation of this need, and the means of providing some measure of control for orderly growth in order to avoid runaway costs for education, can be achieved only by the cooperative endeavor of the school board and the planning board.

With our changing social structure, the struggle to revitalize the decaying structure of our inner cities, and the continuing shortage of energy and resources, this coordination becomes not just important but essential. Added to this is the effect of court-ordered busing on traditional neighborhoods in the attempt to achieve and maintain integration in schools in larger cities. At this point, let me make it clear that I am a strong believer in interracial integration, not just in schools, but everywhere. It is because of this belief that I am completely convinced that court-ordered forced busing of students miles from their homes has been a total failure in gaining effective, harmonious integration. In fact, I would go so far as to say it has been an abysmal sociological experiment that has done far more harm than good to our social structure.

Some of the results leading me to this conclusion are the destruction of the major focal point of vital neighborhoods, the neighborhood school, where kids and parents of all races could, and did, intermingle; the devastating effect on inner cities resulting from the "white flight" to the suburbs, unfortunately motivated by deep-seated bigotry; and the psychological damage to students' mental sense of stability which may well have contributed to our problems of rising crime, an increase in gangs, use of drugs, and teenage pregnancy. Further, the court-imposed methodology of achieving integration by forced busing was a misapplication in that the larger inner cities were the only targets and they have paid dearly because of this myopic approach.

Denver is a perfect example. It is a core central city for a large metropolitan area of suburban incorporated municipalities and was, therefore, the only governmental unit where forced busing was ordered by the court. As a result, Denver has lost population and thousands of students. Its central business district turned into a collection of vacant stores and enough square miles of paved parking lots, primarily serving office employees, to take care of a crowd for a major athletic event. Denver is not alone in this predicament as many other older core inner cities have witnessed the same, perhaps even worse, results.

Be that as it may, it becomes even more obvious that planners, both municipal and school, have had placed upon them a greater responsibility and an interesting challenge in trying to get the biggest bang out of declining bucks, maintaining viability in neighborhoods, and greater coordination of planning for future city and future school system facilities. A glaring example of how destructive and costly a lack of city/school coordination can be is that of San Antonio, Texas. Within the city, there exist 22 separate, independent school districts. This means 22 school boards, superintendents, and school budgets all struggling for adequate financial support.

As the more affluent San Antonio families find their children's schools unsatisfactory, or they respond to their bigotry, they move into another area of the city where they find a more "suitable" school in one of the myriad districts occupied primarily by upper middle class and wealthy residents. In turn, the districts within or near the center city core experience a loss of students, unused classrooms, decreased funding, and fewer teachers. With the help of busing, they ultimately may be abandoned. Should that school structure be at the edge of its district or near a city boundary where growth is occurring, it becomes most imprudent not to preserve the closing school, accept students from the crowded classrooms across the boundary, and keep the school a vital part of the total community.

San Antonio's problem of a multiplicity of school districts is not found in many other places; however, it does serve as a dramatic example of the need for far greater coordination and cooperation between local municipal governments and separately elected boards of education. An even greater argument for this exists where core cities are surrounded by independent local governments and school boards. As the suburbs bulged and schools became overcrowded, the lack of pupils in inner-city schools afforded the opportunity for economies, but the advantage has not been taken. It is foolish for one school located near a municipal boundary to have insufficient pupils to justify it remaining open while another school four blocks away in another jurisdiction is so crowded it is on double sessions. However, this has occurred in many of our metropolitan regions.

At this point, it is appropriate to comment on the sociological inequities of political and educational systems. We have, in most cases, fought to keep schools and the educational process totally independent from the local government of the jurisdiction it serves, under the fallacious belief that this keeps the educational system free from the unsavoriness of "politics." Nothing could be further from the truth. In the many communities with which I have been involved, the politics of a school board election and the implementation of day-today administration has matched, in many cases far exceeded, the politics of local government elections. So-called nonpartisan elections, whether they are the category practiced by government or school districts, exist in name only, not in fact.

While we profess to believe in democratic principles and justice, it takes no great insight to recognize that bigotry still exists, will probably continue to do so, and is a fundamental cause of educational and other imbalances between the inner cities and the suburbs. Efforts in the past to overcome this have not been notably successful, but court decisions regarding general integration, regional fair-share housing requirements, and the necessity for all jurisdictions to provide a full range of housing types for diverse economic levels do lay the groundwork for an increase in integrated neighborhoods. Courts also have begun to look unfavorably on the inequitable system of supporting education from local real estate taxes, which allows a much better level of education in well-to-do communities than in school districts not so well-off financially. For example, the Kentucky Supreme Court a few years ago ordered a complete reorganization of the entire elementary and high school system, including a way educational financial support could be made more equitable for all school districts, poor and rich alike. These factors and many other telling arguments for economic and ethnic integration portend change and give great credence to the thought that city/suburban/rural local government and school planning should go hand in hand in preparation for the future.

DON'T TREAD ON ME (OR MY KINGDOM)!

The organization of the school board, however, results in built-in potential impediments to coordinated planning. In our determination to keep school systems free of politics, we have done everything we can to create the impression that good school administration necessitates complete autonomy and independence, not just in administration but also in school planning. School boards, whether elected or appointed, have often been led to believe that no one else should even consider the question of the location of a school or of its effect on the community. With the expansion of comprehensive community planning, however, planning commissions are finding that the provision and location of schools are factors that cannot be skimmed over or left to a single agency. No master plan is complete unless the school question has been properly related to the general community, its needs, and its potential.

This was something that an Albuquerque planning commission chairman with whom I was involved had not learned. Etched in my memory is the day I attended a public hearing on a zoning amendment held by the commission chaired by this gentleman. The request was for a rezoning to permit a large apartment complex in what was a single-family area. The neighbors were up in arms and out in force. Their spokesperson emphasized the problem of impacting and overcrowding that would occur in the neighborhood school if this project received approval. The chairman began loudly banging his gavel, saying, "You are out of order. School matters have no place in this hearing. The planning commission has nothing to do with schools. That's the school board's problem." It goes without saying that the project was approved; and it can be added that, with outstanding, intelligent friends like this chairman, the community did not need any enemies.

Experience has shown me that rare indeed is the school board that does not appear to resent the action of community planning related to schools. (A noteworthy exception to this is the situation in Portland, Oregon. There, the school board has charged its director of planning with the coordination of school planning and community planning.) There appears to be a feeling that only those elected or appointed to the school board can, or even should be, concerned about the effect that a multi-million dollar yearly budget and a multi-million dollar capital expenditure program for new schools can have on the total community plan. I have seen school boards refuse to permit the planning commission access to enrollment figures and in other ways seek to obstruct the formulation of a master plan. This in spite of the fact that most state planning enabling acts specifically indicate that the expenditure of public funds for any such matter is an element of legitimate concern to planning. Some states even go so far as to mandate referral of all school district real estate and development proposals to the local planning commission for review and recommendation before action can be taken. However, there usually is a provision allowing the school board to overrule any such recommendation by a two-thirds vote of that body. Given a recalcitrant board, the only real advantage to this requirement is that it does provide a greater amount of public disclosure of what is proposed or planned. In extreme cases of uncooperativeness, this attitude has even resulted in litigation between school boards and planning commissions. Fortunately, such cases are rare, and resentment seems most often to arise from simple misunderstanding.

Nonetheless, I have never been able to understand why any feeling of resentment should exist. The responsibility of any board, commission, or agency of a public nature is to the people of a community: its goal is the betterment of the total community. If planning can be used as a means of better locating schools or guiding growth so that orderly tax rates can be maintained, why does it matter whether there is only one agency or several worrying about the problem? The planning commission, of course, has no right to attempt to tell the school board or the educators how to run the schools or what to teach, but it can and should provide wise counsel on the location and priority of construction of buildings, the coordination of school sites with community recreation programs, and the fiscal abilities of the municipality within the foreseeable future.

WHY ARE WE TOO SOON OLD AND TOO LATE SMART?

Comprehensive planning is important to the school problem today more than ever before. As communities spread out in the horizontal sprawl so characteristic of present growth, school systems are swamped with bigger and bigger headaches. Proper advance site selection can often save thousands of dollars not only in land acquisition but in helping to shorten some bus routes and even eliminate others. Zoning and subdivision control are the only two legal means of regulating private land development. If these are coordinated with existing school capacities and plans for future expansion, the resulting sensible and economical approach can save dollars and headaches. Zoning, when based upon a sound plan, can regulate densities of population which, in turn, create demands for schools. While the capacities of school systems cannot be the sole basis for zoning, they can be given weighted consideration in the development of zoning standards. Subdivision design and control can relate community growth to a planned core with easy-to-reach, safe, and convenient school locations at the center. Frequently, needed land for school buildings or school and recreation expansion can be obtained at little or no cost to the community by the adept handling of a major subdivision.

Through cooperative endeavor directed toward comprehensiveness, communities and their school boards can avoid being placed in the situation in which I found a suburban New Jersey township several years ago. This municipality was right in the path of the urban expansion steamroller. While this fact had been known for some time, neither the governing body nor the school board had done much about it. The elected officials felt that planning was unnecessary until conditions got completely out of hand and there was no choice but to institute a planning board and enact a zoning ordinance. By then the population had increased, in a six-year period, from around 3,000 to 16,000. There were only five small elementary schools; all other students were transported to a nearby municipality. Every grade was on double sessions and, in order to correct this within five years, 143 new classrooms had to be built at a cost of between $25,000 to $30,000 per classroom. No doubt they would cost three or four times that now. This is to say nothing of the additional costs for teachers, transportation, and administration. A little advance planning, a touch of school board cooperation, and a bit of firmness in principles on the part of the elected officials would have done much to offset this staggering prospect.

In view of this kind of tremendous capital outlay, yet another reason for planning and school coordination becomes clear. We have seen how sensible planning requires the weighing of each capital expenditure against the total community need. While school needs are vital, the well-rounded community is the one that knows when it can afford schools and when it will be doing more for all concerned by providing other public facilities. In many cases, proper capital expenditure planning does not mean the rejection of school facilities but instead means making certain that such expenditures are properly timed to fit the community's ability to pay. It is an unwise community that blindly ties up its entire bonding capacity in schools because of a fear that they will be needed while letting raw sewage run in the streets for lack of an adequate treatment plant. In the long run, such objectionable conditions will discourage the attractive, ratable-producing growth that would engender sufficient revenues to provide good schools—not to mention good streets, water services, sewers, and parks. Schools, while absolutely vital, are only one part of the total community.

LET'S TAKE AN ASPIRIN—MAYBE IT WILL GO AWAY

I am a firm believer in adequate educational facilities and am always available to vote for an increased salary scale for teachers, particularly since having been a college professor. However, I cannot help but regard the community that stabs out frantically at the school problem, ignoring all else, as similar to an individual treating a persistent headache. The pain is frequently only symptomatic of a much more dangerous ill. The pain can be dulled, but the basic disease goes on unchecked. I always get this feeling when I see school boards appoint citizen study committees who go out and count all the new kids and then extend a straight-line projection to show skyrocketing enrollments for the future—all with little or no consideration of the overall conditions in the community that may affect the rate of growth. While these committees are no doubt well-meaning and sincere, if they are going to work in a vacuum, ignoring comprehensive community problems, they might as well stay home and watch television.

The planning commission that works in a vacuum can, of course, be offered the same warning. No planning agency has the right to ignore the school board or the school problem, nor has it any right to assume a dictatorial attitude. Planning can provide information on the total community that is frequently unavailable to the school board; and, in reverse, no planning commission can possibly know as much about the school problems as the school administrators and the members of the school board. The sensible and effective role for each is complete cooperation and coordination. The planning commission should provide the basis for relating school needs and projects to the master plan. The investigations of land use, population, traffic, and the economic base of the community should enable it to provide valuable counsel in school planning. The school board should be able to see the value of an overall master plan and envision the easier task ahead for it if school plans are part of a general community scheme.

DON'T CONFUSE ME WITH FACTS— MY MIND'S ALL MADE UP

One word of caution to planning commissions: no planning agency has the right by its mere existence to pass upon or review school board plans. A commission unwilling to assume its responsibility to plan forfeits its coordinating position, in my opinion. The purpose of relating school planning to comprehensive community planning is to allow it to be placed in the proper perspective in terms of careful studies and investigations—not to be judged by mere uninformed opinion. The only planning commission in a position to evaluate realistically is one that has at its disposal all of the information needed for an intelligent decision.

Community planning and school planning are important partners in community building. Each has its place, with the responsibility for overall coordination belonging to the planning commission. Neither will be successful without the other. The real element of concern is to make certain that both recognize that they have a common goal, the achievement of which should be uppermost in their minds—that is, making our community a better and more efficient place in which to live. Whether lines of prerogative are slightly crossed in achieving that goal is certainly immaterial.

One final comment regarding the relationship of planning and the schools: school boards and their employees can be of great service to the future of our communities. Because good school planning is dependent upon good master planning, school representatives should insist upon first-rate community planning efforts. If a serious deficiency in planning exists, the public should be informed. One of our most crying needs is for citizens who know what planning is and who can tell the difference between good and bad planning. More discussion of the subject and courses related to city planning, regional planning, and community development should be instituted in our elementary and high schools. When I once suggested this to a well-meaning curriculum planner, she informed me that this was well taken care of already: after all, each civics and social studies class spent one week studying the government of the town. Regrettably, in today's view of modern education, you will have to look long and hard even to find any civics course taught at the elementary or high school level. Few social studies classes offer exposure to community development and the importance of the broad aspects of planning to the future of each of the youngsters.

Let's teach our children that the physical community can be planned; that good planning is comprehensive, long-range thinking; and that it will make their cities finer, more efficient, and more economical. They are smart enough to learn this quickly and then see that poor planning and the lack of planning are stamped just that. They can then build better communities with better schools and, ultimately, a stronger, better nation.

As an example of the influence just an exposure to community planning can have on elementary school children, I would like to describe one experience of mine, the memory of which even now gives me an uplift. During the time that I had my consulting firm on the east coast, the wife of one of my associates was a teacher of the second grade in the suburban community in which our office was located. As a planner's wife, she realized the opportunity she could provide her students in learning something about the role for them to play in their community. After some preliminary discussions and lessons about "My Community" and a brief exposure to the idea of planning for the future of its stores, homes, parks, and playfields, she gave each the assignment of making a planning map showing what they would like to have in the place where they lived. She was impressed by the map results and, especially, by the keen continuing interest the kids had in this kind of project and the way they kept raising questions regarding how a community is planned and who does it. At this point she came up with a great idea.

She called me and told me about her class's work and the kids' interest that she didn't want to squash. She asked if it would be all right, provided she could get the school's permission and the use of a bus, to schedule a two-hour visit to our office by the entire class. This sounded like a wonderful idea to me and I readily agreed. Naturally, we made sure that the office was neater than usual before the day arrived, had numerous illustrations of projects underway, and planned how the children would be divided into small groups, assigned a guide, and given a tour of the four floors of our office. The conclusion would be a gathering in my office where all their "planning maps" would be displayed and discussed, followed by a question-and-answer period. Oh yes, we also had lemonade and cookies.

Everything went very well and everyone on my staff was so impressed with the intelligence, the interest, the explanations of their maps, the sensible questions they asked, that we were all overwhelmed. Actually, several hours of work were lost over the next few days because of the comments on how great the whole idea, the teacher, and the students were. While that was nice, it is not the end of the story. For any number of days thereafter I received calls from mothers or fathers thanking us for having the kids, asking how they could learn more about this planning stuff that "Johnnie" or "Jane" talked about that night at home, or telling us how pleased they were that somebody in the school system had the good sense to know how important it is for kids to know something about their community, what it is all about and how it grows and develops. Two sets of parents actually went to the trouble of making an appointment to come visit our office and more or less see just what their children had experienced. This remains one of the highlights of my consulting experience. Don't tell me that exposure to a "planning attitude" for elementary school children is a waste of time and will not be beneficial in the long run.

CHAPTER

11

Planning and Other Community Development Functions

Few other problems of our times have been more discussed than urban ills and the plight of our cities. Through the years, as society has become more complex, it has become increasingly apparent that all is not well with cities, old or new. Better means for carrying out plans for more livable environments have been constantly sought; but too often the process of comprehensive planning, inasmuch as it is advisory in nature, has been unable to stem the tide of decay or assure improvement without policy support and pragmatic effectuation tools beyond land-use controls. While courts have generally given greater weight to community interests and acted favorably on progressive zoning techniques, this alone cannot change our urban areas.

The evidence of past mistakes that exists in the form of inadequate streets, rundown business districts, pollution, decaying and deteriorating homes, and violence and crime, is all too clear. Major portions of larger cities have become identified as obsolete, depressing, and costly slums. Nor is this confined to one municipal unit in major metropolitan areas. Blight has a way of ignoring political boundaries and spreading across the land like the relentless flow of flood waters. Even in the newer suburban communities and the less densely developed urban areas, blocks of shacks, hovels, or outmoded structures and facilities not only exist, but also, unfortunately, are increasing every day. Thus, we no longer have just an inner-city problem but find ourselves having to deal with a metropolitan and even regional malady.

In recognition of this, as well as the fundamental obsolescence of the inner city and the need for improved housing for the homeless and low-income individuals and families, the federal government attempted to provide financial assistance programs to encourage local government action in housing and general urban development between 1937 and 1982. As discussed in more detail in Chapter 2, some of these attempts failed miserably, either from bureaucratic insistence upon unworkable standardization or because of local ineptness and mismanagement. As we have seen, many of these were short-lived due to their lack of success or the constant changing of administrative policy. With the coming of the Reagan/Bush eras came drastic reduction of aid programs and federal involvement, together with a neglect of domestic policy, all of which left state and local governments with the same ever-increasing problems and inadequate financial capability to provide solutions.

In the 1930s, when the federal government first assumed some responsibility for financial aid to local governments in order to improve urban living conditions, the emphasis was on housing people caught in the "urban trap"; those forced to live in blight and decay and unable to improve their lot without assistance from society. As large urban center cities continued to lose downtown businesses, offices, and theaters, and deterioration and blight hit urban forms other than housing, federal emphasis on housing lessened. The 1954 Federal Housing Act broadened urban renewal to include almost any type of land-use development.

This approach to urban core rebuilding was enlarged in 1974 by the passage of the Housing and Community Development Act (CDA) with its Community Development Block Grants (CDBG) and the Urban Development Action Grant (UDAG) programs. These increased funding for commercial enterprises, including such projects as the Inner Harbor Development in Baltimore and hotels and center city shopping malls in other cities. With the advent of Nixon's "New Federalism" and the move to reduce specific categorical funding and institute forms of revenue sharing, urban renewal was merged into the CDBG program. Existing projects would continue, but new attempts at urban renewal were required to be part of the overall allocation of funds through special revenue sharing or block grant allocation of the CDBG. Thus the longest lasting governmental city rebuilding effort, one that is still with us in some form, has been that of blight clearance and urban renewal.

URBAN RENEWAL OR "URBAN REMOVAL"?

We have had urban redevelopment and urban renewal for 40-plus years. Because these programs will continue to be around and referred to—if for no other reason than the need to pay off the billions of dollars in long-term tax-exempt bonds issued over the years—it seems appropriate to review how they worked and their relationship to comprehensive planning. If there was appropriate state enabling legislation, the local governing body started urban renewal by passing an ordinance creating a local public agency (LPA). The ordinance outlined its purpose and granted authority to clear blighted areas, acquire and sell property, use eminent domain where required, and "renew" selected areas through private enterprise investment or public housing. The LPA could be the governing body if that agency so chose, as could a housing authority or a separate urban renewal authority. The majority of communities opted for the separate agency, which upon creation assumed a semi-autonomous (in some cases almost dictatorial) stature. In a number of instances, this led to conflict between comprehensive planning and pragmatic project planning and execution. While almost all state acts required coordination between planning and urban renewal, they placed the responsibility for surveying an area and certifying it "blighted" with the planning commission. This, of course, caused resentment in LPAs over the necessity to reveal plans in advance and relate proposed reuse of land to a comprehensive plan.

After several troublesome projects resulting from lack of integration and/or bad management that left many cleared areas unused except for parking, Congress tried to overcome some of the problems via the Federal Housing Act of 1954. It was here that the first federal funding for comprehensive community planning was provided and the requirement for a "workable program for community improvement" (WPCI) instituted.

This latter consisted primarily of a statement of "good intention" on the part of the community showing that it had prepared or was preparing a master plan, administrative coordination, reasonable financing arrangements, necessary codes and ordinances, an active citizen participation program, and a real desire to improve itself. The theory and purpose of this WPCI was most praiseworthy, but, as with many other well-intended federal stipulations, local officials and those who were supposed to administer it at the federal level paid it mere lip service in the majority of cases.

As the late Dennis O'Harrow, the highly respected former director of the American Society of Planning Officials (now APA), once said,

"What this country's planning and renewal needs is fewer 'workable programs' and more programs that work." Personally, I continue to be both perturbed and disturbed by the naive idea held by Congress and federal bureaucrats that desirable and high-sounding "guidelines" or requirements can be effectively enforced. We all know what effect a simple telephone call from a member of Congress—one whose home territory has suffered from strict imposition of these standards—can have when placed to the head of a department charged with administering the standards. All of us in the consumer public are naive if we continue to accept this snake oil.

MEANWHILE BACK AT BULLDOZER HEADQUARTERS

Meanwhile back at the office of the local urban renewal authority (LPA), they had probably been going merrily on their way, designating project areas and filing loan and grant applications, the first step in the process. Once an area had been certified as blighted and the Department of Housing and Urban Development (HUD) had processed a loan and grant application, an LPA was in the position to acquire property by either negotiation or condemnation. This done, the LPA could clear the property and sell it to private developers. Once sold, development was required to conform to a reuse plan approved by local agencies and HUD and specified in the project execution application, which was the final phase of submittal to HUD before actual work could begin. Throughout all of this, comprehensive planning and renewal were theoretically cooperative partners, reshaping the urban scene into a more desirable, livable environment. Regrettably, such was not always the case.

Similar to the difficulties that developed between long-range planning and short-range zoning in the past, problems in cooperation between public housing agencies, local public agencies, and planning seemed difficult to avoid. Public housing policies and any program of community revitalization should be an integral part of any comprehensive planning process. Achieving this coordination, however, seems to be as difficult as finding a cure for the common cold. Part of this stems from the amount of autonomy given to housing and renewal authorities and the retention of the idea that planning and the work of the planning commission was *only* advisory. It is easy for an agency authorized to take action to feel that time is wasted if it is taken to relate that action to planning research and study as well as citizen involvement in objective determination of goals.

While this view is myopic and sometimes fatal to a housing or renewal program, its existence can be credited both to the failure of federal and state legislation to recognize a proper role for coordinated planning and to human frailty at the local level. Never have I been able to understand the destructive tendency of men and women—theoretically working for the same ends—to fail to cooperate with each other, building up instead a resentment against the imagined interference of an advisory agency. As planning is more public-participation oriented, it would be easy to say that the base of this is partly an unwillingness to bother with an informed public rather than just ego-centered parochialism. Any intelligent member of any other public agency, whether it be housing authority, urban renewal authority, library board or school board, should realize that a close relationship between any one of their special projects and the comprehensive planning process is desirable. The more successful the individual project, the more credit will be due the sponsoring agency. Yet many communities are sitting with half-finished or abandoned urban renewal projects, newly created slums in housing projects, or other mislocated public facilities, resulting largely from petty squabbling among local agencies all supposedly existing to service the same public.

OTHER PLAYERS IN THE GAME

With the shift in federal policy away from financial assistance programs, a severe recession throughout the country, and the resultant downturn in state and local government budgets, the focus has now switched from community development to economic development. The danger this poses to long-range planning and meaningful land-use regulations already has been discussed. What needs to be pointed out now is that this has brought new players into the game. Planning commissions and planners need to recognize the effect that these increasingly visible organizations can have on planning policy and on the tools that have been developed to guide the shaping of future urban form. This is not to suggest that antagonism is inevitable between economic development policy and planning policy, but rather only to emphasize the need for establishing a cooperative relationship between the two interests that is supported by the governing body.

Economic Development Agencies

Economic development commissions and departments have existed in many states, regions, counties, and municipalities for a goodly number of years, but never have they enjoyed the position of importance gained over the last decade. In earlier years, most such agencies were adjunct organizations of chambers of commerce and were composed of volunteer members from the business community. They might be provided staff assistance by the parent group or have their own staff consisting of an executive director and a secretary. Now all that has changed. The chambers of commerce may still have their economic development outreach, but more and more governmental units have created an agency for this purpose within their organizational structure. Whether inside or outside of government, no longer are such agencies staffed by only two or three employees, but have grown to the point of employing one to two dozen or more people. In some few cases, the name of the planning department has been changed to the department of planning and economic development. From the standpoint of cooperative interrelation this approach is commendable as it does appear to recognize how closely tied together planning and economic development always should be.

During my research visits around the country, however, I found that the most common practice was to either create a separate governmental department or a semi-autonomous public/private partnership agency financed by both the local government and the private sector. In some cases, as in Baltimore, Memphis, and San Diego, the cities actually contract with the economic development commission to serve as their specialists in that area. Because these agencies seek out prospective developers, they are usually the first community contact for those interested in securing approval for a project there. This automatically places the development commission or department staff in the position of performing an initial-stage planning role, with some carrying this on to the final plan and a tentative agreement with the developer.

This is true in San Diego to the point that the planning commission and its staff are not sent the material for their review and comment until the staff of the Center City Development Commission has worked with the developer on an acceptable plan, design criteria, and negotiated terms, and the project has been approved by the development commission board. The development commission does not have to accept the planning commission's recommendation and I was informed that, should a conflict arise between these two agencies, the mayor and council would support the development commission. The converse of that was found in Charlotte, North Carolina. The Charlotte Uptown Development Corporation is an excellent example of a broad-based, representative, nonprofit economic development agency. Its board, 16 in number, comprises representatives from the city council, county commission, residential community, corporate sector, chamber of commerce, and nonprofit agencies. To assure coordination with the city, Charlotte's city manager and planning director also serve on the board. The corporation's staff and the city/county planning department work together very closely. When a prospective developer stops by the corporation's office wanting to discuss a possible project in the center city, that developer is told by the executive director to go see the planning department first, then come back to see us. The results of such cooperation and coordination are plainly evident in the Uptown Charlotte area.

Business Promotion Organizations

Another type of association interested and involved in development that relates to planning is that of independent private sector business and commercial groups. Usually these organizations are the result of a stimulus from one or more business owners in a particular area of the community who encourage others with similar interests to band together to preserve, revitalize, and promote improvement in their area of concern. Such associations can be very beneficial, not only in their target areas, but also by contributing to improvement in the quality of life of the entire municipality, provided they are willing to work in close harmony with the overall planning and zoning functions of the entire community. They offer another opportunity for effective planning leadership to prove itself by showing an eagerness to work with such groups to assure that their objectives, actions, and end results are in keeping with the comprehensive plan's proposals for land-use development in their sector of the city. At the same time, planners should assume the responsibility for gaining support for their endeavor from the local government, even to the point of financial assistance if that is feasible.

The objective of most of these business associations is not just a one-shot, clean-up and fix-up endeavor. It is to create the framework for a continuing cooperative effort to improve the business potential of their own neighborhood community for the long-term. This calls for the willingness of the affected business people and other landowners in a designated area to be willing to in effect "tax" themselves over a period of time to provide the needed financial base to pay for full-time administration and the needed community improvements. This can best be done by having a successful vote of all property owners in the designated area approving the creation of a "development district." Such a district is given the power to levy a yearly charge, above taxes paid to the government, to be used solely for the betterment of the district. If the district covers a large area, but has one or two streets with the greatest concentration of commercial and business enterprises, a graduated rate of charge, decreasing as the distance from the focal core increases, usually is applied.

Although not all existing business promotion associations are financed in this way—some rely on association dues from members—organized development districts have increased steadily over the last two decades. They can be found in cities all across the country. One of the early ones can be found in New Orleans, where the chamber of commerce organized a downtown development district with a surtax to pay for additional police protection, refuse and garbage collection, and other municipal services as well as the promotion of the downtown area. Denver has the 16th Street Mall Improvement District, with efforts now underway to enlarge it as a development district; the Uptown Partnership in the East Colfax Avenue area; the Lower Downtown District; and the Cherry Creek Business Improvement District in the Cherry Creek North area and around the new Cherry Creek Mall.

Mention should be made of three other business associations that are funded as privately supported, nonprofit groups. The first, the Greater Baltimore Committee, was a most important cog in the creation of Charles Center and the Inner Harbor, both urban renewal projects. It has continued to help keep business development alive in the inner city. The others are the San Diegans, a private, nonprofit business group, and the Central City Association, both in San Diego and both playing influential roles in how that city has developed. The history of these groups, however, shows that there was no effective cooperation between them and the city planning department. In Baltimore, the same can be said about cooperation between the mayor and council and the Greater Baltimore Committee.

Historic Preservation Organizations

Over the years, interest in historic preservation has grown throughout the country. Unfortunately, during boom years when new buildings are thrown up almost overnight, some of the most important aspects of the history of our society have been lost. Perfectly sound historic office buildings and residential structures are demolished in defiance of public support for historic preservation and the work of historic preservation organizations. It is vivid proof that, in American capitalistic society, the value of the dollar is far more important than the preservation of our heritage. The most disgraceful thing is seeing what has happened to a city like Denver in just the last two decades, and it is not the only one. In the early '70s, the city began to experience a fantastic office building boom. At times there were as many as 15 building cranes towering over construction sites in the downtown area. Those high-rise structures stand as memorial tombstones for the destruction of dozens of unique, sound historic structures.

Even as we moved into the '80s, the speculators still were convinced that the time of $750 to $1,000 per square foot prices of building lots in the downtown area would never end. But it did and several of those new owners, many of whom had already demolished an existing building or buildings, now owned a barren, vacant parcel of land. Others were stuck with structures—whether residential, business, or office—long ago vacated by tenants who left downtown or found other locations. Then came the parking lot, a cardinal signal of creeping paralysis. As the depression (referred to in politically correct circles as the "slight recession from which we are steadily recovering") continued and actually worsened, landowners in bankruptcy or on the brink thereof continued to defy such agencies as Historic Denver. Probably in a desperate move to gain lower taxes and under their banner of "private rights of the landowner," they added to their carnage in downtown Denver.

What has all of this to do with planning, you may ask. That should be followed immediately with the question, "Where were the planners and planning during all this?" Then there is a third, even more telling, question. What about the "planning attitude" of the elected officials, the policymakers, during this period? In the answer to those questions lies the chronicle of the downfall of downtown Denver into what exists today. First of all, before the building boom actually started, Denver officialdom was the epitome of an "all growth is good, regardless of the consequence" city. From 1970 until 1982, the only reason the planning department existed was because a section in the city charter required its existence. All zoning matters were, regrettably, placed in the hands of a separate zoning department that held all planning in low esteem. The zoning for the central business district was, and still is, replete with enough bonus and incentive credits to allow developers of any new structure to double the stated allowable square footage of the existing floor area ratio requirement (10:1)—and they did! Under those conditions, why even hesitate to tear down a building exuding character, still in good condition, that was 50, 75, or more than 100 years old? Even if some "kooks" thought that it had historic significance, you had the backing and approval of the mayor and the governing body.

This was the time that the major damage was done and word got around that Denver is ratable crazy and you can do anything you want to do to make the greatest amount of profit. Before casting too many stones, look around your town or city. Did it do a lot better or not? Apparently, people in Denver did just that and said "enough" in 1982. As a result, a young Hispanic man with some degree of vision for the city's future defeated the leader of the old regime for the mayor's office. Soon thereafter, a rebirth of the planning department occurred and a new, dynamic planning director came on board. The planning process did improve a great deal, but the people who voted in the new administration overlooked one big, important key to turning a decadent city around. Most of the members of the previous city council were reelected and the few newcomers shared their lack of understanding and support for planning—no "planning attitude."

The planning director and his much improved staff labored long and hard during the eight-year tenure of the new mayor. There were a number of innovative and beneficial planning projects and proposals put forward with some effectuation. One of the more important achievements was successful rezoning of the one remaining historic area, Lower Downtown or LoDo as it is known, in such a way as to provide much greater protection for its preservation and revitalization. With a major national developer considering a new inner-city shopping center and looking at the LoDo area, there is speculation that the center of the city's retail complex may well shift from the relatively new 16th Street Mall strip to the LoDo area. While this may sound very exciting to the landowners in LoDo, there is a real danger that, should this occur, a large section of the business area the mall was designed to serve may become a forgotten sector, considered impossible to revitalize and upon which the city and developers have turned their backs, but which won't go away.

During the '70s, planning and historic preservation were not even on speaking terms, since collaboration might interfere with the rush to become the Wall Street of the West. Without backing from the administration, no planner could dare to suggest the advantages of being in agreement with and closely cooperating with those supporting historic preservation. During the '80s, the communication and cooperation between planning and preservationists did increase, causing some mutual success stories.

With the help of some of these people and others concerned about the city's future, the greatest accomplishment of the planning department and its director during this period was a complete revision of the outdated master plan and adoption of a superior comprehensive plan by the planning commission and unanimous vote of the city council. Regrettably, the mayor of eight years decided not to run again in 1991 and the planning director, whose effort to achieve a desperately needed total revision of the antiquated zoning ordinance was thwarted, also resigned.

In that 1991 election, Denver voters again made history by electing the city's first African American mayor and, fortunately, elected to the city council some people displaying at least a little understanding of the importance of planning. In a surprise move, the new mayor decided not to hire anyone trained primarily as a planner, but instead named a skillful woman who had been a practicing architect and was then serving as president of Historic Denver. Even though some practicing planners in the state were upset and expressed strong objections, many other people saw it as an opportunity finally to achieve a very effective working relationship between planning and historic preservation, something for which every planning department and its leadership should strive. Whether this will be the case in Denver, only time will tell.

The important point of this discussion has been to try to emphasize the advantage when both planners and historic preservationists recognize their common interests, form a coalition of strength concerned about both the past and the future, and communicate and cooperate to help each other.

Many other individual local government functions concerned with community development and their relationship to planning could be discussed in the same detail here. These would include codes and code enforcement (many communities have now placed these in their planning or community development department), social welfare programs other than housing, cultural endeavors and maintenance, and fiscal management. Rather than do so, let me repeat that only through an understanding that well-functioning comprehensive planning must be the hallmark of any successful government can effective, economical municipal management be achieved. Coordination and cooperation among various individual or independent functions is recognized as essential if the entire operation is to succeed—or survive. Good, efficient government is just as dependent upon good business administration as is IBM, General Motors, or AT&T. An effective, dedicated mayor or council member recognizes this and will give top priority to seeing that all community development-related functions are based upon and coordinated with the comprehensive planning process.

IT'S THE IMPACT THAT MATTERS

Before leaving the subject of coordination, it is appropriate to discuss another means of making planning effective and more people-oriented. During the earlier days of the plethora of federal programs affecting community development, the Environmental Protection Agency institutionalized the idea of environmental impact studies, officially known as Environmental Impact Statements (EIS). As is the usual practice of the federal government, the "carrot and stick" approach applied. If there is federal money involved where an EIS is required, not only must it be completed, but it also must meet with the approval of the appropriate federal agencies—or no federal handout. The decrease in federally funded programs has not caused the EIS requirement to disappear from the scene. There are still a number of programs where federal dollars are contributed to state and local projects that require a filed and approved EIS. Among these are highways, mass transportation, airports, water reservoirs, sewerage facilities and even what is left of some of the urban renewal projects.

Some states and many communities began to realize the value of the EIS program in aiding them to better gauge the effect of development on the environment, provide greater public disclosure, mitigate excessive impact, and encourage increased community involvement. This is the theory behind the impact zoning technique now utilized by communities in various parts of the country. Simply stated, an EIS used at the local level is a means of saying, "O.K., so you are planning a project in our jurisdiction. Now tell us all about it, and while you are doing that, show us just what effect it will have on our public facilities and services, our environment, and our community character." If really carried to its fullest potential, the use of the EIS technique can be a very powerful tool for effective planning, community development-related coordination, and successful citizen involvement.

In essence, the environment impact idea has been the principle of the Planned Unit Development (PUD) provision in many zoning ordinances for a goodly number of years. A developer seeking PUD approval has to (or should have to) present much of the same type of information as is required in applying the EIS technique to local zoning. The resort community of Breckenridge, Colorado, has been using EIS zoning for a number of years and its efforts are discussed in more detail in Chapter 13. Generally, the community has developed a very complete list of effect factors. Each proposed development is scored on its degree of compliance with or impact on each factor. A minimum total score is required for approval; if the project fails to attain the minimum, the developer must come up with changes and improvements that mitigate and alleviate the problems, or no approval.

A PIONEERING ATTEMPT

As early as 34 years ago, some of us in the planning consulting field were urging our client communities to abandon rigid, traditional zoning classifications. We recommended that they reduce the number of zones or districts, but allow certain more intense uses in specified areas based upon their impact on the proposed location and the entire community. In 1958, I recommended just such an ordinance to Chesterfield Township, then a semi-rural farming community in New Jersey. There was to be only one zone—residential/agricultural—and all other uses were to be subject to a special application, public discussion and hearing, and an analysis of the impact on the immediate neighborhood, the surrounding area, and the entire township. This proposal would have required all developments, other than those in the single-family residential/agricultural zone, to submit the same kind of thorough plans and information that is required in the PUD and EIS zoning practiced today and upheld in numerous court cases.

Chesterfield officials, including their 82-year-old township attorney, liked the idea and adopted the ordinance. Unfortunately, one landowner who just didn't like the idea of any zoning took it all the way to the New Jersey Supreme Court. At that time, the court was horrified by the ordinance not having the usual number of use classification zones, as well as the idea of impact measurement, and threw it out. Before I retired from teaching, I used to tell my classes that one of the things of which I am most proud is the fact that I wrote the basis for a zoning ordinance based upon the now very acceptable principle of determination of allowance by measurement of impact on environment and the general area, and it was the only zoning ordinance ever to be declared illegal and unconstitutional by a unanimous vote. Oh well, it's nice to know now that it was not such a bad idea.

Granted, the present EIS has come a long way from original attempts at impact zoning; however, the idea is the same. Any major project today, particularly if federal funding is involved, can be subjected to such an impact analysis prior to the granting of approval, and such analysis is often required. Analysis provides the planning commission with a good opportunity to relate to a master plan and to take full advantage of the coordination of planning. For illustration, let us assume that the agency responsible for potable water production and delivery is planning a major new filtration facility. In the old days of "business as usual," they probably wouldn't have even bothered with more than a cursory check with the planning commission. Now federal funding is involved and an EIS is mandatory. While federal laws do not say that the planning commission is to be sole judge and jury on the EIS, the commission certainly can use the fact that submittal is required to exercise its proper role of coordinator and involver of people. There is no reason that the commission can't be the agency responsible for seeing that an objective, impartial EIS is prepared or at least have the organization preparing it responsible to the commission rather than the proposer agency, which obviously has a vested interest.

Such an EIS would provide a thorough analysis of the impact of the facility on water resources, water quality, land use, traffic, community or neighborhood character, open space, wildlife habitat, the capital improvements program and budget, and fiscal ramifications for the municipality as well as taxpayers and water users. In general, the question of what this will do to our ecology and environment would be answered. By seeking a review of the EIS by other affected agencies, the planning commission not only fulfills its role as a coordinating agency but also enhances this role in the eyes of others, thus furthering the possibility of truly successful comprehensive planning. By insisting on open meetings while the EIS is being discussed and by promoting public meetings and hearings on the project, the commission can involve more of the public and encourage citizen participation, again strengthening the planning process.

This same approach can be used by the planning commission in reviewing a request for rezoning to allow a more intensive type of use.

A developer proposing a change to allow an apartment complex in what is now a zone restricted to single-family units can be required to underwrite the cost of an impartial EIS. A real estate broker seeking a change to allow land to be used for a shopping center or an industrial park should expect to follow the same procedure. The advocate of a major planned unit development can and should be asked to present a thorough analysis showing similar information. Almost any major project can be analyzed better as a result of the requirement that the developer or agency must prepare and submit an EIS.

I hope it is unnecessary to emphasize the fact that the value of an EIS is dependent on its being prepared independently and not by the proposing agency or individual. Either the planning department staff or a consulting firm responsible only to the planning commission should be used. The cost for this can be appropriately assessed to the proposer, and many communities do so. This is done in some cases by obtaining an estimate of the costs and requiring that sufficient funds be deposited in escrow by the advocate to insure payment upon completion. The idea of the EIS and the appropriate method of its handling are all important points that should be remembered in considering the tools for effective planning and the involvement of concerned citizens.

More and more we hear the idea that planning is, or should be, total involvement of all of us in community development. It is a certainty that citizen involvement, the trademark of community development professionals, is essential to the planning process in a democratic society. In these days of an astronomical national debt that continues to rise geometrically, a continued depressed economy, and an almost total lack of a national domestic policy, one of the greatest unmet needs of most people is stability—stability that can come from a sense of "community" and a feeling of being involved in that community. An insistence upon increasing the coordination and cooperation of all community development functions within any jurisdiction is one of the essential means of developing a greater sense of community, of improving the feeling of stability. The growing recognition that planning with involved citizen support is the most vital tool for beneficial future community development is something all of us should seek to strengthen and increase for our own survival. How successful we are will have great bearing on our environment and the livableness of our communities in the future.

CHAPTER

12

The Citizen and Planning Action

Many people, whether they are members of planning commissions or just interested citizens, have a sincere desire to get more out of planning. They want to understand it and to find out how it can help their community. Where no planning commission exists, this interest is frequently in how to get others interested and how to get started. Even if there is a planning commission, the individual members or an interested citizen may justifiably feel that more should be done or that things should be done better. There may be a real need to secure better understanding and wider support. All of these things are important to a successful planning program. Far too many established commissions lack sufficient energy or curiosity to seek continually to improve themselves and their programs. It is up to the interested individual to make sure that this does not happen or that planning is not delayed because of a lagging program. The truth is that each and every citizen has a responsibility to see that the community is doing the best that can possibly be done to shape its future. Unfortunately, many of us choose to forget or to ignore this simple fact.

KNOWING WHAT'S HAPPENING MEANS THAT WE CARE

Even where a commission exists, we can ill-afford to sit back and relax, assuming that everything is being cared for properly. Though most of the members may be conscientious people—and many commissions are doing a good job in the interest of all of us—still we need to be concerned about their work and the quality of the planning they are doing. We should not permit ourselves to be lulled into a false sense of security by the mere existence of a planning agency, for its program may be less than adequate for the needs of the area. It is one thing to have the machinery technically established and something else to be sure that it is functioning well and doing the best job that can be done.

Far too many myopic or ill-motivated politicians, when pressured by citizen demands to initiate planning action they did not support, have made planning ineffective by simply "going through the motions." They kill effective action by appointing the politically faithful, or they try to starve programs to death through lack of funding. I have seen such people anticipate a strong demand for planning they considered undesirable and quickly move to block any hope of good results by creating and/or supporting sham programs that they call planning. I know of an entire county that is being sold short by just such a move right now. What its officials are passing off as planning has no more resemblance to true planning for the common good than a peanut has to the Rocky Mountains. The general public, because it does not know any better or does not care enough, accepts this and, in the long run, will pay for it.

Any of us who is the least bit interested should know whether there is a master plan and, if there is, what its proposals are and what is being done about them. Is the plan being used to review propositions put forward by various departments of the administration, by council, and by developers? Is it truly a blueprint for building a future community? Is it truly being followed? How current is it in terms of the changing conditions of national, state, and local trends and other forces that may affect it? These are but a few of the areas about which we all should make sure we are aware. To better gauge the quality of the planning being done or to assist in organizing new activity, a great deal of help is readily available to assist individuals or groups. Educational materials can be obtained from many sources, both on a national and local level.

ASSISTANCE—ASK AND YE SHALL RECEIVE

As interest in environmental protection and concern about the quality of the future urban form we are building has risen, states are creating or enlarging existing state planning agencies. A further impetus for this has been the recognition by some states of the large void created by the exodus of most federal government aid programs for planning and community development; a need that, fortunately, they have realized that they must fill. With more state agencies concerned with environmental problems, better coordination of planning, and the promotion of economic development, those citizens interested in planning, planning commissions, and planners will find more informative publications and general planning and development information available from the appropriate state agencies. These should provide information on the job of a planning commission, the comprehensive plan, zoning subdivision controls, and capital improvements programs. Such assistance can be very valuable in either organizing or improving the local planning process and in educating the general public more about why well-done planning is valuable to them and how they can get involved.

In addition to state agencies, regional planning organizations, councils of governments, and state leagues of municipalities frequently have publications and materials related to planning and community development. Do not overlook the possible available help to municipal planning endeavors from many counties that have their own planning commissions. California counties long have been leaders in planning activities, as have several Maryland counties near Washington, D.C., Westchester County in New York, and Bucks County in Pennsylvania. All have established reputations not only for innovative action but also for their excellent publications.

Another valuable source can be the state or regional chapter of the American Planning Association (APA). These exist in all parts of the country and are organizations composed of professional planners, local officials, allied professionals, and interested citizens. For a nominal yearly fee, membership in a chapter is open to all. Those simply interested in the future of their community and how to become better informed about planning are most welcome to join. In addition to regular meetings, newsletters, and other publications, many of these chapters conduct planning commission workshops and one or more general conferences on planning matters each year. Two of these chapters have recently published excellent treatises on the rudiments of the planning process. The first is *Planning Concepts for the Citizen Planner* from the Illinois Chapter of APA, and the second, from the Virginia Chapter, is titled *Planning in Virginia.* Also, the Colorado Chapter has published *Colorado Land Planning and Development Law, Fourth Edition,* a 638-page compilation of Colorado laws, including appropriate statute and court case references. Perhaps it won't appeal to the neophyte planning-interested citizen, but it is a veritable bible for professional planners and attorneys in Colorado.

I add one final word on the value of membership in the national APA to call attention to some of the services provided by that organization. First is the most valuable monthly magazine, *Planning,* that contains interesting and informative articles about the planning function and issues affecting it. Other services include information about planning for the media, a job placement service, the Planners Bookstore, and the Planners Press, which publishes numerous books on planning, zoning, and related subjects, including three previous ones by this author. In addition, individuals, planning commissions, and governing bodies who are members can subscribe to the *Journal of the American Planning Association,* a scholarly quarterly on planning research and theory; the Planning Advisory Service, a research and information service on specific planning problems; *Land Use Law & Zoning Digest,* an update of zoning information and land-use law cases; *Zoning News,* a four-page monthly newsletter that monitors trends in local land-use controls; and *Environment & Development,* a monthly newsletter devoted to environmental planning. All are available at reduced cost to members. A national planning conference is held yearly in a North American city, where APA members and nonmembers gather to exchange information with each other and hear informed speakers on many subjects pertaining to planning and land-use regulations. Readers, both individuals and local government agencies, are encouraged to take advantage of APA membership as a means to be better informed on all matters related to community development.[1]

COMMUNITY RELATIONS: TRUE DEMOCRACY

Even though we have talked a great deal about information, materials, and knowledge, there are those who have said that community planning or development action is about two percent technical knowledge and 98 percent public or community relations. Even though this is not entirely true of good planning, it is true that the success of any planning program is greatly dependent on the nature of community relations. Many of the elements of a master plan are recommendatory in nature. Even those proposals that can be enacted into legal tools, such as the land-use plan through the zoning ordinance, must be understood and supported or they will never get past the idea stage. In a democratic society, there is no stronger deterrent to the enactment of any proposition, regardless of its merit, than a well-organized, vociferous group of objectors whose ringleaders have thinly veiled motives for wanting to see a proposal killed. The only solution to this problem in planning is to have people dedicated to the practice of good community relations and to informing as many citizens as possible of the merits of planning proposals.

This should be taken even further, especially if what is true in your community is the same as I have seen in so many others, where few, if any, people in favor of planning or zoning proposals or against attempts to weaken them attend any public meeting or public hearing. It is always the "aginners" who turn out in large numbers. The local planning leadership should work to rally those who are interested in and dedicated to progressive planning and strong land-use controls to attend such public meetings and make their support or opposition known. A well-working planning commission will have developed a cadre of supporters with the assignment of mobilizing supportive and informed participation rather than permitting the "aginners" to convince the hearing body that everybody in town feels the same way they do.

No community should undertake planning until it knows what planning is. This may seem like a hard and unnecessary statement, but I have become firmly convinced that it is necessary not only to say it, but to repeat it often. Let me emphasize that in a different way by repeating that unless there is a *planning attitude* in the community on the part of the elected officials and those who elect them, planning will solve no problems, save no money, and be of little value in any other way. Frankly, I think it is time professional planners, planning commission members, interested citizen groups—all of us—begin shouting this from the rooftops and stop letting this inescapable truth be swept under the rug or hidden in the closet.

The community that simply goes through the motions of the master planning process with little knowledge of what is involved is doing itself, as well as planning, a disservice. I was informed in one locality that no one would ever get planning started again, as they had tried it once and it had failed. Mind you, now, the statement was that *it* had failed, not that the *community* had failed. An investigation disclosed two very interesting facts. First, the thing called planning had consisted of a political, inept commission that had hired a nearby and handy fringe operator who claimed to be a planner. No effort was made to find out about planning or to engage in a community relations program. The so-called master plan consisted of a poorly prepared zoning map and a few proposals for new streets and roads. In this case, it was actually a good thing the public had risen up against it.

The second discovery was even more interesting. It seems that the mayor at the time this plan was prepared had been completely opposed to planning as a hindrance to his political patronage system. A local civic group had steamed up a demand for a planning commission and crammed it down the governing body's throat. The mayor then carefully set about the premeditated murder of planning by making certain that all of the wrong things were done. The resultant revolt proved just how successful he had been. At last report, the mayor was still very happily enthroned in an ever-growing political kingdom and was very profitably selling crackerbox houses on inadequate lots as a sideline.

While this case is a study of purposeful disruption, there are many communities that innocently fall victim to the same fate. These are the ones in which planning suddenly catches on as a good thing to do but about which absolutely nothing is known. This scenario was frequently activated in the days of federal aid by the knowledge that the neighboring community had obtained some of that "free money" available for planning assistance. Naturally, the innocents did not want to be left out. No thought was given to the meaning of the process, what was involved in it, or the responsibility that went along with the opportunities available through planning. These were things to worry about later.

I have a vivid recollection of one municipality whose officials approached our consulting firm in just this frame of mind. In spite of all I could say, they were determined to get on the gravy train without even reading the timetable to know where it went. They applied for aid and were accepted by a state agency that, for one reason or another, had no time to ascertain the preparedness of the community before federal aid was granted. The results were predictable but sad. As soon as planning got beyond the basic data collection stage and into policy-making and decision making, the local officials began to say that they had no idea that this type of work was involved. Reports were unread, and, by the later part of the project, five meetings were called before a quorum of the planning commission could be assembled even to discuss the master plan proposals. Needless to say, little was accomplished by this planning program. Here again, if more people had been informed, and if even a few had understood the process, the story could have been very different.

IT'S NOT MUCH OF A PARTY IF NOBODY COMES

An informed public is essential to the organization of planning, as well as to the effectuation and activation of plans. Any type of planning activity attempted in a vacuum will in all probability fail. A well-informed citizen or commission member is aware of this and is ever alert to avoid the obstacles presented by an uninformed citizenry. In many instances, the advice of an experienced professional planner can be of great assistance in making certain that community relations are well-organized. At the same time, it should be remembered that the responsibility of community relations cannot simply be passed over to the professional. His or her job is to render technical advice, not to relieve local officials of their obligations.

In any community relations activity, whether it is selling the idea of a planning commission or putting across recommendations for zoning changes, there are a number of things that should be kept in mind. The first principle is that the more citizens who can be made to understand the broad concepts and purposes of what is being attempted, the more likely is the chance of success. Far too many communities leave informing the public to chance or ignore it entirely under the mistaken theory that there will be less trouble that way. This leaves the rumormongers a clear field and an opportunity to fill the minds of people with false information. Once an individual has become convinced of something, even though it is based upon less than the truth, it is much harder to win that person over. A planning commission should seek to get as many people as possible involved and to convince them of the merits of its proposals.

Once this principle is accepted, the next question is what work of the commission should be put before the public. The answer to this, of course, is all of it—including information on what good planning is and can do. Forums and discussion meetings on the need for planning and the role it plays in government are a good means of gaining early support. In addition, press releases and discussions of the job of planning are important. The community should know just what the commission can and cannot do, and should not expect too much or accept too little. Once a planning program is underway, time and effort invested in community relations for the purpose of explaining the master plan and its purpose will pay big dividends. Zoning principles and purposes and the function of the zoning board of appeals are matters that can use plenty of explaining and public examination.

The more that is presented publicly in this fashion, the better informed both the members of the commission and the people will become. Naturally, any education or community relations program must have behind it well-informed commission members, elected officials, and technicians. Each matter presented to the public must be supported by careful study, and the results must be presented in clear language. The manner in which the material is presented, whether in the press, radio, television or public meeting, is also important. A good design or an attractive report can go a long way toward selling its contents. A poor presentation can sometimes lose support for an otherwise desirable proposal.

Throughout any program of community relations, it is important to be aware of the various publicity aids available. Primary among these is the press. An active, aggressive newspaper can be a valuable ally in furthering planning. Press releases should be prepared from time to time to aid reporters and editors in getting to the heart of what you are trying to do. The press should be encouraged to attend planning commission meetings, and its assistance should be actively sought. Radio and television are media that have a great influence on our public. I frequently feel that we are missing a golden opportunity to explain good planning by not having more programs on radio and television. In many cases, in the smaller communities particularly, stations welcome the chance to air programs with a local flavor. An additional opportunity has now appeared with the ever-increasing numbers of local cable TV systems, many of which are required by their franchise grant to make one or more channels exclusively available for governmental and community affairs programs. A surprising number of people watch these local programs. Their availability provides an excellent opportunity for more exposure to planning information and general public education on what the process is all about.

Public meetings and forums are also an excellent means of explaining planning. These need not be special meetings; local civic organizations can be asked to schedule a discussion of planning. The program chairperson of the Lions, Rotary, or Kiwanis Club is usually only too happy to know where a suitable topic and speaker can be found for a meeting. Other groups that should be kept informed include granges, fire companies, unions, women's clubs, and church organizations. They all can aid if informed, and, at the same time, many helpful suggestions and comments can be forthcoming.

In order to be able to tell its story, the commission should have some material for broad distribution. If an individual is able to take something away from a meeting, the possibility of his or her thinking further about it is increased. The material distributed should be carefully prepared and carefully chosen. This is not meant to imply that the public is entitled to know only certain things, but that most citizens will not, in my experience, bother to read bulky documents. They are interested in facts, figures, and conclusions. They like to have their theory digested for them: the more concise the material, the more effective it is likely to be. Appropriate items for public distribution include:

1. Facts and figures, particularly those that show reasons for concern, needs, or conclusions. Population growth, land use in acres, school enrollment figures, and economic details are all of interest.

2. Findings and conclusions. These are the real heart of the matter and should be carefully stated.

3. Summaries. Almost all of the work in planning can be summarized in a concise manner without losing its full significance. The preparation of a summary of a technical investigation will, in many cases, help the commission members themselves understand the work.

4. Maps. A self-explanatory map of a phase of the planning program can be very helpful. Care must be exercised, however, to make certain that no map is ever distributed that may be misleading or subject to easy misinterpretation. A good example of this would be a map showing proposed streets or roads before the alignments have been definitely and precisely established.

5. Ordinances. These are naturally a must for distribution. Often a simple explanatory statement attached to them can aid in offsetting emotional objections. It should always be made clear to the public that all ordinances will be subject to a public hearing before being adopted.

It is equally important to recognize that certain things should not be distributed, either because they will not be effective or because they are certain to create trouble. The planning commission should not work in secret, and all of its study should be available to those interested in the full details, but those who are truly so interested are few. The material distributed should *not* include:

1. Technical tomes. Planning theory is all right in its place, but its place is not in the local barber shop or at neighborhood get-togethers. Formulas for appropriate amounts of commercial frontage per 100 population or theories about the amount of traffic generated by two-story warehouses in the Mid-Atlantic states have little effect on hardheaded landowners.

2. Long, involved reports. Staff or consultant reports may have to be long and detailed to examine all facets of a problem. This is for the commission's information and use, not to be broadly distributed. Don't expect the public to review any report of more than a few pages.

3. Material about which the commission members disagree. While a healthy divergence of opinion is a good thing, the commission should make certain that the basic principles presented in material that is distributed have been generally agreed to by the members.

4. A technician's report as a technician's report. This simply means that the quickest way to kill a planning study is for the planning board to sit back and receive a report, not to become a part of it, and to distribute it as the report of a professional. The technician is valuable only if used in an advisory role by the board. The material distributed must be accepted as the conclusions of the members of the duly appointed local body, arrived at with professional advice.

I MAY BE PERFECT, BUT I STILL NEED ADVICE

Many communities find their planning program can be greatly aided by the use of citizen advisory committees. Citizen committees usually are appointed by the mayor or the commission chairperson and should work directly with the commission. They can be helpful if properly organized and properly used. They can also be deadly harmful if created just for the sake of having a committee by that name, or if they are not properly handled. The question of whether a citizen advisory committee can be beneficial is a local problem to be evaluated by each community.

If the decision is made to have such a committee, as much care should be exercised in selecting its members as in the selection of the members of the planning board. Members should be interested citizens motivated by a genuine desire to help improve their community. While it would be impossible to organize any group of people who would all agree, it is not necessarily good to put the most vociferous objector to planning on the committee just for the sake of appeasement. Such a move has frequently backfired. All members of the committee should know that their responsibility is to work constructively with the commission, and all should be willing to do so. The members should also be selected to give the broadest possible representation from interest and geographic viewpoints.

An advisory committee can be used both as a sounding board for planning proposals and to perform certain tasks in conjunction with planning. The committee will be most effective when there is a definite program for its activity. Meetings should be well-organized, and the purpose of the committee clearly defined. Be as specific as possible and assign definite tasks to the committee. Never permit a citizens' group to feel that it has been formed just to get a group of people together or simply because the commission wanted someone to rubber-stamp its action. Great care should be exercised to make certain that the committee does not wander aimlessly off on its own, and particularly that it does not become a mere front for political ambitions.

A word or two should be said here about the upswing in neighborhood activism. In both large and small cities, numbers of property owners bound together by a sense of commonality—whether by the threat of a new freeway or the intrusion of a large apartment complex into a single-family area—have organized neighborhood councils or people's action groups to protect their interests. While some of these quickly dissipate with the resolution of the crisis, many others become permanent, effective forces within the community structure. The latter are increasing in numbers and planning must now take them into account. In point of fact, there are many who believe that, if planning is to be anything other than elitist control of resources, not only must it take into account neighborhood opinion and neighborhood organizations, but it must start there as well. Recognizing this, a number of cities maintain a list of registered neighborhood organizations and provide their president or registered representative with a copy of all planning commission and zoning board agendas and reports on action taken. This has proved to be an excellent way to open the door and encourage neighborhood interest and cooperation.

It is obvious that, if we are to maintain a true sense of democratic action, we need to reexamine our governmental structure and devise ways for more meaningful citizen involvement. One way of doing this would be through a carefully structured program for involvement of neighborhood councils in all decision making. Although this may appear unwieldy, it may be necessary to avoid complete takeover of local government by special interest groups.

No planning program is going to be successful and no planning commission can say it is functioning properly unless there has been recognition of this grass-roots movement. It must be shown also that careful attention is being paid to neighborhood planning and the desires and wishes of neighborhood residents. As noted in previous chapters, the format of the master plan is changing to that of a policies plan emphasizing goals and objectives concerning the kind of community people want to see. It is only logical that the rudimentary sources for determining those goals and objectives lies in the neighborhoods and the structured organizations of those who feel a sense of common concern. The proper use of neighborhood planning techniques can well replace the need for a formalized citizens' advisory committee, which frequently turns into a mirror image of the establishment or the power structure. At the very least, any formal organization of an advisory committee should be firmly founded on the principle of adequate representation and involvement from each identifiable neighborhood.

NOW LISTEN HERE, YOU BUREAUCRAT

This brings us to methods of formalizing citizen input through public meetings and required public hearings. Please note the purposeful differentiation. Public hearings are always required by statute, and many officials make the mistake of limiting citizen involvement to these alone. Public meetings are for discussion and the give-and-take of information. They can be held anywhere at any time but should never be held without adequate notice and publicity. Neighborhoods are an excellent locale for constructive and beneficial citizen meetings. Public hearings, on the other hand, are rather rigidly structured as to advertising, posting of notices, and the manner of reporting. More and more courts, when faced with ruling on the reasonableness of municipal action concerning planning and land-use controls, are requiring that a complete transcript of any official public hearings be provided for their review. I feel that the conduct of both public meetings and public hearings is one of the most vital and important aspects of local government and of planning, and one to which too little attention has been paid. The manner in which these are conducted often determines the success or failure of a proposal or a plan. A tremendous responsibility thus rests upon the commission or agency, in particular the chairperson, for the conduct of each meeting or hearing.

I have been present at dozens of these and have been amazed by the differences between them in various communities. One of the things that has bothered me most in the last few years is the deteriorating decorum of those who attend. Manners, courtesies, and just proper conduct seemingly are forgotten or left at the door when people attend public hearings. I am sure that in many cases, if a movie were made, some of the individuals involved would find it hard to believe later that they were viewing themselves. I saw one hearing at which six rather large police officers lined the walls to maintain order—and it turned out to be fortunate that they were there. In many other hearings, invectives, profanity, and inhuman conduct have become commonplace.

Some of this results from the increasing frustration over non-responsive government, and some comes from observing the effectiveness of protest movements and politics of conflict rather than compromise. While this is not the place to discourse on the general morals and code of conduct of the American people, it is important to note that, in many cases, such objectionable occurrences can be avoided by the manner in which the hearing or meeting is conducted. An efficient but firm chairperson who knows his or her business makes certain that the meeting never gets out of hand.

In zoning, both the zoning commission (which in many cases is the planning commission) and the governing body must conduct a public hearing before taking action. The zoning board of adjustment has to conduct a hearing before granting a variance. Newer zoning ordinances also require a hearing in conjunction with special exceptions, special use permits, or planned unit developments within the ordinance. The use of the planning commission as a review agency and the conductor of the hearing is becoming more common where special provisions such as these exist. In addition, the public hearing is required in connection with the adoption or change of the master plan and the approval of a major subdivision. As mentioned in an earlier chapter, in the case of urban renewal, several public hearings are necessary, including one by the planning commission concerning the declaration of blight. Capital improvements programs and budgets necessitate public hearings by both the planning commission and governing body before becoming official. This type of public involvement also may be required for many other functions of local government.

In all cases, it should be remembered that the hearing has one purpose and one only: to permit the public to express its views officially in an orderly and constructive fashion. These views should be formulated in advance of the hearing by ample publicity and public meetings. Any material to be acted upon, together with supporting documents, should be readily available, published in the local paper, and generally explained to inform the public thoroughly before the hearing. Maps and material needed for reference should be on display and easily accessible.

The meeting itself should be well-organized. The chairperson, the key individual in the procedure, should present an opening statement setting forth the purpose of the meeting and the rules under which it will be conducted. It should be made absolutely clear that the hearing is neither a debate nor a political forum. Some additional suggestions may be helpful in keeping your public hearing on track:

1. Before scheduling any public hearing, the responsible agency should have carefully studied the issues and should have its own house in order. No members of any commission, board, or agency should be permitted to sit in a public hearing until they can personally attest to the fact that they have studied the new zoning ordinance, reviewed the master plan, or are otherwise thoroughly aware of the case up for discussion.

2. The chairperson of the meeting should very carefully make a statement at the very beginning concerning the conduct of the meeting. He or she should explain just how the hearing will proceed and should make it clear that decorum and order will prevail. It should also be made clear that the agency conducting the meeting will not engage in lengthy discussions or debates with anyone. The purpose of holding the hearing is to listen to the views of the citizens of the community and then to evaluate the entire matter at a later date.

3. A secretary or stenographer should be present to take down careful notes, and, if possible, verbatim reporting should be provided. This not only ensures an accurate record but helps to keep the speech-making to a minimum and the language above approach.

4. The subject under consideration should have been made public sometime prior to the meeting, and there should be no necessity for any formal presentation during this meeting. Instruct each person to give his or her full name and address and state his or her views as briefly and quickly as possible. Usually it is better to give all of those speaking *for* a particular proposal an opportunity to speak first, followed by all of those opposed.

5. Upon the conclusion of each individual's statement, the chairperson should thank the speaker politely and assure the speaker that expressed views will be considered, and then move immediately on to the next person. No cross-examination or prolonged argumentative questioning of the commission members should be permitted.

6. Upon the conclusion of the statements by the public, the chairperson should again thank all for their interest and attendance and assure them that their views will be carefully studied and that the entire matter will be given full consideration by the body concerned. It is very important for the chairman to tell those in attendance that they and the general public will be apprised of the hearing body's decision as soon as possible. The meeting should then be adjourned. Careful study should be given to the record after it has been typed, for frequently the written word is subject to a different interpretation than speech.

7. The agency conducting the hearing should keep in mind that there are many things necessary for consideration other than the expression of personal views. A public hearing should supplement the data-gathering, analysis, and discussions that have preceded the hearing, but at no time should the public hearing simply supplant this qualitative analysis. Above all else, the agency should remember that it is appointed or elected to represent not only the 50 or 60 people present at the hearing but also the other thousands of citizens of the community who did not attend or who did not express themselves publicly.

This last comment is an extremely important one. Time and again I have seen sound, desirable proposals killed by a wild and vocal group of 10 or 20 people. It is up to the hearing body to make certain that the opposing opinions expressed are indicative of a general feeling within the community and not just the expression of a narrow and selfish interest. The public hearing, if it is properly conducted, can be a valuable means of ascertaining public opinion.

EVERYBODY OUGHT TO GET INTO THE ACT

We have all heard that "you can't fight city hall." This has been (and is) true in many cases, but only because of the lack of an informed public, ineffective approaches, or disorganization. There is nothing more effective for quickly changing the mind of a public official, especially an elected one, than a sizable number of well-organized people who, through objective discussion and data collection, have gotten their act together. Having sat in the position of a city manager, serving an elected commission both before the public and in private discussions, I have seen the results of such action. Unified, well-founded public opinion is still the most effective weapon in participatory democracy. The problem with most of us is that we don't want to bother with other people's opinions or with obtaining a consensus; we just want to see our own views reflected in every action taken. When we don't, we resort to the old American pastime of griping about "them" and what idiots and crooks "they" are. This all may be good for the blood pressure and personal satisfaction, but it leaves a lot to be desired in shaping community policy or winning the day for "our side."

This is not the way to be effective as a concerned person; indiscriminate griping has never solved many problems or gotten much accomplished. Citizen action need not be negative or in opposition to something proposed. Many times, positive things have taken place because of the foresight and determination of persons with no other concern than a genuine interest and caring. Parks have been built, open space preserved, libraries established, and planning agencies created because someone who cared would not take no for an answer.

On the western side of the city of Albuquerque, the land rises from the Rio Grande River to what is known as the West Mesa. In full view, as a scenic backdrop for the city along the western horizon, majestically protruding from the mesa, are five extinct volcanoes. Around the volcanoes in the early '70s was nothing but sand, rocks, tumbleweeds, and rattlesnakes; but, as usual, developers began to think about the opportunities offered by the site. The volcanoes and the area were not only scenic; there was considerable historic significance attached to them. Indian artifacts and signs of earlier cultures, rare organic materials, and some unusual vegetation abound in the area. No one had thought much about all of this until development became a possibility. Then most seemed to accept the idea that rape by the developers was inevitable (after all, it had happened almost everywhere else in the area). Not so one marvelous, gentle, but determined woman, Ruth Eisenberg.

Coming to Albuquerque from Chicago in 1968, Ruth, being a concerned individual, had immediately involved herself in learning about the city and trying to do what she could to make it better. Just to learn, she sat in on a class called "Creative City Watching" in the University of New Mexico's School of Architecture. Once she asked the professor what she could do to help put a stop to the rapidly vanishing attributes of the city and was thrown this challenge: "Do something about the volcanoes." In all probability, that professor did not think what the ultimate result would be or even that he would hear again from Ruth about the issue.

I must shorten the story unfairly, for there was a lot of frustration, dogged determination, research, arguments, and head-knocking thrown in between. But I recall with a great deal of pleasure the day when Ruth, with the equal persistence and help of the first woman ever elected to the city commission, turned over the deed to the land (880 acres) upon which stood three of the five volcanoes. The story doesn't end there. Ruth, who kept on her almost single-handed fight, later succeeded in snatching the other two out of the path of exploitative development and placed all of the remaining 440 acres, including the other two volcanoes, in public ownership. There is still the opportunity for further enlargement into a major park and open space to be enjoyed by all, and there now exists a guaranteed protection of an irreplaceable scenic vista for the entire city.

Almost ironically, some of the "establishment" that fought her the hardest joined hundreds of others in attending "An Evening at the Volcanoes in Honor of Ruth Eisenberg," at which the mayor dedicated the new amphitheater to be named for her at the base of one of the volcanoes. Don't ever let anyone tell you that sincere interest and concern together with a determination to do something will not be effective. Ruth Eisenberg is living proof to the contrary.

The amazing thing is that most elected officials, as well as appointed commission members, welcome clear expression of formulated group opinion and agreement and will respond to it almost always. The obstacle is getting any group of two or more to reach that agreement or formulate a collective opinion, assuming it does not involve merely an issue that can be blown up into an emotional crisis. From my brief experience in politics, I have learned that the "pros" in the game quickly master the primary rules of all successful politicians: always postpone action on any controversial issue; don't take a position publicly until you see how the wind is blowing; and always look for, even encourage, dissension and disagreement among members of any delegation. An understanding of these gives a clue or two as to how to make citizen action more effective. In brief, a credo for doing so might run like this:

1. Make sure you have a real issue, not just a personal ax to grind.

2. Once you believe you have an issue, check it out to see how inclusive of others it is and make certain that it is a valid concern, not just something founded on rumors.

3. If there is no neighborhood council already in existence, get others together who should be interested and find out if they are informed and have some facts, not conjecture, to further inform them.

4. Assuming the issue is genuine and has held up through discussion and interest arousal, program carefully how you are going to get your act together.

5. Pick out any expertise in your group and get members to take responsibility for data collection, analysis, and presentation preparation. If possible, supplement this with aid from other citizen action groups, advocacy agencies, or community design centers that are usually connected with colleges and universities (all of these exist in many cities.)

6. Organize and plan your strategy, your timing, and your approach, making certain that you stay away from emotion and stick with facts. Avoid threats and implied intimidation.

7. As soon as you have enough data to begin to formulate a position, assign effective individuals to personally contact key local officials and members of the "power structure," if they are known. No one in a position of influence or decision making likes to be surprised.

8. Get the troops out for the presentation, but be sure you have them well informed and under strict orders to stick with the "game plan" of your presentation. An effective maneuver is to have the opening speaker ask all those interested in this issue and being represented to stand up. Keep them standing for a few minutes so that the "pros" can get a good idea of the head count.

9. Proceed with your informative and persuasive presentation, keeping it as concise as possible. Have graphic materials and visual aids to help make points. Prepare something to leave with the hearing body, but keep it short and in summary form. Interestingly, one of the least effective things to leave is a petition. Too many of these have been shown to have been signed by those who will sign anything without knowing what it is about. There is no effective substitute for personal appearances.

10. Get a decision or get a definite timetable for action. Follow up and make certain that commitments are carried through. If and when favorable results occur, don't forget to thank those who caused them to happen.

These are but some of the things to remember in making sure that the planning and day-to-day issues in your community are reflective of the true representative will of the people. The important thing is to overcome that old bromide of not being able to fight city hall and to recognize that people working together can and do make a difference. Just as in all matters of local government, this is essential for good planning. Even though planning done *for* us may help in correcting some mistakes from the past and in solving some problems, it is a more satisfactory solution and comfortable feeling to know that what is being done under the aegis of planning is being done *by* and *with* us.

Planning for the future of our communities is vital to you and to me, and we are vital to good planning. I have tried to emphasize that point and to provide some touchstones for a better understanding of the process. Each of us, an individual citizen, is the key to the future of our communities, whether they be large or small, urban or rural. If we remain interested and inquisitive, overcome discouragement and frustration, and are well informed and involved, we will have better places to live, work, and play—the kind of environment we all want and must have. If instead we leave our future to chance or the exploiters, we have no choice but to take the consequences. We will have little justification for complaining about pollution, inconveniences, disorganization, high taxes, or loss of community quality.

We must remember that our community, our society, will be, for better or for worse, what we make of it as individuals—by putting it all together collectively in our system of government. We have the responsibility to make it the best that we can, but to do so also makes good sense for each of us now and for those to come. No sector of organized society can long afford to be without the best possible planning for the best possible community of tomorrow. It just might be the most important issue facing us, not just for our comfort and convenience but for our very survival.

NOTES

1. For further information contact the American Planning Association, 1313 E. 60th St., Chicago, IL 60637.

CHAPTER

13

Some Things to Think About

In a concluding chapter, it seems wise to look back at some of the things that have been said regarding the planning process of the past and reflect on how the process may be called upon to help solve current and future problems. No one is clairvoyant enough to look ahead with any degree of accuracy. If we could, we might have avoided having to cope with automobiles on streets designed for horse and carriage. Looking ahead, who can say what strides will be made by technology in the abatement of pollution within five years? On the other side of the coin, however, there are those who say we have played out the string on the ability of technical improvements to save us from ourselves and our seemingly destructive tendencies. Whatever the case may be, the best we can do at any given point is to anticipate and to plan based upon as much information as we can gather, an intuitive analysis of the obvious trends, and careful observation of the signs that can be read from our social system. From then on, it is a matter of making the best value judgments possible.

And the making of sound value judgments as a collective society, as a government, particularly as it relates to the future, is where the going gets tough in our divisive, capitalistic society. We seem to be imbued with a philosophy that, as far as government action is concerned, it can and should be only reactive, not proactive. We do not involve ourselves in prevention or protection, only correction. We don't lessen the number of carbon monoxide-producing engines on the streets until the accumulated pollution makes it so unhealthy that it is necessary to declare a crisis, and then the action taken is only a temporary stopgap measure. We don't take seriously the problems of survival, lack of adequate housing, the deep-rooted feeling of social and economic injustice in the inner cities until we have several incidents such as in Newark and Los Angeles's Watts in the '70s, and again in Los Angeles in 1992, as well as Miami and other cities. Even when these disasters occur, our attempts at solutions are like fighting a house fire with a garden hose and, together with hollow promises seldom fulfilled, usually result in further distrust and anger. We sit placidly by while our governments—federal, state, and local—largely controlled by special interest pressure groups, fail to take effective future-oriented action dealing with the myriad of domestic issues and problems threatening the very existence of our present society. It has become a certainty that there is no effective pressure group protecting the interests, well-being, and quality of life of the general public.

Thus, it seems that we are psychologically conditioned to crisis reaction instead of anticipatory positive change. This does not have to be the case: I still have hope that enough of us will adopt a proactive stance to see that change will occur. Equally, I believe the process by which this can be accomplished is collective societal planning. This is, at the same time, the greatest challenge and opportunity facing us today.

In the preceding chapters, we have seen how today's planning evolved, how governmental activity in this area has grown, and how some of the earlier tools have been found to be in need of change, although their fundamental principles remain sound. Some of those major changes—such as the requirement for available public facilities being concurrent with new development, and the growth of impact fees and/or exactions—already have been noted. Probably the most notable change is that we no longer have the plethora of federal government financial aid programs, some of which encouraged and provided incentives for local planning that, at least, had to meet some level of standards set by federal agencies. If the state and local governments had accepted this responsibility after the abdication of the federal government, that change could have been all to the good. Regrettably, with the exception of some six or seven states, assumption of the responsibility for assuring local planning, not to mention the quality of that which is done, has not as yet been evident. However, as has been indicated, a trend for doing so may have been started. Whether this trend materializes is a matter that could have far-reaching effects for planners, planning commissions, and local governments. It should be given careful attention.

In community or individual decision making, we can make only the best possible value judgment in determining what action we take. Prior to that, however, we need to do some preparatory thinking about what we may have to face and the problems we may find. Anyone concerned about long-range planning or even immediate problem solving would be badly mistaken not to examine past patterns, statistics, and predications of trends in order to anticipate how best to avoid or, if necessary, deal with troublesome situations. This approach also provides the opportunity to take advantage of innovative techniques that can assist future planning as they are developed. For what it may be worth, what follows is the Smith synopsis of readings, from a rather cloudy crystal ball, of some of the major items that are becoming and/or will become issues requiring planning involvement. This list is surely not all-inclusive nor is it the sole responsibility of planners or planning to single-handedly deal with these challenges and magically produce solutions. They are, however, key issues that will have to be faced by decision makers and planning can be a valuable tool in dealing with them effectively and intelligently.

MANAGING GROWTH

Theoretically, the primary purpose of planning through the years has been that of managing growth. We have looked at the major tools available for doing this and referred to some of the successes and failures in using a comprehensive plan and other tools as a reference base in shaping future urban form and reshaping that which already exists. At the time the second edition of this book was published, the term *growth management* had begun to appear as representing a relatively new technique used by a few cities to better relate population increase to the capability of the community to provide essential facilities and services within its budget limitations.

Now, the idea of local growth management has become widely practiced in a number of states and local communities. The original motivation for adopting growth management, quite frankly, was to control and slow down population growth that threatened to outstrip a community's financial capability. Along with population caps or limiting the percentage of building permits each year, provisions for cluster zoning and planned unit development requirements were the primary features of earlier growth management ordinances. As a result of successful legal challenges to the enactment of specific population caps, they are now very rare. However, cluster zoning and planned unit development remain standard and accepted practices in zoning and other types of land-use control legislation founded on the growth management idea. Over the past few years, communities have developed and experimented with new techniques for implementing this basic idea. It has been an interesting and innovative process.

NEW TECHNIQUES FOR MANAGING GROWTH

A continuation of growth pressures in both large cities and small communities, the reduction of federal financial aid, the imposition of mandated service requirements on local governments by federal and state agencies, and the financial crunch on local government budgets logically led to a search for new means of meeting the rising costs of public facilities and services. Such pressures also continued to encourage economic development in a serious recession. The answer most thought reasonable, based on the growing acceptance of the philosophy that private development should pay its own way, was to impose impact fees and/or exactions on private developments. The impact fees assessed would pay for the costs of adding or improving public services resulting from the impact of the development.

This simply is an expansion of a practice long followed in regulating subdivision developments: requiring the developer to pay for, or post an adequate guarantee to pay for, infrastructure, drainage facilities, streets, curbs and gutters, sidewalks, fire hydrants, street lighting, landscaping, street trees, and other services and amenities within the development. Exactions can also be required and used in this way, but more often represent expectations by the local government of what is necessary to make an applicant's project part of a successful growing community when finished. There usually is more negotiation between the government forces and the developer in the exaction process, which certainly can lead to a greater possibility of a compromise. In some cases exactions have been used to assist in dealing with a major problem in a jurisdiction not directly related to the development, such as housing for those with very low incomes or the homeless. This practice raises some possible legal questions regarding coercion of or contracting with the developer and should be approached with extreme caution.

The several states that have recognized the value of good planning, and have begun to mandate action by local governments, have recognized the necessity and logic of private development paying its own way. They have authorized, in some cases mandated, the levying of impact fees by local governments. A great deal already has been written here about the strong, but controversial, concurrency provision in Florida's 1985 (amended in 1992) Growth Management Act, which states that all public facilities and services necessitated by a development must be in place before final approval may be granted. Related to concurrency is the spreading popularity of the adequate public facilities (APF) requirement referred to by Douglas R. Porter, president of the Growth Management Institute, in an article entitled, "The APF Epidemic." Porter indicates that a survey made in 1990 by the League of California Cities showed that 30 percent of all California communities utilized this technique as a means of managing growth. He goes on to point out some serious concerns about using APF without a firm commitment from the community to assume its responsibility for some financial role in implementing planned public facilities.[1] With the swelling controversy surrounding this issue, it behooves planners and local officials considering or using this approach to make certain there is some form of a public/private partnership evident in the ordinance and the comprehensive plan. In our litigious society, major legal challenges are sure to come.

OTHER EXAMPLES OF GROWTH MANAGEMENT TECHNIQUES

Management of growth by government, which by necessity means regulating the private use of land, always generates strong opposition, but it is becoming more and more essential in our complex, self-destructive society. Doing it successfully is always a byproduct of a broad, informed, committed public support base, without which success will be extremely difficult, if not impossible. Nevertheless, there are states and local governments where, out of a sense of place and community as in Oregon, or out of crisis as in Florida even before Hurricane Andrew, growth management techniques have worked and more than proved their worth. In the most successful places, there has been an acceptance of government responsibility for developing and implementing well-designed infrastructure plans and meaningful capital improvements programs.

According to Doug Porter, two small California cities, Tracy and Carlsbad, have approached growth management in the right way and have been successful. Both undertook studies to determine the amount of growth and the quality and character for which they were looking. Tracy took the positive approach of accepting local governmen' responsibility for adequate public facilities. Through a public/private partnership, a $240 million capital improvements program was adopted to provide for the orderly expansion of those facilities to accommodate the anticipated new development in the build-out of the city. This was followed in 1987 by the city's adoption of two detailed specific plans, one for residential and one for commercial projects. The specific character of the plans provides the methodology for managing development together with mandating a limit of 1,200 residential units per year.

Carlsbad, facing a boom development onslaught, adopted a City-wide Facilities and Improvements Plan that was ratified by the voters in 1986. A measure such as this can be changed only by popular vote. The legislation devised three optional methods for financing: two involve developer financing, while the third is accomplished by assessment district, special benefit district, or city-backed bond issues. The city retains responsibility for financing major improvements such as sewage treatment plants and administrative facilities. Carlsbad's program has been in effect for four years and has constrained development somewhat, but it has been met with favor by local builders and developers.[2]

TWO DIFFERENT APPROACHES THAT WORK

As previously mentioned, the town of Breckenridge, Colorado, gained national publicity for its growth management program in effect since 1978. Essentially, it is based on the Environmental Impact Statement (EIS) procedure mentioned previously. An applicant for development approval must prepare a very complete application showing the possible impact of the project on six major areas of concern: community development, natural environment, site suitability, economics, sociocultural values, and services and facilities. Points are assigned for the extent to which the proposed project meets acceptable impact conditions. Applicants falling below the total required for the permits must meet with the planning staff and work out a way to mitigate excessive impact factors. In all instances, the planning commission may rehear a staff decision and the town board may rehear a planning commission decision. Two complete booklets, *Breckenridge Development Code* and *Town of Breckenridge Application,* provide the developer and the community with the details of the process.[3]

One of the more innovative methods of growth management has been instituted in Fort Collins, Colorado. Called the Land Development Guidance System (LDGS) it was developed during 1980-81 by then-Planning Director Curt Smith and staff members Joe Frank and Ken Waido, together with consultant Bob Komizes. After much discussion it was approved by the planning and zoning board and adopted by the city council as a city ordinance in 1981. Unlike so many of the others, this is not an attempt to limit or stop development, but rather is intended to guide development, provide flexibility in use and design, and yet maintain the adopted goals and objectives regarding the physical, social, economic, and environmental development of the city. After voters in 1979 turned down a ballot referendum that would have artificially limited housing starts, the city government began to look for methods of managing growth in a positive way. The guiding principle in this search was the decision made by city officials that the real issue wasn't how much new growth to allow, but how to assure its quality.

Using the adopted Land Use Policies Plan as a guide and working with citizen groups, the planning director and his staff developed a system to regulate land development beyond that provided by the traditional zoning approach and, in addition, could achieve the following objectives:

• The orderly, positive development of Fort Collins;

• Encouragement of infill and higher density development to curb leapfrog development that requires expensive expansion of streets and utilities;

• Encouragement of mixed use of land, placing work, home, shopping, and recreation closer together to help decrease the number and length of vehicle trips, thereby reducing air pollution and wasteful energy use;

• Emphasis on community goals like energy conservation, protection of the environment and low-income housing;

• Provision of increased amenities and higher quality development.

In the face of the tsunami bent on stopping or restricting growth, found in so many cities similar in characteristics to Fort Collins, this approach is refreshingly unique. So much so that it has been endorsed as a reform model of conventional zoning and labeled the product of a progressive, creative community. The city has been presented an Innovations Award from the Ford Foundation and the John F. Kennedy School of Government at Harvard University, as well as several other state and national awards for the LDGS. There is no question that it is a tremendous challenge to continue to make this approach achieve its objectives, maintain economic viability, and build an even better quality of life for the community. To fully meet it, the community will have to overcome some still existing "no growth" opposition; continue to increase public support of the LDGS beyond these first 11 years; ensure that the quality of elected officials, the planning and zoning board members, and professional planning staff remains equally high; and make certain that a planning attitude is further nurtured among city residents over the coming years.

Under Planning Director Tom Peterson's leadership since 1986, the city has come a long way in charting a nationally recognized path for more flexible land development than traditional zoning can provide. Peterson stresses that *guidance* is the key word in the system's name. That this philosophy seems to be working is exemplified by several successful completed projects. The major question remaining is whether they convert the NIMBYs (see Glossary of Planning Terms) or, at least, hold them at bay over the years ahead. Five to 10 years from now, an analytical study and community profile of a city somewhat similar to Fort Collins that has maintained a policy of restricting growth could prove to be most intriguing and enlightening.[4]

Around the country, a potpourri of other provisions aimed at growth management, including attempts to control or stop growth, have been enacted. Some have been well-conceived and effective while others can be termed discretionary or simply hoping to create an apparition to scare developers away. A listing of these includes: limiting utility extensions, public-private development partnerships, density reductions and downzoning, refusal to annex, and transfer of development rights (TDR). TDR is not a new technique. The concept has been around for more than 30 years, but it still is not generally understood and is relatively sparsely used. It has been enacted in some places to help preserve historic structures, preserve open space, and regulate density to encourage development in established or planned future service areas where a higher density of development is desired. A more complete explanation of TDR can be found in the Glossary of Planning Terms.

We end the discussion on growth management with this quote:

> Even the worst systems can teach us lessons, however. First, there is no substitute for sound planning. Effective growth management programs invariably rest on the four cornerstones of planning; comprehensive planning, zoning (in all its forms), subdivision regulations, and capital improvements programs.

> But no matter what term is used, growth management has a fundamental purpose. It links and coordinates the basic components of planning to place public officials in a more influential position in the development process. Experience shows that public capacities to manage growth effectively are limited more by political constraints than by technical know-how. Somehow planners must find ways to surmount those political pressures (particularly the scourge of NIMBYism) to put their knowledge to work.[5]

THE TAKING DILEMMA

Since the inception of governmental regulations regarding the use of private land and structures, debate and litigation have questioned the extent to which private land may be restricted by police power ordinances and when a community has crossed that fine line between reasonable limitation and inverse condemnation. It is an accepted legal principle that government may reasonably restrict private rights, including the use of land, as long as such action can be shown to be necessary for the public health, safety, and general welfare. It is the use of this last term that has been the major bone of contention for land-use restrictions. Just what is general welfare, and can it be defined so that even two people can completely agree as to its meaning, much less hundreds or thousands, especially as it applies to private land?

There are a number of police power enactments that few of us would disagree are in the interest of general public welfare as well as protection of public health and safety. These include such areas as normal police department functions, traffic control, animal control, building codes, sanitary codes, and plumbing codes. However, when a police power action even appears to result in denying a landowner *all* reasonable use of land, the charge of an illegal "taking"—condemnation without compensation—will certainly be made. This has been the cardinal principle of zoning since it first began. However, recent challenges and resultant U.S. Supreme Court decisions, instead of clearly defining a taking, have only served to cloud the issue further, inviting even more heated legal arguments. What is evident is the trend of the present Court toward stronger support of any kind of private property rights, regardless of the reason for the regulation. This shines like a lighthouse beacon, warning of danger to future planning and zoning measures aimed at environmental protection, strict floodplain development control, and the establishment of areas of critical state concern where limitation of development may be desirable and in the public interest.

Cases pertaining to the question of taking are not new to the U.S. Supreme Court. Some go back to the 1880s, long before zoning became a land-use control tool. However, until the change in the makeup of the Court begun during the Reagan years, U.S. courts have generally upheld the rights of government to restrain or prohibit land uses that would be harmful to the public interest. Sensing a changing attitude that favors private rights over the safety and well-being of the general public, owners and developers have steadily increased their challenges based upon arguments that they unfairly and illegally have been denied the use of their property. While over the years there have been a number of cases filed in both state and federal courts charging taking and seeking compensation, three have reached the Supreme Court since 1987. These have resulted in extremely important opinions that could be interpreted as a potential threat to the very principles upon which planning and zoning are founded. It is these three that will be mentioned briefly here.

The cases are officially captioned *First English Evangelical Lutheran Church v. County of Los Angeles* (107 S.Ct. 2378), *Nollan v. California Coastal Commission* (483 U.S. 825), and *Lucas v. South Carolina Coastal Council* (112 S.Ct. 2886). Examination of these cases reveals that each can be said to have a fundamental basis for government action taken to assure protection of environmental features, although less in *Nollan* than the other two. *Nollan* was an attack on state regulatory controls concerning public beach access and *Lucas* dealt with coastal protection. *First English* was directed at a county government's establishment of a "moratorium" with no established time limit preventing development in a floodplain area.

The *First English* Case

In *First English*, two natural disasters came together to create a problem the county sought to solve. The church owned a 21-acre campsite with some structures thereon, all provided for the benefit of handicapped children. It was located within the Angeles National Forest and along the Middle Fork of Mill Creek. A major forest fire occurred in 1977, denuding some 3,860 acres of high ground above the natural drainage basin in which the campsite was located. The following year, a torrential rain storm flooded the basin area, including the campsite, and took the lives of 10 people, fortunately, none of them children. The county immediately moved to adopt a "temporary" ordinance creating a floodplain zone in which it prohibited the reconstruction of existing structures and construction of new ones. Some time later, the ordinance was made permanent and revised to permit some reconstruction provided strict building code provisions were met. With these revisions, the church could have rebuilt some of the structures, but chose to proceed with a suit it had already filed against the county.

After the California courts rejected the plaintiff's arguments, the case was heard by the U.S. Supreme Court, which in a 6-to-3 decision ruled that the plaintiff had suffered the loss of "all use of its property," even from the temporary ordinance, and could be entitled to compensation for its loss. The Court then sent the case back to the California Court of Appeal for a determination by that court as to whether there had been a taking under the state's law of property. In June 1989, the appeals court reconsidered the case and again found that there had not been a taking (258 Cal. Rep. 893).

The *Nollan* Case

The decision of the U.S. Supreme Court in *Nollan* followed quickly on the heels of *First English.* In 1972, California voters approved a Coastal Act that included a coastal plan, detailed land-use regulation, the establishment of the California Coastal Commission, and the requirement for permits from the commission for development along its 1,000-mile coastline. To carry out this mission, the commission sought to encourage public access to the beach and restrict residential and commercial development in its area of responsibility.

The Nollans owned a lot that contained a beachfront bungalow. They wanted to tear this down and construct a two-story house on the property. As a condition of granting a building permit, the commission required that the Nollans file a deed granting permission for the public to cross the part of the beach to which they had title above the high tide line. They refused. Attorneys for the Nollans filed suit against the commission, arguing that the state was attempting to take some land that belonged to them without just compensation. The coastal commission argued that this was necessary to maintain adequate public access between parks and beaches that were public, and that such requirement had been agreed to by 53 other coastal property owners. The California courts found in favor of the commission.

The U.S. Supreme Court rejected all the state's arguments and determined that the commission's insistence that the Nollans deed land to it would constitute a taking. Justice Antonin Scalia wrote the opinion adopted by the majority of the Court. It contains a number of disturbing comments indicating troubled days ahead for those supporting environmental planning for conservation purposes as well as restrictive action taken in the name of protecting the "general public welfare." This is best indicated by one of Justice Scalia's statements in the opinion:

If it [the state] wants an easement across the Nollans' property, it must pay for it.

The *Lucas* Case

David Lucas, a building contractor, bought beachfront lots numbered 22 and 24 in Isle of Palms, South Carolina, in 1986, paying almost $1 million for them. The history of the area is one of being under water, out of water, and altered by coastline changes, erosion, and shifting sands. In 1988, Hurricane Hugo invaded the area, destroying one home and damaging more than half of the others. The house on lot 23, between the two lots owned by Lucas, was turned a number of degrees off its foundation. As a result of the damage to the properties and the beach, South Carolina passed the Beachfront Management Act of 1988. It was drafted with restrictions intended to protect both lot owners and beachfront residents all along its coastline, including the area in which Lucas's lots were located, and to assist in controlling erosion of the beach itself. A setback line was established for all future development based on the past patterns of flooding and beach erosion. The setback line established in the area of Lucas's lots was such that development of his property would be prohibited.

Lucas filed suit against the South Carolina Coastal Council, charging that this effected a taking of his property without just compensation, in violation of the Fifth and Fourteenth amendments to the United States Constitution. This action was taken before the state amended its Beachfront Management Act in 1990, allowing a waiver of the setback requirement for those who owned property in the protected area prior to passage of the act. Lucas failed to apply for a waiver although he had ownership of the lots two years before the waiver provision was enacted and he had not applied for a building permit at any time before filing suit. In spite of this, the South Carolina trial court agreed with Lucas, indicated that the act had made his land valueless, and ordered that he be paid $1,232,287.50, reflecting his original investment plus interest. This decision was reversed by the Supreme Court of South Carolina, and the attorneys for Lucas were granted a U.S. Supreme Court review.

During opening arguments, Justice Sandra Day O'Connor pointed out that, in other takings cases in which all administrative remedies had not been exhausted, a majority of the Justices had declared those cases "not ripe" for their consideration. Nevertheless, the majority opinion, again written by Justice Scalia, dismissed this as not applicable in this case. By a 6-to-3 vote, the Court overturned the Supreme Court of South Carolina's decision, declared that the law resulted in a taking of the Lucas property, and remanded the case to the lower court with instructions to reconsider it based upon the state's common-law principles of landownership and nuisance. The law firm of Robinson & Cole, in one of their helpful publications, has provided an excellent summary of the meaning of this case to both governmental units and property owners:

> This issue has divided the Court in past cases decided in favor of the government, and the *Lucas* majority expressed doubt about the continued vitality of these cases. If in the future the Court is willing to consider whether a property owner has been deprived of all economically beneficial use on only a portion of his property, the "total takings" rule announced in *Lucas* may take on great significance. In that event, the takings equation might shift toward compensating property owners whenever all development is barred by government regulation on a segment of property recognized under state law. Without further judicial extension, however, the *Lucas* decision may be limited to those rare cases where government has deprived a property owner of virtually all value on an entire tract of property.[6]

It is important to note that in all three of these cases the Supreme Court placed emphasis on the wording of a state's legislation pertaining to property and nuisance as a basis for determining whether government can deny the use of any property without having to compensate the owner. In other words, the long-standing zoning principle regarding a taking has not changed; however, the old philosophy that the burden of proof was on the landowner has been changed by this Supreme Court. Now, when all use is denied on private property, the burden of proof showing the existence of nuisance and definite necessity for preserving and protecting public health and safety is now placed on the government attempting to do so. This is something that planners and governing bodies in every state should look into carefully with their legal counsels and legislators to determine if their present laws on property ownership would meet, or could be made to meet, the guidelines laid down by the U.S. Supreme Court.

NEW FEDERAL ACTS OF NOTE

There are three recent federal legislative acts about which all planners and local governments should become aware because they have a far-reaching effect on local and state policy making and planning. The first of these is The National Affordable Housing Act of 1990, about which much already has been said. It is mentioned again here only to emphasize the need to make certain the utilization of it does not allow a return to individual, pragmatic projects of urban renewal years and that comprehensive planning is used as the base for coordination of individual programs.

THE CLEAN AIR ACT AMENDMENTS OF 1990 (CAAA)

The Clean Air Act Amendments were signed into law by President Bush in November 1990. The significance of this legislation, if strictly enforced by federal authorities, can be enormous to state and local governments in terms of costs, administration of requirements, and overall community development. It is another example of well-intended legislation lacking consideration of the overall effect on local governments, and without any attention given to how local governments will pay the cost. The House Energy and Commerce Committee chairman, Rep. John D. Dingell (D-Mich.), called the revised act the most complex, comprehensive, and far-reaching environmental law that any Congress has ever considered. According to him, it is going to affect virtually every human activity. There are 11 "titles" in CAAA, covering everything from Urban Air Quality to Worker Benefits. Title I, Urban Air Quality, contains a far-reaching listing of regulations mandating action by urban areas for which they will have to pay, especially for the reduction in ozone-depleting chlorofluorocarbons and carbon monoxide.

Enforcement of CAAA's provisions comes through sanctions and penalties imposed on states, urban areas, and local governments that remain in the nonattainment category (failure to meet federal standards for carbon monoxide, ozone, and sulphur dioxide), withholding even federal funding for highways and transportation. States with nonattainment areas were required to submit a revised State Implementation Plan (SIP) by November 1992. The Environmental Protection Agency (EPA) has prepared and distributed a "policy guidance" statement explaining how the agency will interpret and implement the required and discretionary areas under Title I. EPA places the primary responsibility for attainment in meeting the minimal standards on the states, and noncompliance can result in more stringent measures added to the state's SIP; however, these sanctions may not be imposed if the state has implemented its SIP properly, even though nonattainment may continue. The matter is complicated even further by the requirement that if a part of a Metropolitan Statistical Area (MSA) or a Consolidated Metropolitan Statistical Area (CMSA) receives a nonattainment classification, the entire MSA or CMSA will fall under the applicable pollution control requirements.

Certainly, there is much more in this demanding legislation that could be discussed, but for our purpose only one other question seems to be important. That concerns the influence this act can have on comprehensive planning, economic development, and urban growth areas. Assuming disciplined enforcement by state governments, sanctions, and additional requirements by EPA, the effect could be far-reaching on local or metro area land-use development and the general economy. Stationary source requirements are such that they could well have a substantial affect on the willingness of businesses and industries to locate in urban nonattainment areas. The act itself states: "nothing in this Act constitutes an infringement on the existing authority of counties and cities to plan or control land use, and nothing in this Act provides or transfers authority over such land use." These are relatively meaningless words that can be interpreted in many ways. Such purported reassurance will not be heart-warming to speculative developers, major industries, and even existing nonconforming businesses and industries that are in total compliance with local zoning and other land-use regulations.

The total enforcement of the new requirements could mean that formerly unregulated small businesses such as laundries, dry cleaners, metal fabricators, bakeries in shopping centers, and other multi-use urban structures may now find themselves having to comply with stiffer and more expensive measures to meet pollution regulations. Having to face music that appears as discordant as this, including the overall increased requirements for urban air quality, air toxics, stratospheric ozone, and enforcement could cause business developers and small business owners to shun presently polluted and noncomplying communities. It is important that planners, planning commissions, and local elected officials learn the CAAA changes and their state's SIP, and determine their impact on present land use, future land-use planning, land-use regulations, and present pollution abatement programs.

In no way has any of the above been written with the intent of opposing more stringent standards and enforcement measures designed to fight pollution and improve our air quality. I do criticize federal government-mandated action without a realistic determination of local governments' financial ability to take that action or to give adequate consideration to the effect such legislation will have on our economically strapped, sometimes almost bankrupt, cities and metropolitan areas. This writer has been, is, and will be a strong supporter of ways to overcome the pollution disaster in which we have enveloped ourselves and would be in full support of any federal legislation to do so, provided it had any chance of being successfully enforced and had a workable financing scheme. The reason for including the CAAA here has been to alert readers to how its provisions may affect their own lives, as well the community in which they live, and perhaps to start cooperative efforts to ensure that we do have cleaner air without breaking the financial back of local government.

THE INTERMODAL SURFACE TRANSPORTATION EFFICIENCY ACT OF 1991 (ISTEA)

Continuing the policy of returning federal programs to the states, Congress passed and the President signed the ISTEA legislation in 1991, just one year after CAAA became effective. In all likelihood this act will prove even more far-reaching in its effect on future land-use planning and urban form building than CAAA. This is because the legislation is designed to focus on regional or areawide transportation planning and development under the guise of turning transportation programming over to the states and local governments. For years, the U.S. Department of Transportation (DOT) has attempted to encourage coordinated transportation planning by funneling federal financial assistance through regional agencies, frequently Councils of Governments (COGs), with authority to review, discuss, and forward a recommendation to DOT. Together, CAAA and ISTEA can strengthen this trend of an increasing federal emphasis on regional agencies, referred to as Metropolitan Planning Organizations (MPOs), that began with the transportation act of 1962. Under both of these acts, MPOs have been given additional power in the distribution of federal funds. Contained within ISTEA is some $6.5 million for so-called "demonstration projects" (a politically correct name for old-fashioned "pork barrelling"), authorization for $151 billion over five years for roads and highways, and an innovative $24 billion Surface Transportation Program for mass transit projects. A question remains, however, whether or not the membership and staff of most MPOs or COGs can change from tacit, nonpolitical statistics-gathering agencies to groups that can deal effectively with controversial issues related to allocations between regions and local governments. Even more important is how coordination will be accomplished and whether local governments will have any role in this other than through the MPOs.

Transportation planning is required by CAAA to advance clean air goals in the existing 29 regions classified by EPA in the nonattainment category. MPOs are required by CAAA's Section 176(c) to show consistency between the emissions projections in their transportation plans (TIPs) and in the SIP currently approved by EPA. This will necessitate coordination between land-use planners and traffic engineers, and there probably will be a need for land-use planners to provide projections of trip generation on an area-by-area basis in their development plans. Approval of future development based on acceptable estimated trip generation, at best only a guess, is certain to cause some heated arguments among the involved professionals, to say nothing of the affected developer.

To raise yet another question, ISTEA will not allow federal transportation funds to be used in nonattainment areas for the purpose of increasing the capacity of a highway. Does this mean funds can be used to build a new highway or increase capacity of an existing one in an area that has met its attainment standards, yet funds will be denied to surrounding regions classified as nonattaining for those same improvements, so that we will have highway improvement by sectors, leaving existing bottlenecks to simply add to the pollution generation? The only answer seems to lie in the fact that ISTEA is telling MPOs, planners, and governmental officials that they must place the emphasis on reducing vehicle miles traveled rather than simply trying to comply by the reduction of tail pipe exhausts.

Again, there is much more to these complex pieces of legislation, especially ISTEA, that could be pointed out here. The details of both are something for which MPOs, COGs, county and municipal officials, planning commissions, and planners need to become familiar, and discuss with legal advisers, in order to determine the extent of the effect of both acts on their future planning and development. For the conclusion here, I would say that the objectives of both are desirable, provided the acts are properly enforced, but the problems of achieving those objectives are going to be shocking, expensive, and of tremendous influence on both comprehensive long-range planning and the resultant building of the urban form.

DON'T SLAPP ME OR I'LL SLAPP BACK

SLAPPs—Strategic Lawsuits Against Public Participation—represent an attempt at intimidation by some members of the development community to discourage public opposition to their projects. The tactic usually followed is this: After a proposed project is submitted to the planning commission or governing body, is opposed strongly by residents, and is turned down, extremely modified, or restricted, the developer's attorneys seek out the leaders of the public opposition and file a punitive action suit against them. In several cases, civil suits seeking financial judgments have been filed against individuals who have circulated petitions or printed material or spoken out publicly in opposition to the project. These suits charge everything from restraint of trade to spreading unfounded rumors and misinformation. They are primarily nuisance suits and almost always are thrown out of court by judges. Nevertheless, the potential of such suits for frightening citizens into stopping the exercise of their constitutional rights is great in a number of areas of activity in addition to land development. As a result, Denver University Law School Professor George W. Pring and sociology Professor Penelope Canan have instituted a nationwide Political Litigation Project study at their institution. They also are writing a forthcoming book, *Getting Sued For Speaking Out In America*. My plea is for concerned citizens not to be deterred from fully exercising their constitutional rights because of the possibility of such a suit and to continue to stand up and fight. A way should be found to assess punitive costs against any individual, corporation, or organization filing such a suit if the case is thrown out of court or ruled against by a judge. This would put a very quick end to this harassment tactic.

The fact that we have become such a litigious society also has contributed to the increase in these nuisance and intimidation court suits, some extending to the point of being completely ludicrous. A case in point, one that has not been thrown out of court yet, came to my attention while visiting Weslaco, a Southeast Texas town near the Mexican border with a population of 19,331. The city has a moderate-sized airport, which it is planning to expand by lengthening one of the runways. At the same time the Weslaco Mid-Valley Airport Board was making preparations for the expansion and seeking federal financial assistance for the project, the Weslaco Independent School District Board needed a location for a new school and was negotiating with John F. Dominguez, a retired district judge, and his wife, Sylvia, for the possible purchase of a 20-acre plot of land next to the airport boundary. The Dominguezes' land had an appraised value of $47,685 and had been offered to the school board for $180,000. The board agreed to the price and voted to purchase the land; however, no contract was signed nor had any formal agreement been made between the parties.

In the meantime, Walter H. Baxter III, a retired general and former chairman of the Rio Grande Chamber of Commerce, had just finished a term on the airport board. At the December 1989 public meeting of the airport board, he informed members that the land was directly in the flight pattern of the airport and raised the question of danger from a possible airplane crash on the school or the land around it. Three other members of the airport board later supported Mr. Baxter's concern. The school board called off negotiations and indicated they would not buy the land.

In 1990, a suit was filed in state district court by Mr. and Mrs. Dominguez against the City of Weslaco and the members of the airport board individually. One defendant named in the filing was a past member of the airport board and two others were not board members when discussion about the land purchase and the decision not to buy the property took place. It should be noted that all members of that board are unpaid volunteers. The suit charged damages to real property, loss of economic opportunity, personal injury, pain and suffering, and mental anguish. Before the suit was filed, Mr. Dominguez claimed that the stress over calling off the sale had caused him to suffer a brain hemorrhage and a heart attack.

The case did not come to trial until April 13, 1992 when it was heard over two days without a jury by a "visiting" (also retired) District Court Judge Joe E. Kelly. The opinion, which consists of three double-spaced pages, found for the plaintiffs and awarded the tidy sum of $6,541,184.00 for actual damage, exemplary damages, and interest of 10 percent per annum. Judge Kelly ruled that Mr. Baxter's statement before the school board was false and that this constituted an attempt to use private property for public use without compensation. In other words, a taking! In order to stress just how far-fetched some of these nuisance cases can become, the major portion of the judge's opinion is included verbatim as written:

The court after listening to the evidence and reviewing the pleadings is of the opinion that the Plaintiffs shall have the relief they requested in the following manner: IT IS ORDERED ADJUDGED AND DECREED that Plaintiffs have and recover from the Defendants jointly and severally the following sums of money:

For lost wages	$ 8,700.00
For personal injury, pain and suffering and mental anguish of John Dominguez	$ 1,200,000.00
For mental anguish of Mrs. Sylvia Dominguez	$ 300,000.00
For loss of consortium to each Plaintiff	$ 400,000.00
For reasonable and necessary medical expenses of John Dominguez	$ 42,596.00
For damages to real property	$ 192,000.00
For loss of economic opportunity	$ 20,000.00
TOTAL	$ 2,163,296.00

IT IS FURTHER ORDERED that the damages found above are in the same amounts and for the same elements as a result Plaintiff having proved each theory of liability, any one of which justifies this award of damages

IT IS THEREFORE ORDERED, ADJUDGED AND DECREED that Plaintiffs have and recover from the Defendants jointly and severally the sum of $2,163,296.00 as actual damages. It is further ordered and the Plaintiffs recover from the Defendants jointly and severally the sum of $4,326,592.00 in exemplary damages.

IT IS FURTHER ORDERED that Plaintiffs are entitled to prejudgment interest at 10% per annum, which is the rate authorized on this judgment after entry, as to all actual damages except lost wages and medical expenses from 6 months after December 12, 1990, until the date of the signing of this judgment which amount is $51,296.00; and hereafter the judgment shall bear 10% interest on all damages, exemplary and actual. All relief not expressly granted, is denied. All court costs of this proceeding are assessed against the Defendants, jointly and severally.

Now that is a real example of Texas "justice" and a perfect example of SLAPPs. You can believe that after learning of this decision the entire population of Weslaco was up in arms, especially when the rumor started that compliance with this judgment would "cost every taxpayer in Weslaco $744." As a result, on August 9, a mass meeting was held in front of city hall, where all citizens were invited "to come and pray for justice." This they did by the hundreds. Prior to this trial, in early 1992, the Rio Grande Valley Chamber of Commerce became convinced that southern Texas was the site of too many lawsuits in which excessive damage judgments were being rendered. Citizens Against Lawsuit Abuse (CALA) was formed under the chamber's leadership, and through flyers, direct mail, and word-of-mouth began a campaign based on these two slogans: "The civil justice system is simply out of control" and "It seems that the Valley's 11th Commandment has become Sue Thy Neighbor." By the time of my visit, they had incorporated as a nonprofit 501(c) (3) organization and had collected a war chest of $258,000 to raise citizen awareness about excessive injury and damage litigation and the exorbitant awards being made by judges and juries. CALA seized upon the Dominguez case as its rallying point to further arouse public support for its mission of "making liability laws fair for all of us." Their full support was pledged to the Weslaco cause.

Although CALA has the approval of a great many people, it also has stirred up a hornet's nest among trial lawyers in the Valley area as well as other parts of Texas. Many attorneys argue that the charges of excess awards are unfounded, that by creating this attitude CALA is causing chaos in jury selection, and is prejudicing jurors against making fair and justifiable awards. All of this is best summed up by a quote from Harlingen, Texas, attorney Randy Whittington—who does both plaintiff and defense work—which appeared in the *Houston Chronicle* on August 2, 1992.

> To me, the citizens-against-lawsuits movement is designed in large part to prejudice juries, to create a belief in their minds that lawsuits are frivolous until proven otherwise, to create a mind-set that no one is entitled to a significant amount of money in a jury verdict, and so there is a bias created in the minds of the jury before they even get in the courtroom.

One wonders just how Mr. Whittington feels about the judge's award in the Dominguez case.

The differences in viewpoint among CALA, its supporters, and the attorneys will liven up discussion through the winter months, especially in the Valley area of South Texas. In the meantime, the City of Weslaco, including members of the Weslaco Mid-Valley Airport Board individually named in the Dominguez suit, have succeeded in petitioning for a new trial in the federal court system. The suit now will be heard in the U.S. District Court in Brownsville, Texas, sometime in the future. It is interesting to note that the attorneys for the plaintiffs are now seeking to amend the Dominguezes' original petition to raise the award from $520,000, the amount originally sought in the petition submitted to generous Judge Kelly, to $9,692,000. So goes the litigious life in South Texas.

Apparently Mr. Whittington, CALA, and the people in Weslaco are unaware or fearful of the best possible remedy against these intimidating SLAPP suits. It is simply that of a SLAPP-Back lawsuit. An excellent paper entitled "Strategic Lawsuits Against Public Participation (SLAPPs): An Overview," prepared by Jeffrey A. Benson and Dwight Merriam provides a thorough discussion of both SLAPPs and SLAPP-Backs from which the following is taken:

> A party who is SLAPPed need not turn the other cheek. He (or she) can SLAPP right back. Professor Pring argues that the SLAPP-Back, a subsequent counterclaim or countersuit for damages by the SLAPP's target, is the most effective long-range tool for discouraging SLAPPs.
>
> There are a number of legal grounds for a SLAPP-Back:
>
> 1) violation of U.S. or state Constitutional rights;
>
> 2) federal and state civil rights statutes;
>
> 3) abuse of process;
>
> 4) malicious prosecution and other state law torts.
>
> Each of us has a stake in our communities, and on occasion we get upset when we hear of a change taking place or an agency being run inefficiently. We all want open space somewhere in town, good schools, a decent police force, and clean water. Factors such as these keep our quality of life acceptable. It is our ties and commitment to the community which makes us speak out about problems and potential solutions. SLAPP suits are nothing less than an attempt to make us all afraid to speak up about those problems and to punish us when we do. They are a threat to both free speech and to informed decision making by our leaders. While there is no panacea to such litigation, courts and the legislatures may wish to examine this issue more closely and step up efforts to protect legitimate exercises of the First Amendment.[7]

FEARFUL FACTS FOR THE FUTURE

In the second edition of this book, written in 1979, I stated that even if the drastic measures represented by California's Proposition 13 were not emulated in other states, my crystal ball told me that the money crunch in financing governmental services was real and was going to be around for a long time. The amazing thing is how accurate that prediction was. Thirteen years later, not only have other states established limits on the amount that taxes and overall spending can rise yearly, but even more have tried. In 1992, Colorado voters were faced with a proposition (Amendment No. 1), placed on the ballot by referendum for the third time in five years, that would hamstring state and local officials' taxing and expenditure powers far more than Proposition 13 has done in California. This time voters approved it. Colorado is rife with decaying infrastructure, declining maintenance of parks and other public places, and needs additional law enforcement and a number of additional detention facilities. Yet the taxpayer rebellion remains alive and well, even after the evidence from California of what over-burdensome limitation can do.

The one thing about which you can always be sure of in Colorado is the unpredictability and inconsistency of voters. Along with this Amendment No. 1 ("Taxpayers' Bill of Rights" as it was called) were nine other petition-generated constitutional amendments. Just prior to the election, pollsters were predicting a defeat of the tax limit proposal. Little did they know! With a large turnout of 75 percent of the registered voters, the measure garnered 53 percent of the votes cast. To emphasize this "thou shall not tax us" attitude, a measure to increase the state sales tax by one cent to aid education and another providing a voucher system with freedom of choice for secondary schools (including parochial) were defeated. Further, the state's national reputation suffered from an intolerant vote prohibiting any community from adopting an ordinance making illegal any discrimination against gays or lesbians. This latter action invalidated existing ordinances protecting their rights in the home-rule cities of Denver, Boulder, and Aspen.

In a bit of irony, the voters who stifled state and local revenue by passing Amendment No. 1 and defeating the two measures to aid school financing and provide school reform, then joined with others to overwhelmingly beat down all five proposals that would have allowed limited gambling in 36 more communities and three counties. At the same time, the majority of voters favored requiring all lottery money to be used only for parks, recreation facilities, and open space and not allowing the legislature to spend any lottery funds for prison construction and other capital expenditures as was done in the past. Finally, in a splendid show of compassion (for animals, not for humans) the majority approved an amendment prohibiting the hunting or killing of mother black bears during the spring season.

It would take a most talented pundit to determine the psychology behind the erratic voting pattern in this election, but a large role would have to have been played by dislike of all government, hatred for the Denver metropolitan area, and bigotry. Regardless, the fact is that Colorado, just poised to raise itself out of a recessionary period, now must face state and local governments hog-tied in attempting to deal with present and future needs for public facilities and services. One of the more ludicrous comments concerning all of this after the election came from some local "wag" who, after discussing Colorado's increase in criminals, the lack of prison facilities in which to keep them, and the cut-off of money to build more, said, "Hey, why not take all the criminals and feed them to the black bears!"

If revenue sources are limited and funds for government general operating expenses, facilities, and services are inelastic, the answer can lie only in the "fool's gold" of gambling (and its concomitant problems) or in one of two traditional areas: new sources of revenue or cuts in services. It appears unlikely that taxpayers will permit these new sources simply to be other methods of taxation and even more unlikely that the federal government and states will relinquish the taxing base they have zealously protected over the years. This can leave the almost illegitimate children of our governmental structure, the municipalities, in the unenviable position of reducing services or having to go more and more to "user charges." Carried to the extreme, this would mean that you and I would be charged a fee when our garbage is collected, the street is swept, we call the police, or need the fire department. These fees would have to be sizable enough to provide the basic financial support to keep these services in operation.

This difficulty of remaining solvent, perhaps even remaining afloat, is something for which I see no happy solution in sight. It is why so many communities are making the mistake of accepting, even encouraging, anything that comes along that even pretends to be an economic development shot in the arm. This is also why we have had the rush to impose more and more extractions and impact fees regardless of whether courts will find them justifiable and legal. The present move to push for freedom of choice in schools and subsidized vouchers stems from the shameful way we have neglected our schools and the quality of education of our children, especially in the inner cities. And what are we doing about all of this? Is there a hue and cry for better leadership and more efficiency in government at all levels? Are there involved people who understand that the degradation of our cities and towns by shoddy development only exacerbates the ultimate decline of the overall economic base upon which survival is so dependent?

And where are the planning commissions and planners in all of this? This is a time when voices of concern should be heard loudly expressing the importance of planning for the future and stabilizing and protecting the present with an insistence upon strong and more effective leadership in government, appointed bodies, and even the planning profession. It is the time for meaningful education of the public on the valuable role of collective, organized, present and future planning in assuring protection of the quality of life and the economic viability of every unit of government. Planning by itself will not solve all of our present economic problems. But people working together for the future of their community through the planning process is the strongest tool we have available to make sure that we are not just going to sit around and see the things so important for the future of society—our community—go to hell in a handbasket.

We are coming into a new era of governmental financing that can and should mean an increasingly important role for careful planning, not reduced planning department budgets, as is happening far too often. Every available dollar is going to have to be prioritized and used to produce the most good for the total community (a theory that is supposed to have been in effect for some time but that some of our governments seemed to have overlooked). The maintenance of existing capital investments in museums, libraries, streets, and sewer systems will be a struggle in any budget, and new capital improvements programs will require even more justification of the essential need for each project.

Thus the challenge to planners and the planning profession has never been greater. We need to believe in ourselves, believe more than ever in community planning, and prove to this country that we are capable of rising up and meeting this challenge. Having done so, then we can truly call ourselves a profession.

NOTES

1. Douglas R. Porter, "The APF Epidemic," *Urban Land* (November 1990), p. 36.

2. Porter, "Facing Growth With a Plan," *Urban Land* (June 1992), p. 18.

3. For information contact: Town of Breckenridge, Department of Community Development, P.O. Box 168, Breckenridge, CO 80424.

4. For information contact: Planning Director, City of Fort Collins, 281 N. College Avenue, P.O. Box 580, Fort Collins, CO 80522-0580.

5. Porter, "Looking Back," *Planning,* (July 1992), p. 15.

6. Robinson & Cole, "U.S. Supreme Court Decides Lucas v. South Carolina Coastal Council," *Land Use and Environmental Section* (July 9, 1992), pp. 1-3.

7. Jeffrey A. Benson and Dwight H. Merriam, "Strategic Lawsuits Against Public Participation (SLAPPs): An Overview," paper presented at ALI-ABA Land Use Institute (August 1992), pp. 884 and 848.

Glossary of Planning Terms

Included below is a brief discussion of some of the terms that anyone interested in planning has heard or will hear about in the future. No attempt has been made to include all of them. It is hoped that those left with unanswered questions will contact persons involved with their own local planning commission and/or planning staff and perhaps become better acquainted with this activity that greatly affects our individual lives.

American Institute of Certified Planners (AICP) The present organization for qualified professional planners as part of the APA structure. To become a member requires passing an examination after having gained some practical experience in the planning field. The number of years of experience required to take the examination can be reduced to two years if the applicant has a graduate degree in planning from an accredited planning school, to three years with an accredited bachelor's degree, and to four years with any other graduate or undergraduate degree. Those having no college degree desiring to take the examination must have eight years of planning experience. All members of AICP must be members of APA. AICP provides its own published materials and information to its members. Governance is by a separate board of commissioners elected by the AICP members.

American Institute of Planners (AIP) Founded in 1917, this was the organization of professional planners in the United States until AIP consolidated with the American Society of Planning Officials in 1978. Membership required passing a test of planning competence after having gained experience though planning practice. AIP had standards for schools teaching planning that had to be met before an institution could be included in the list of recognized schools of planning. AIP published the AIP Journal, Practicing Planner, and AIP News.

American Planning Association (APA) The present "umbrella" organization resulting from the merger of ASPO and AIP in 1978. Its purpose is to encourage planning activity, provide information on the field of planning, conduct research, maintain and seek to improve the standards of planning practice, and serve as a clearinghouse for information for its members. Members include professional planners, government officials, planning commissioners, planning educators, and interested citizens. Membership is open to anyone who would like to be involved in and informed about general planning activity in the United States and other countries. A subsidiary organization, the American Institute of Certified Planners is open to professional planners who have passed certification tests (see definition above). APA publications include *APA Journal, Land Use Law & Zoning Digest,* Planning Advisory Service reports, and *Planning* magazine. The Planners Press, located in the Chicago office, is APA's publishing arm where books, pamphlets, and other materials on planning are published each year and made available through the Planners Bookstore. APA has two offices: at 1313 East 60th Street, Chicago, Illinois 60637, and at 1776 Massachusetts Avenue, Washington, D.C. 20036.

Central Business District (CBD) A designation given to the innermost core of an urban area. There are no fixed standards for determining the physical demarcation of the CBD other than the area of the more intensified retail, commercial, and office concentration in the central core. While suburban and regional shopping centers have drained away the vitality of many CBDs, they remain that sector of the community with the greatest public investment in utility installations and operational service costs. They are an essential element in maintaining the health of an urban core.

Community Development Block Grant (CDBG) A term resulting from the passage of the Housing and Community Development Act of 1974 (Public Law 93-383). Under this legislation, the various community development programs administered by the Department of Housing and Urban Development were consolidated into a single block grant system. These included the formerly categorical (stated purpose) funding programs for urban renewal, model cities, neighborhood facilities, open-space land, and basic water and sewer facilities. Within the guidelines adopted, local governments were given greater discretion as to where the money would be used. A principal purpose was to strengthen the ability of local government to "determine the community's development needs, set priorities, and allocate resources to various activities." State governments were eligible also. Grants were 100 percent funded without requiring a local match, although there were stringent requirements that had to be met for approval, including a housing assistance plan (HAP). Most of this act has now been replaced by the provisions of the National Affordable Housing Act of 1991 discussed in the text.

Capital Improvements Program (CIP) The systematic organizing of the capital needs of a governmental unit into a plan for meeting those needs over a set period and within financial capabilities of that unit. Considered to be a vital part of master planning, the CIP sets forth the essential facilities and service mechanisms necessary to support future growth and development as well as serve the existing population. Included are planning for future streets, water and sewer facilities, parks, libraries, museums, police headquarters, city halls, and all other "capital" expenditures to be funded from public tax support or dedicated revenue funds. These expenditures usually are financed by bonds sold by the governmental unit and repaid over a fixed period from tax sources, primarily the real estate property tax. Ordinary or routine maintenance expenditures should never be made part of a CIP and should be taken care of through the general operating fund budget. The CIP should be the basis for the capital improvements portion of each year's adopted municipal budget.

Cluster Development (Density Control Development) A design technique permitted by many zoning ordinances allowing clustering of residential units on a smaller land parcel per each unit than is specified as the minimum lot size for an individual unit. The controlling factor is that the normal average density for the zone must be maintained. If the zoning permits three units to the acre but requires a minimum lot size of 12,000 square feet, a developer's plan could be approved in which the units are "clustered" on individual parcels of only 6,000 square feet provided the density of three per acre is maintained. The remaining land is utilized for common open space or public use. The technique encourages innovative design and planning, saves development costs for the investor, and provides green areas and open space in common ownership for the residents. Some more sophisticated ordinances also use this same principle in planning for commercial and industrial development.

Council of Governments (COG) Organizations of local governments officially banding together to work on common regional problems, issues, and planning. Membership in a COG comprises elected officials appointed by the governing bodies of the individual governmental units. There is usually an executive director and a professional staff. COGs were originally started as an alternative to formalized metropolitan government and a means of cooperative regional planning in such matters as land use, transportation, air quality control, and delivery of services. In federal government legislation these are referred to as Metropolitan Planning Organizations (MPOs). COGs have become clearinghouse organizations for federally aided programs (in effect, almost subsidiary branches of some of the federal departments). In the past, local governments' federal grant applications were submitted through them for coordination clearing (A-95 Review) with any similar proposed projects of other governmental units and with adopted master plans, prior to being forwarded to the appropriate federal agency. In recent years, many COGs (or MPOs) have become the transportation planning agency for their regions and administer Department of Transportation programs and funding as well as many programs of HUD and the Department of Health and Human Services (HHS). With the Clean Air Act Amendments (CAAA) and the

Intermodal Surface Transportation Efficiency Act (ISTEA) now law, COGs (or MPOs) have been given a significant increase in both responsibility and authority.

Environmental Impact Statement (EIS) Created and instituted as a requirement by the establishment of the Environmental Protection Agency (EPA), the EIS has now become one of the most potent tools in the planning process. An EIS consists of a detailed analysis of the impact of a proposed project upon the total environment—natural and man-made—within the general vicinity of the project or in an affected area of any distance. For example, a challenge based on potential environmental impact led the EPA to reject one of the largest proposed water projects in recent years, Two Forks Dam in Colorado. Curtailment of logging in Oregon resulted from environmentalists protesting the continued destruction of the habitat of the spotted owl, declared an endangered species. Communities are discovering that a requirement similar to the EIS to measure the impact of all major projects (not just those that are federally funded) is a useful means of making certain that good planning principles are followed and that quality and character of areas beyond the project site are adequately protected.

Eminent Domain The power of government to acquire property for public use for which the owner must receive "just compensation." This an important tool of planning and is vital in capital improvements planning. An example might be that a master plan shows a location for a new fire station on a parcel of land that is privately owned and now vacant. The property can be acquired by the governmental unit through negotiation and purchase, or, if this is unsuccessful, it can be "taken" through the use of the "condemnation" process under the right of eminent domain. Compensation is set by appraisals or, as a last resort, a condemnation court. Many special districts (autonomous authorities, school boards, water districts, etc.) and public utilities have been granted the "right" of eminent domain by the federal government and the states.

Gentrification A word that is increasingly used in reference to what some consider to be a meaningful social dilemma, especially in older inner-city areas. In simple terms, this refers to the trend of the return of the "gentry," or well-to-do, to inner-city residential areas, resulting in a displacement of lower-income persons, many of whom were renters. Older neighborhood homes are becoming more attractive to persons of means, usually without children, as city living is again becoming more desirable and acceptable. The displacement of the poorer families creates a problem of finding adequate and affordable housing for them and begins the transformation of what probably has been a heterogeneous area back into a homogeneous one. A major, but more extreme, example of this is now occurring in what is referred to as Lower Downtown, or Lo-Do, in Denver. Originally built as a warehouse, wholesale, and office area of four- and five-story buildings, but experiencing decline and neglect over the years, it has been designated a historic area by the city and a revitalization plan has been developed. With ground having been broken on the construction site for the new Coors Field major league baseball stadium and the pending move of Elitch Gardens' Amusement Park to Lo-Do, the area has become the "hottest" renovation sector in the city. The conversion of the upper floors of many of these older structures into residential lofts started some two or three years ago and the successful sale and rental of such units has made this practice almost epidemic. Unfortunately, many of the older boarded-up, vacant buildings and the area underneath the 20th Street viaduct, now being torn down for the new baseball stadium, were providing minimum shelter for large numbers of the legitimately homeless and indigent transients who now are forced to seek other refuge in the city or elsewhere. Some may say that this result is good riddance, but it certainly contributes to worsening a serious social problem with which we are now faced.

Department of Housing and Urban Development (HUD) This agency was established in 1965 as a cabinet-level department. All housing and many of the urban development programs were consolidated into the department. HUD is the agency that administers the provisions of various housing acts passed by Congress over the years, including urban renewal, federal aid for planning (Section 701 Program), open-space, neighborhood facilities, and basic water and sewer facilities programs. Under former President Nixon, these were combined and transferred into special revenue sharing or block grant federal measures called Community Development Block Grants (CDBG) awarded to qualified communities. While some CDBG funds remain to be expended, the primary HUD programs have now been included in the National Affordable Housing Act of 1991.

Local Public Agency (LPA) With the demise of urban renewal as it was practiced from 1948 to the 1980s, this term has become somewhat passe and is included here as a historical note. LPA was what federal legislation called the local governmental agency designated as the one responsible for administering all programs for urban renewal in any local jurisdiction. LPAs could be the local governing body, a housing authority, or a separate urban renewal authority, depending upon the desires of the policy-makers. Due to the potential for controversy and conflict in the handling of an urban renewal project, most municipal units chose to go the semi-autonomous urban renewal route. The majority elected to create a separate urban renewal authority as their LPA.

Model Cities Program This is another historical inclusion. It was part of the Demonstration Cities and Metropolitan Development Act of 1961 that proved to be a miserable failure in social programming attempts. It was designed as a prototype program for the purpose of attacking physical, social, and economic ills in specially selected areas of approved cities. Federal money was used for housing rehabilitation, street and utility improvement, job opportunities, and welfare projects such as child-care centers, dental clinics, meals for the elderly, etc. The theory was that if you could put one neighborhood back on its feet, the cities would then extend such programs into other neighborhoods. A self-determining "Model Cities" neighborhood board was elected to participate in the allocation of the available funds. The program did not live up to expectations due to power struggles within neighborhoods, the divisiveness created between areas, and politics in general. Funds for the program were reduced drastically by the Nixon administration, and the categorical funding was eliminated by revenue sharing and the Community Development Act.

NIMBY This is the acronym for "Not In My Back Yard." It is an attitudinal mind blockage that crops up like flowers in springtime when a planning or zoning change is proposed either by a developer or local officials and is found objectionable by some residents in the immediate vicinity of where it would be located. In some extreme cases, an issue like this can extend to an entire neighborhood and even beyond. The generators of Nimbyism can range from a townhouse proposal for a large, long-time vacant lot in a single-family residential area that kids have played on for years to the conversion of a large residence into a group home, or even the construction of a place of worship, regardless of belief. Isolated commercial stores such as a 7-Eleven or the expansion of any commercial zoning can fuel a Nimbyism attack. The opposition statement usually goes something like this: "Now I am certainly not against providing housing and care for mentally retarded children, but not in my (our) backyard. It just should be put somewhere else where it is more appropriate." All of this is not intended to suggest that there are not times when planning or zoning changes, proposed either by government or private interests, deserve to be opposed. There certainly are occasions where strong opposition is most appropriate. Rather, it is to indicate that there are times when "me-ism" takes over and blocks out any possibility that there might some merit in a proposed change that could result in a benefit to the bigger picture—the total community.

Planning Accreditation Board (PAB) The PAB is a cooperative undertaking sponsored jointly by three organizations: Association of Collegiate Schools of Planning (ACSP), AICP, and APA. The planning accreditation program reflects an assumption that all parties to the planning enterprise—practitioners, educators, students, elected officials, and citizens—have a vital stake in the quality of the nation's programs of planning education. Responsibility for accreditation policy is shared jointly by AICP (primarily representing the interests of planning professionals) and ASCP (primarily representing the interests of planning educators). The AICP Commission and the ACSP Executive Committee each take action on PAB-proposed amendments to criteria and procedures. The APA board is asked to provide consent for the amendments, in accordance with its representation of students, elected officials, and citizens (in addition to practitioners and educators). The PAB's principal responsibilities are to evaluate and reach decisions regarding applications for accreditation, and to discuss and propose appropriate policy changes to enhance the role of accreditation in furthering academic excellence. The PAB also provides assistance to schools apart from the accrediting process. The PAB is composed of eight members: three ACSP representatives, four from AICP, and one citizen planner from APA.

Planning Attitude Anyone reading this book will recognize that the writer has a very strong penchant for the term "planning attitude." It seems only fair, then, that I should try to provide a definition in more specific terms of just what this conjures up in my mind. By whatever term it is identified, the most important element necessary for the planning function to work in American society is an infusion of concern about the future of the city along with an understanding of and support for the community's role in guiding and directing building for the future. That is a "planning attitude." Without it, the existence of a planning function in name is just that—a name—and can best be termed "lip-service planning."

Police Power The power (or right) of government to restrict and regulate private rights pertaining to property and person for the public good. Such an action must be reasonable and in the interest of public health, safety, and/or general welfare. Some examples of police power regulations are animal-control ordinances, building codes, traffic codes, zoning ordinances, and subdivision regulations. The use of police power reasonably restricting land use does not require that the owner of land be compensated.

Planning, Programming, Budgeting System (PPBS) The PPBS is a management system used by some governments that attempts to combine its three listed functions into a process under the direct responsibility of the chief administrative officer. As stated in "Management Policies in Local Government Finance," a publication of the International City Management Association, the PPBS "organizes goods and personnel into groups in order to carry out a defined purpose. . . . Specifically, the use of PPBS requires: (1) analyzing the objectives of city government spending and how well these objectives are being met; (2) carrying out detailed multiyear planning; and (3) setting up the necessary programming to present data in a form that can be used in making major decisions by the department heads, the city manager or other chief executive and the finance officer. . ."

Planned Unit Development (PUD) The original idea of the PUD concept was to allow greater flexibility in planning, design, and even mixed use than could be achieved by traditional zoning in the development of large parcels of land. As an illustration, a 100-acre tract might have three or four fixed zoning areas (or perhaps even only one) and rigid requirements (e.g. commercial only, apartments, single-family). The developer of the tract, by using the comprehensive master planning technique for the entire parcel, could request consideration of intermixed uses (apartments or offices over commercial, townhouses mixed with apartments, compatible employment generators near residential) under standards adopted in a PUD ordinance or zoning amendment. If approved by the planning commission and the governing body, the developer could build out the parcel over a period of time in accordance with the approved plan, which would be superimposed on and supersede the existing zoning requirements. The use of the PUD is a way to amend a zoning ordinance in accordance with a complete, coordinated plan of development for acreage parcels rather then piecemeal changes or variances of zone regulations. The Fort Collins Land Development Guidance System uses a similar technique, although it is not confined only to larger parcels. It is important to remember that the first step is the development and adoption of a carefully conceived PUD amendment to the zoning ordinance, my preferred method of using this technique.

701 Program While the 701 Program is also a thing of the past, reference to it for other reasons seems worthwhile. It came into being as part of the Federal Housing Act of 1954. This was the entry of the federal government, for those readers too young to know about it, into financial grants for comprehensive planning purposes by local governments. Through approved state agencies, funds were made available to municipalities to pay for planning studies and plan development, first on a 50-50 basis and later on a 75-25 match. This was the "carrot" portion of the "carrot and big stick" approach of the 1954 act that greatly increased local planning activity and master plan preparation—some good and some bad.

Transfer of Development Rights (TDR) The TDR idea has been around for quite some time, but still is a controversial and difficult process to gain support for and administer. In theory, it is a system of land development control wherein rights or development units are assigned to each parcel of land based upon planning studies that establish urban growth areas based upon the availability of public facilities and services and set density control factors. These rights are separable and may be transferred to other parcels, thus they are marketable. A piece of land may be unsuitable for intensive development for environmental reasons or any number of other conditions, yet lie in a zone where such development is permitted. By use of TDR, the owner of the property can be compensated from private sources for the usable rights, which are then transferred to other land more suitable for intensive development. This technique also can be used in preserving low-density development and/or agricultural and open space while concentrating intensive development in existing or planned urban service areas. The transfer of air rights has been effective in retaining low-level historic buildings in the central business district. It allows the transfer of these rights obtained by the difference between the height of the existing structure and the height limitation established in the zoning ordinance. Once development rights are transferred, the decreased utilization right becomes a restriction of the future use of the originating property and runs with the land.

Workable Program for Community Improvement (WPCI) Another "old-timer," but somewhat similar to the Comprehensive Housing Affordability Strategy (CHAS) in the National Affordable Housing Act of 1991. WPCI was a provision of the 1954 Federal Housing Act that initiated the requirement of measurement criteria for determining community action for improvement for any local government seeking federal funds for urban renewal. Seven items of evaluation were included. The first and most fundamental one was that there be a comprehensive master plan for total future development. The WPCI had to obtain federal approval before funds would be released for an urban renewal project. This was the "big stick" scenario that resulted in a large increase in the number of local planning commissions and master plans. The WPCI also began the federal insistence on citizen involvement in planning and urban renewal activity. The similarity to CHAS comes from the requirement for a CHAS to be submitted by states and local jurisdictions and approved by HUD before becoming eligible to receive funding through the HOME Investment Partnership Act (HOME) or any other funding under the Affordable Housing Act.

Appendix A

EXCERPTS FROM

1989 DENVER COMPREHENSIVE PLAN

FEDERICO PEÑA
MAYOR

Richard Deane
Chairman, Denver Planning Board

Philip Milstein
Lee White
Co-Chairmen, Comprehensive Plan Advisory Steering Committee

William Lamont, Jr.
Director of Planning and Development
1983 - 1990

Frank Gray
Director of Planning and Development

VISION

An overall plan for a great city must answer the question "what do we really want this city to be, and to become?" This isn't a simple question. Any city and its people are both the beneficiaries of special opportunities and, in a sense, the victims of special circumstances suggested by a particular history and geography. The core of this Comprehensive Plan lies in our attempt to agree on Denver's purposes for the future, to think through the effect of Denver's special inheritance on those purposes, and then to apply our consensus in specific plan suggestions.

The fundamental thing we want Denver to both be and to become is a city that's livable for all its people: a city in which they can learn, move about, work and play in safety and comfort, with pleasure and pride, and in a spirit of openness and opportunity.

It is essential that living quality for all the people of Denver be perceived as this plan's central purpose. The question "does this action improve the quality of life for people?" is the challenge the plan poses to future civic leaders.

If livability is at the heart of the plan, a number of associated purposes become easier to define:

- A Denver that is focused on the quality of life for all its people must be a Denver that is economically healthy, with a broad mix of good jobs. Livability and economic development are permanently linked -- neither improves without the other.
- Such a Denver must be a city that shows real commitment to providing equal opportunity to all its citizens to share in its livability. Whether the concern is adequate housing, excellent education, convenient mobility, solid family life, public health, or diverse recreation, Denver must be a city that cares and shares, with compassion and equity. Particular priority must be given to educational excellence at all levels, for the quality of education is the cornerstone of a city's spirit and capacity to progress.
- To be ever more livable, Denver must be built to a human scale, and to inviting standards of attractiveness. This means that in the design of our physical surroundings, such as buildings, streets, parks, and neighborhoods, priority should be given to people's mobility and convenience. And this should not be a city in which "beauty" is an after-thought in the built environment.
- In regard to its physical environment, Denver must be especially sensitive, for our spectacular natural setting is the foundation of both this city's economy and livability. Clean water, clean air, clean parks and streets, protected mountains and open spaces must be abiding goals.
- Denver must also build on its strong endowment of a first-class cultural environment. The arts, humanities, and educational institutions are vital to both attractiveness and economic health, and to that special "spirit" of a city.
- Denver must continue to carefully preserve its historic heritage and its cultural and ethnic diversity. Both livability for residents and invitation to visitors lie in our Western heritage, ethnic mix, neighborhood "color," and in the depth of the differing cultural traditions among the people.

The most promising ethnic and cultural model for the future Denver lies neither in the extreme of the blandly uniform melting pot nor in that of the rigidly fixed mosaic. Rather this must be a dynamic community which preserves the best of its heritage while enabling social as well as physical mobility.

- Denver's future depends on its being a successful regional partner. With limited exceptions, Denver isn't going to grow any more by adding land, but by being smarter and more innovative in building on its present base. An era of destructive competitions between Denver and its regional neighbors must yield to mutual strategies which emphasize the core city's advantage, attraction, and accessibility as the cultural and financial center of the Rocky Mountain West. Interdependence, not competition, must become the dominant theme of the regional political dialogue.
- Denver must capitalize on its unique geographical opportunity as a national transportation and communication center, being both the gateway to the Rocky Mountain recreation and natural resources empire, the nation's greatest and most central port of the air age, and the most populous Western intersection of the interstate highway system.

This Comprehensive Plan for Denver makes, then, the central proposal that the city and its neighborhoods first and always be developed for the living quality they offer people, both those already here and the many more sure to come. In putting people first, Denver must attend to their economic health and equality of opportunity, the human scale and beauty of their physical surroundings, their historic heritage and cultural diversity, and the excellence of both their physical and cultural environment. As essential to economic health and hence to livability, we emphasize Denver's unique role as the leading partner of the mountain West region, and as a national center of transportation and communication.

In the nature of any planning effort, compromises must sometimes be struck between purposes where they conflict. But if the balancing question at the point of compromise is "which decision will do the most to enhance the living quality of the most people," the Denver that emerges in the years ahead will be the city we really want it to be, and the one our heirs will thank us for.

DISCUSSION

The 1989 Denver Comprehensive Plan is by far the broadest, most inclusive plan in Denver's history. The vision demanded a plan of great scope, but it was immediately recognized that if the plan was to be anything more than a public exercise in theoretical city planning, it must include a very strategic element -- that is, an element capable of being quantified, consisting of understandable and achievable short term goals and timetables, subject to implementation strategies and monitoring techniques and within the financial capabilities of the City. The Action Agenda of the 1989 Denver Comprehensive Plan is designed to meet these criteria.

There are two very basic assumptions underlying the Plan and the Action Agenda. First, the citizens of Denver support its content and expect it to be aggressively implemented. Second, they expect the City's actions to be consistent with the Plan and the Agenda, or, if the elected representatives believe it to be appropriate or necessary, they expect the Plan to be amended through an open public process. In short, the Comprehensive Plan should not be ignored.

The achievement of a financing structure capable of supporting this aggressive planning rests in part upon the improvement of Denver's economy as set forth in the Economic Activity Chapter. We must move ahead with the critical public projects such as the new Denver airport and the completion of the Convention Center. And the City must develop the organization and skills that, in cooperation with the private sector, will result in primary job creation, a favorable small business environment and the climate which will support the needed public revenues and expenditures.

The following financing, implementation and monitoring strategies then, constitute a process to achieve the Core Goals of the Plan and to address these financing issues.

ACTIONS

IMPLEMENTATION

The public support for the 1989 Comprehensive Plan which developed during the preparation and adoption process, should be built upon to generate support for the Plan's implementation.

Based on such support, the City Council and the Mayor must act to assure implementation of the Comprehensive Plan.

IM-A-1 Request the City Council to adopt the full Comprehensive Plan and the Action Agenda as its priority strategic legislative agenda.
Timing: Completed, October 1989

IM-A-2 Request the Mayor to adopt the Comprehensive Plan and to include the Action Agenda in the City's annual work program.
Timing: Completed, October 1989

IM-A-3 Request the Mayor to require that cabinet members adhere to the Plan, or recommend changes to the Plan if deemed appropriate.
Timing: FT

IM-A-4 Request that a clause stating consistency with the Comprehensive Plan be included by the Council in all appropriate ordinances. Request that the Council consider a change to the Comprehensive Plan in instances where the Council feels legislative acts are appropriate that are at odds with the Plan.
Timing: FT

IM-A-5 Advocate better in-depth press coverage and awareness of planning and urban design issues to assist education and awareness throughout the community, including a regular urban affairs/urban design column in the newspapers and regular urban affairs issues programs on radio and T.V.
Timing: FT

IM-A-6 Initiate a Denver Zoning Study, supported by the Mayor, City Council and Planning Board, to perform a comprehensive review of Denver's Zoning Code and procedures. The study should be reviewed by the Planning Board for possible charter and/or ordinance changes, if any, and appropriate recommendations should be made to the Mayor and City Council.
Timing: FT

MONITORING

The Denver Planning Board's role should be expanded to include the responsibility of monitoring implementation of the Comprehensive Plan and the Action Agenda. The role of City Council in approving Planning Board members and Council's participation in policy matters before the Planning Board should be enhanced. In particular, Council members should be encouraged to participate on Task Forces working on special projects and subarea plans.

IM-A-7 Request the City Council and the Mayor to approve the Planning Board's statement of its role and its policies simultaneously with the adoption of the Comprehensive Plan, as well as to approve any amendments to such role and policies in the future.
Timing: FT

IM-A-8 Request the City Council to approve the Mayor's appointments to the Planning Board.
Timing: FT

IM-A-9 Establish a monitoring system to permit the Planning Board to monitor implementation of the Comprehensive Plan and report on progress to the Mayor and Council. Use the Action Agenda as the basis for measuring the success of short-term work programs.
Timing: FT

IM-A-10 Review progress on implementing the Action Agenda, review the core goals and develop the 1990-1991 Action Agenda with updated goals and new actions. Request Mayor and Council adoption.
Timing: FT

FINANCING

Financing is an integral part of the Plan. The recommendations of the Plan are ambitious but are intended to be implemented over time. As mentioned earlier, the actions contained in each Action Agenda will have an estimated cost and suggested source of funding whenever appropriate. This typically means allocating existing budgets and funds so that the Plan is not entirely dependent on finding new funds for implementation. But in addition, the Plan makes the specific recommendation that the City begin to develop other sources of funding to help implement some of the Plan's more ambitious long-term recommended actions. Attention must also be paid to expenditures, ensuring that the City is providing services in the most cost effective manner possible and that capital investments will serve the City's long term needs.

It is also important to point out that the financing described in the Action Agenda represents only those fast-track actions that are anticipated taking place in the following months. Other actions from the larger Plan will be implemented simultaneously and will also require reallocation of or creation of new funds. However, it is anticipated that the Action Agenda will have the greatest detail concerning funding for the Plan.

IM-A-11 Evaluate the overall system of financing City services and investments including the potential use of other taxes and sources of revenues that would be more sensitive to the nature of Denver's future growth and economic base.
Timing: FT

IM-A-12 Evaluate the four basic funding sources for City improvements and maintenance to assure a balance among the four and to assure each is funded at a level sufficient to meet the City's needs. The four sources are:

General Fund - sufficient to avoid maintenance functions from being moved to the Capital Improvements Budget (e.g., park or street maintenance expenditures).

Capital Improvements Budget - sufficient to keep the City's improvements in good repair, and not push annual maintenance needs into bond issues; and

Bonding - sufficient and frequent enough to provide for the large expenditures which fund new or major redevelopment projects; evaluation should also include the establishment of priorities for the use of bonding capacity.

Enterprise funds - should be revised regularly to assure they generate sufficient funds to develop, maintain and operate their respective responsibilities without reliance on any assistance from the General Fund on Capital Improvements Budget.
Timing: FT

IM-A-13 Consider the assessment of development fees on new development as well as developing clear policy statements as to the fees to be charged and infrastructure improvements required of redevelopment projects. The fees would be tied to the amount and cost of development and should be reviewed annually. Administrative procedures could be used to carry out the annual update. Among others, consideration should be given to the adoption of traffic impact fees, parkland dedication, fees and development requirements for new development and a reevaluation of costs that are a disincentive to redevelopment.
Timing: FT

ACTION AGENDA

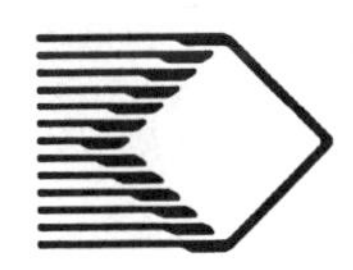

THE FIRST 24-MONTH PLAN FOR ACTION EXTRACTED FROM THE 1989 DENVER COMPREHENSIVE PLAN

TABLE OF CONTENTS

HOW TO USE THE ACTION AGENDA

This is the Action Agenda component of the 1989 Denver Comprehensive Plan. The Action Agenda is a "business plan" based upon the 10 Core Goals identified in the Comprehensive Plan as top priority for action. As such, the Action Agenda is organized thematically (e.g., improve air quality) whereas the actions underneath each goal were written functionally (e.g., education, mobility, housing). A Core Goal may draw actions from several different functional chapters (e.g., the Core Goal of Air Quality will have actions from chapters on Mobility, Air Quality and Environment and Land Use).

The actions in this agenda were selected from the larger Comprehensive Plan because they are actions that the City and other organizations must take by 1990 to advance the City toward its Core Goals. While they in no means represent the entire Comprehensive Plan, they do represent a clear fast-track agenda for the City.

Each action is identified by an alpha-numeric code that describes the functional chapter in the full Comprehensive Plan from which it was drawn. This coding system provides the reader with an easy cross-reference system for the Plan. The first indicates the location – the chapter name. The next letter indicates the type – whether it's an Action (A), Objective (O) or Policy (P). The number is the sequential order in which they were written within the chapter of the full Comprehensive Plan. See the example below that was taken from Core Goal #1 – Stimulate the Economy – in this document. A full list of abbreviations follows the example.

EA-A-10 *Streamline permitting processes, implementing one-stop permitting.*
The "EA" means the Economic Activity chapter.
The "A" means it's an Action.
The "10" means it's the 10th Action in the Economic Activity chapter.

List of Abbreviations

Abbr.	Resource Component Chapter
UD	Urban Design
NE	Neighborhoods
HO	Housing
RS	Retail, Services & Employment
EA	Economic Activity
MO	Mobility
AQ	Air Quality and Environment
ED	Education
CA	Culture, Arts and Leisure
HS	Human Services
GO	Governance and Metropolitan Cooperation
IM	Implementation

Abbr.	Type
A	Action
P	Policy
O	Objective

VISION STATEMENT AND CORE GOALS

An overall comprehensive plan for a great city must answer the question, "What do we really want this city to be, and to become?" This isn't a simple question. Any city and its people are both the beneficiaries of special opportunities suggested by a particular history and geography. The core of the Denver 1989 Comprehensive Plan lies in our attempt to agree on Denver's purpose for the future, to think through the effect of Denver's special inheritance on those purposes, and then to apply our consensus in specific plan suggestions.

The fundamental thing we want Denver to both be and to become is a city that's livable for all its people. A city in which they can learn, move about, work and play in safety and in comfort, with pleasure and pride, and in a spirit of openness and opportunity.

It is essential that living quality for all the people of Denver be perceived as this Plan's central purpose. The question "Does this action improve the quality of life for people?" is the challenge the Plan poses to future civic leaders. In too many cities plans are made and decisions taken without livability being the upfront test, but for the most part this has not been historically true of Denver, and we hope it never will be.

If livability is at the heart of our city plan, a number of associated purposes become easier to define.

These have been identified as Denver's 10 Core Goals — goals that are absolutely essential to maintaining and improving Denver's quality of life.

Core Goal #1 — Stimulate the Economy
Core Goal #2 — Beautify the City and Preserve its History
Core Goal #3 — Protect, Enhance and Integrate a City of Neighborhood
Core Goal #4 — Educate All of Denver's Residents With Excellence
Core Goal #5 — Clear The Air, Now
Core Goal #6 — Meet Expanding Transportation Needs, Efficiently, Cleanly, Economically, Innovatively
Core Goal #7 — Help the Disadvantaged Help Themselves
Core Goal #8 — Revise Land Use Controls, Streamline Procedures
Core Goal #9 — Celebrate the City's Arts, Culture & Ethnicity
Core Goal #10 — Share Resources and Responsibilities in the Metropolitan Area

This Comprehensive Plan for Denver makes, then, the central proposal that the city first and always be developed for the living quality it offers its people, both those already here and the many more sure to come. In putting people first, Denver must attend to their economic health and equality of opportunity, the human scale and beauty of their physical surroundings, their historic heritage and cultural diversity, and to the excellence of both their physical and cultural environment.

In the nature of any planning effort, compromises must sometimes be struck. But if the balancing question at the point of compromise is "Which decision will do the most to enhance the living quality of the most people," the Denver that emerges will be the city we really want it to be, and the one our heirs will thank us for.

CORE GOAL #8

Revise Land Use Controls, Streamline Procedures

Denver is a developed city with limited vacant land and a state restriction on growth through annexation. With these restrictions, Denver has been forced to focus inward and make the best use of the precious land it does have, unlike other cities which have abandoned their core areas for opportunities on the edge of their boundaries.

To assure the desired development of Denver and to retain and attract to Denver families of all economic means and to protect the stability and quality of its neighborhoods and its economy, the City Government must review and revise its zoning, development standards and administrative procedures which in the past have inhibited such activity and benefits.

Review of codes and procedures.

IM-A-6 Initiate a Denver Zoning Study, supported by the Mayor, City Council and Planning Board to perform a comprehensive review of Denver's Zoning Code and procedure. The study should be reviewed by the Planning Board for possible charter and/or ordinance changes, if any, and appropriate recommendations should be made to the Mayor and City Council. (See also UD-A-56, UD-A-71, NE-A-7, NE-A-19, CA-A-23 and CA-A-24).
Suggested Responsibility: Denver Planning Board
Timing: Begin in 1989

UD-A-66 Review and revise the Sign Code and develop procedures for implementation and enforcement.
Suggested Responsibility: DPO
Timing: 1989

UD-A-65 Adopt the revised billboard ordinance, minimizing the size, numbers and permitted locations of billboards;
Suggested Responsibility: DPO, Zoning Admin., City Council
Timing: Completed, Spring 1988

NE-A-23 Expand code enforcement and sensitively target a selected number of neighborhoods.
Suggested Responsibility: Zoning Admin., Building Dept., Clean Denver
Timing: 1989

UD-A-58 Evaluate building codes requirements and administrative procedures, including inspection and enforcement, to:
- Remove incentives for demolition;
- Adopt reasonable code requirements for historic features; and

• Include a representative from the Landmark Preservation Commission on the Chapter 31 Board and develop educational materials about the Chapter 31 process and how it applies to rehabilitation work on historic properties.
Suggested Responsibility: DPW
Timing: 1989

UD-A-59 Evaluate development requirements, such as traffic and fire codes, to support renovation and adaptive re-use of historic buildings and to promote the historic urban design elements of the neighborhoods.
Suggested Responsibility: DPO
Timing: 1989

EA-A-10 Streamline permitting processes, implementing one stop permitting.
Suggested Responsibility: Mayor's Office, Building Dept., Zoning
Timing: Spring 1989

EA-A-11 Adopt the Uniform Building Code.
Suggested Responsibility: Building Dept., Mayor's Office
Timing: 1989

EA-A-12 Update building, fire and health codes, using simplified standard codes wherever possible and review administrative procedures.
Suggested Responsibility: Building Dept.
Timing: 1989

NE-A-26 Appoint a Task Force to review the City's building codes and initiate changes which facilitate mixed use projects and preservation of existing buildings and avoid conflicts with adjacent jurisdictions.
Suggested Responsibility: Mayor's Office
Timing: 1989

Streetscape design guidelines.

UD-A-25 Develop streetscape design guidelines that reflect Denver's historic urban design legacy of tree lawns and street trees and that reflect the conditions of different types of streets and business areas.
Suggested Responsibility: DPO, Parks Dept., ASLA, AIA, DPW
Timing: 1989

Development fees.

IM-A-13 Consider the assessment of development fees on new development as well as developing clear policy statements as to the fees to be charged and infrastructure improvements required of redevelopment projects. The fees would be tied to the amount and cost of development and should be reviewed annually. Administrative procedures could be used to carry out the annual update. Among others, consideration should be given to the adoption of traffic impact fees, parkland dedication, fees and development requirements for new development and a reevaluation of costs that are a disincentive to redevelopment.
Suggested Responsibility: DPO, Budget and Management
Timing: 1989

Planning Board role.

IM-A-7 Request the City Council and the Mayor to approve the Planning Board's statement of its role and its policies simultaneously with the adoption of the Comprehensive Plan, as well as to approve any amendments to such role and policies in the future.
Suggested Responsibility: Planning Board
Timing: 1989

Planning Board appointments.

IM-A-8 Request the City Council to approve the Mayor's appointments to the Planning Board.
Suggested Responsibility: Planning Board
Timing: 1989

There were a variety of reasons why Denver, like other cities, ignored and in places destroyed the river system. Flooding and intermittent flows were two reasons. But the recent construction of the Platte River Greenway and Cherry Creek pedestrian and bicycle systems demonstrate renewed interest in using and restoring the waterway system.

There are recommendations in these paragraphs as to how Denver can capitalize on this interest and turn the waterway system into a highly used and visible amenity.

ISSUES AND OPPORTUNITIES

While there is an established park system in the city, it does not take good advantage of the creeks and rivers. There is little access to or open space development along these waterways, even though they are distributed throughout the city. Access is further restricted by the location of railroads and highways along the Platte River and subsequent industrial development which separated residential neighborhoods from the river.

Similarly the location of rivers and gulches has tended to divide neighborhoods within the city; it will take significant effort to knit these parts of the city together.

Air pollution collects in the natural bowl created by the river system. The river banks and water quality have been degraded by pollution and inappropriate storage and industrial uses. Other gulches have been enclosed in culverts or drains, destroying their natural qualities.

In the past there have been significant flooding and floodplain issues, but particularly since the devastating flood of 1965, these have been alleviated to a large extent by dams and other control devices. Still, some floodplain issues remain to be corrected on private property along the rivers and creeks.

The draft Parks Master Plan documented the degree of deficiency of parks and open space areas in the core city; the developed nature of the city's neighborhoods makes it difficult and prohibitively expensive to purchase the large parcels that are needed within some neighborhoods. The redevelopment of obsolete industrial uses along the Platte, providing additional access points to Cherry Creek, and redevelopment of Stapleton provide new opportunities to regain access to waterways and to provide open space and parks along them. Parks along the Platte in particular, would be very close to the homes of many Denver residents, and areas poorly served by parks now.

The successful efforts of the Greenway Foundation and other adjacent jurisdictions, developing and maintaining trails along the Platte River and cooperation between the City, the Greenway and U.D.F.C. District can be expanded to other projects and areas of the city.

OBJECTIVES AND CONCEPTS

Citywide and regional open space system

The draft plan envisions a citywide system of natural open space, primarily based on existing rivers and gulches -- a series of interconnected loops of open space with multimodal trails tying into the regional network. This "natural" open space system will be integrated with an improved existing system of parks, parkways, and boulevards. Denver's open space system will be the heart of the regional system. Cooperation with neighboring jurisdictions through which these waterways and parkways continue, will be required for the vision to come to fruition.

Taken to its fullest, the urban and natural open space system creates an interconnected network of parks, recreation facilities, parkways, boulevards, and bikeways closely related to the neighborhoods. It will link activity centers and public buildings. By the quality of its connections and the location of its open space and recreation facilities, it will reduce the dependence on the automobile to reach parts of the system.

In addition to improved urban pedestrian facilities and bikeways, parkways and boulevards, proposed new trails and open space loops are the following:

East: Platte - Cherry Creek - Highline Canal - Sand Creek - Platte; a variation is to use Buchtel Boulevard or to take the Highline Canal through Lowry to Stapleton.

West: Platte - Sanderson Gulch - Bear Creek - Platte; other variations would be to go from Marston Lake - Fehringer Ranch - Bear Lake or a loop involving Weir Gulch and Public Service Company right-of-way.

Existing open spaces will be made safer and more enjoyable by landscaping, clean up and redevelopment of activities along river and

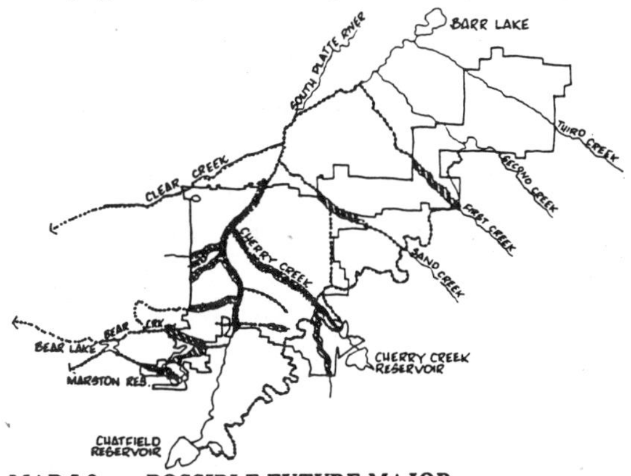

MAP 5.8 POSSIBLE FUTURE MAJOR OPEN SPACE LOCATIONS

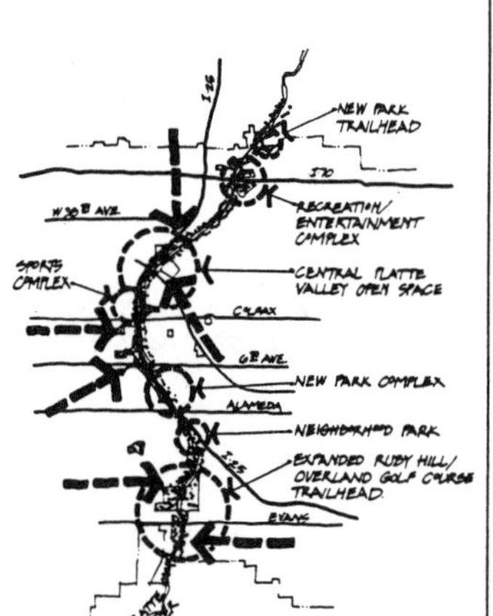

MAP 5.9
PROPOSED PLATTE RIVER
OPEN SPACE SYSTEM

creek banks and the addition of "people" amenities. New open spaces will be added to the system. The character of open space can change, for instance, from very urban along Cherry Creek at the shopping center and in downtown, to very natural along Sand Creek.

Throughout the system, opportunities should be sought where the presence of water, and people's access to it, can be increased. Perhaps alternative methods of regulating flows along the Platte River and Cherry Creek would increase the water flowing in those channels. Fishing ponds, lakes, canoeing and kayaking courses and other water amenities could be added, with proper safeguards for public safety.

An attractive, accessible open space network will improve the look and feel of the city; it will give residents a pleasant way to get to parks, both close by and through out the city. Not only will it benefit residents, but these are the types of amenities that attract visitors and new residents.

Platte River "String of Pearls"

The long term vision calls for the Platte River to be the focus of Denver's natural open space system. The entire length of the Platte River should be redeveloped to become a high image open space corridor, a "string of pearls" with major new parks serving the heart of Denver, interspersed with nodes of urban activity. Water should be celebrated and wildlife and vegetation added. Open space connections to adjacent neighborhoods via the numerous gulches could provide access to the new parks. In other words, the Platte River will change from being a divisive element in the city to one uniting neighborhoods on the east and west sides.

By adding parkland and open space, the city can overcome existing deficiencies as well as address future park needs. The cities of Montreal and Oakland and our own Greenway have demonstrated that open space, when properly designed, can pass through industrial areas and be pleasant places. The vision calls for reinforcing the strong industrial and employment areas, making them more attractive and productive. The City will encourage smaller office/ warehouse/showroom businesses and other nonpolluting employment activities that are compatible with the neighborhoods and which can capitalize on a landscaped setting.

Over time, housing should replace the old industrial uses in selected areas. Existing neighborhoods and housing close to the river should be protected and new housing added.

The street grid system should be completed where possible to meet the river's edge; open space and special activities could be developed as focal points at the east - west arterial river crossings.

(Please also see Chapter 9 for detailed recommendations on the redevelopment of the Platte).

Improving existing open space links

In addition to redeveloping the Platte River corridor, a high priority is to improve Cherry Creek as an amenity. In the Downtown and Central Platte Valley this could involve shops, more pedestrian facilities, landscaping plazas and so on. Restaurants, shops, plazas, water features and open space along the creek banks will be part of the improvements being made to the

Cherry Creek Shopping Center. And further east, improved pedestrian access and parks will enhance the remainder of the Creek.

Open Space in other parts of the city

New open space corridors should be obtained in developing areas, such as Sand Creek, First Creek and Second Creek in the northeast. Critical wildlife areas should be preserved along these open space corridors; opportunities to reintroduce wildlife to existing areas should be explored. It is also important that the regional system be protected from urban development, especially connections west to the mountain parks via Clear and Bear Creeks.

Other utility and railroad corridors are suitable as open space corridors, e.g., Buchtel Boulevard, West 12th Avenue; trails should be developed along these, and they should be developed as integral parts of the open space loop system.

POLICIES

UD-P-3 Gulches, rivers, creeks and substantial drainageways, irrigation ditches and other waterways normally should be developed and maintained as recreation and open space amenities for the enjoyment of Denver residents. The City should preserve critical wildlife habitats along these waterways and should reintroduce habitats where appropriate.

UD-P-4 Except in unusual circumstances (as determined by the Wastewater Management Division and the Urban Drainage and Flood Control District) gulches, drainages or rivers should not be culverted, filled in or put into drains. Should this be deemed unavoidable, structures should be designed so as to be aesthetically pleasing and if possible, usable for recreation.

UD-P-5 The City should seek to remove or mitigate floodplain problems using techniques that will allow continued use of private land, that maximize recreation use and are visually appealing.

UD-P-6 The City should continue to work with other entities such as the Greenway Foundation, U.D.F.C. District and adjacent jurisdictions, e.g., surrounding counties and private developers, to develop the area's rivers, waterways and their environs as connected open space trails for recreation use.

UD-P-7 Creeks and other waterways in developing areas must remain in open space, with sufficient land retained in public ownership on either side to permit access to and along the waterways.

UD-P-8 The City should work with the railroads, utilities and R.T.D. to obtain public access along abandoned or active rights-of-way as appropriate; the City will seek to ensure the development of multimodal trails in conjunction with any transit systems built in these corridors.

STRATEGIES AND ACTIONS

Expand Open Space And Park Land Along The Platte River

(See also following sections)

UD-A-2 Acquire initial park parcels in the Central Platte Valley - Denver Common, Rockmont.
Timing: FT

UD-A-3 Design the flood control measures and create a special district to implement such measures to remove land in the CPV from the floodplain.
Timing: FT

UD-A-4 Evaluate the suitability of parcels along the Platte River for new parks; develop a plan for phased acquisition.
Timing: FT

UD-A-5 Inventory critical wildlife areas in the city that should be preserved.
Timing: FT

Improve Gulches And Open Space With Trails And Attractive Landscaping

UD-A-6 Improve open space and park areas to provide more usable areas for people along Cherry Creek, especially at the Cherry Creek Shopping Center.
Timing: FT

UD-A-7 Complete plans for the Cherry Creek Creekfront and implement a pilot project.
Timing: ST

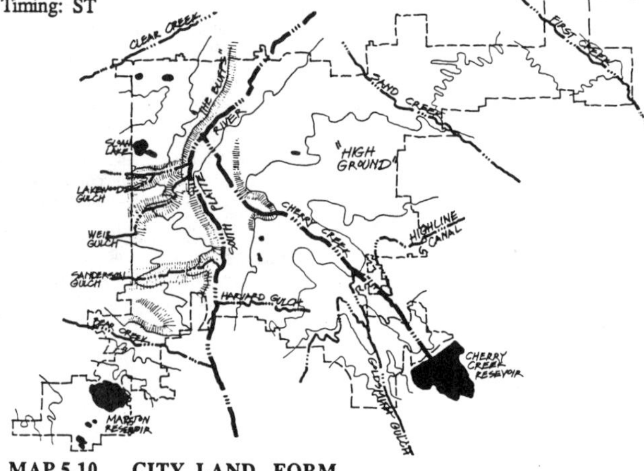

MAP 5.10 CITY LAND FORM

UD-A-8 Reopen culverts and improve gulches on a selected basis to provide neighborhood linkages where feasible; begin with segments identified through the neighborhood planning process, or working with neighborhood organizations, e.g., portions of Weir Gulch in Barnum and Barnum West, or Lakewood Gulch.
Timing: ST

UD-A-9 In development plans being prepared, designate land along Sand Creek, First Creek and in Lowry as part of the natural open space system; develop mechanisms to assure open space is actually preserved.
Timing: LT

2. TOPOGRAPHY AND MOUNTAINS

Denver is the gateway to the Rocky Mountains. The mountains are more than the backdrop to the city; they are probably the element that most influences the city's image and lifestyle. Denver has extensive assets in its mountain park system, which it acquired in the 1930's, including Alameda Parkway leading from the city to the foothills, Red Rocks amphitheater, and over 13,000 acres of park land.

There is a tradition of locating parks in the city on sites with vantage points for viewing the mountains. Panoramic views of the Continental Divide and the plains, long views of specific peaks such as Long's Peak, Mt. Evans and Pike's Peak; and short range views to the downtown skyline or State Capitol have been key elements in the design of the park system. This has led to the adoption of mountain view preservation ordinances, originating at parks and public buildings.

Preserving views heightens people's enjoyment of the city and preserves the city's unique character.

See Draft Parks and Recreation Master Plan for more information on the Mountain Parks.

ISSUES AND OPPORTUNITIES

Denver's mountain parks are an asset underused by Denver residents. It is difficult for the City to justify expenditures for mountain park development and maintenance when its revenues are inadequate to maintain the urban parks and when nearly two-thirds of the mountain park users are not Denver residents. Financing questions could jeopardize retention of these park areas. There are many park sites and acres of public land controlled by different agencies and scattered throughout the near mountains. But there is little coordination on planning, publicizing or maintaining these assets. Discussions among affected agencies have begun recently in an effort to promote use and make maintenance more cost effective.

Further development of the mountain park lands could supplement park space available to Denver residents and give less mobile or less wealthy residents opportunities to enjoy the mountain environment. Capitalizing on the mountain park potential and views could also help attract tourists.

Index